CONTENTS

REPORTS

POETRY

THE POLAR MUSE *following p. 32*

with contributions from
Lucy Hamilton, Sarah Howe, Rod Mengham,
Drew Milne, Redell Olsen, Andrea Porter,
Lucy Sheerman, Rebecca Watts

ARTICLES

REVIEWS

A CELEBRATION OF EAVAN BOLAND
Edited by Jody Allen Randolph and Michael Schmidt
with contributions from

Cover image: a portrait of Eavan Boland as a child, by her mother, the painter Frances Kelly (1908–2002).

Subscriptions (six issues):
£39.00 ($86.00) individuals
£49.00 ($105.00) institutions
to P N Review, Alliance House,
30 Cross Street Manchester M2 7AQ UK
Trade distributors:
CENTRAL BOOKS LTD, 99 Wallis Road, London E9 5LN
email magazines@centralbooks.com
Copyright © 2014 POETRY NATION REVIEW
All rights reserved
ISSN 0144-7076   ISBN 978 1 84777 189 6

General Editor MICHAEL SCHMIDT
Co-ordinating Editor HELEN TOOKEY

EDITORIAL ADDRESS:
Michael Schmidt
St John's College
Cambridge
CB2 1TP

Manuscripts should be sent to the editorial office
and cannot be returned unless accompanied by a
self-addressed and stamped envelope or, for writers
living abroad, by an international reply coupon.
Typeset in Ehrhardt
by XL Publishing Services
Exmouth, Devon
Printed in England
by SRP Limited, Exeter

Eavan Boland is a poet of rivers, of the Iowa River and of the Thames, of the Hudson and particularly of the River Liffey. 'O swan by swan my heart goes down / Through Dublin town, through Dublin town' she wrote in 1962, when she was eighteen and had already begun her journey. *New Collected Poems* read chronologically traces a development now incremental, now momentous. The distance between the young Irish poet composing 'Liffeytown' and 'The Liffey beyond Islandbridge' and the poet of *A Woman Without a Country* is instructive. Her stable yet evolving example is useful to poets and readers; stage by stage she writes her way into a resistant tradition she values. That resistance proves energising. She writes now, as she has for four decades, in a space she has cleared for herself and for other poets and readers.

Her poems are never instrumental: truthfulness is not, as in Adrienne Rich, whose work she fervently advocates, primarily to the moment. Feminism she says is 'an enabling perception but it's not an aesthetic one. The poem is a place – at least for me – where all kinds of certainties stop. All sorts of beliefs, convictions, certainties get left on that threshold. I couldn't be a feminist poet. Simply because the poem is a place of experience and not a place of convictions…'.

Although Eavan, unlike Donald Davie and C.H. Sisson, was never an editor of *PN Review*, she has for more than three decades been part of its editorial consciousness and conscience. It would have been a different journal without her. Many of her major poems, essays and interviews have appeared in these pages. Beyond that contribution, she is an advocate, alerting me to younger Irish writers and American poets – among them Louise Glück, Jorie Graham, Bridget Pegeen Kelly and Kay Ryan – whose work I needed to know. As an editor I could not do without her. As a reader also, and a friend these almost forty years. And so we gratefully mark her seventieth birthday in these pages. Jody Allen Randolph and I invited contributors to respond to work that they most value. Eavan herself contributes the title sequence of her new collection, an eponymous essay, and a major new interview.

In *PN Review* 2 (1978) Stan Smith reviewed her early collection *The War Horse*. Published by Gollancz, the book cost £2. Smith's review included John Montague's *A Slow Dance* (Dolmen Press via Oxford University Press, £1.75) and Seamus Heaney's *North* (Faber, £1.25). It was the first time her name was mentioned in these pages, a time when Heaney was news and Dolmen Press was still a major purveyor of Irish writing, and when poetry collections cost £2 or less.

Eavan made the first of her own more than forty contributions to *PN Review* seven years later (*PNR* 41) with the poem, 'Listen. This is the Noise of Myth':

This is the story of a man and woman
under a willow and beside a weir
near a river in a wooded clearing.
They are fugitives. Intimates of myth.

The poem at once tells and reflects upon its story, then enjoins us boldly:

Look:

the scene returns. The willow sees itself
drowning in the weir and the woman
gives the kiss of myth her human heat.

That human heat, applied from without, elicits from the intimate and from the narrative itself an answering heat. Evoking elements of myth, legend and history, Eavan's poems revive their inherent human heat: poetry as a restorative act, acknowledgement, justice done, sometimes through narrative, through objects in a defining context, or through silences and gaps which the reader must fill.

A gap she revisits in her own life is located in childhood, exiled from Ireland. The idyllic worlds of some of her Irish contemporaries are for her remote: hers is more a labour of reclamation. Much of her childhood was spent abroad where her father was a diplomat. She was brought up in London from the age of six to twelve, and she was not happy. 'Some of the feelings I recognise as having migrated into themes I keep going back to – exile, types of estrangement, a relation to objects – began there.' When she did return to Ireland, attending Trinity College, Dublin, she encountered the 'genderless poem' that was expected of the woman writer. Her complex engagement with her contemporary culture began in earnest. In time, she broke away physically and imaginatively. 'I went to the suburbs. I married. I had two children.' Her experience was not accounted for in the poetry around her. '*Night Feed* is the book I could have been argued out of, if I had let myself listen to what was around me.'

In the suburbs she discovered 'that what went into the Irish poem and what stayed outside it was both tense and hazardous for an Irish woman poet.' Irish women have to negotiate from being objects in the Irish poem to being authors of it. 'I began to know that I had to bring the poem I'd learned to write near to the life I was starting to live. And that if anything had to yield in that process, it was the poem not the life.'

The challenge has changed, but what she said about *Outside History* (1990) remains a challenge to herself as to her readers. 'Here I was in a different ethical area. Writing about the lost, the voiceless, the silent. And exploring my relation to them. And – more dangerous still – feeling my ways into the powerlessness of an experience through the power of expressing it. This wasn't an area of artistic experiment. It was an area of ethical imagination, where you had to be sure, every step of the way – every word and every line – that it was good faith and good poetry. And it couldn't be one without the other. There is very little technical experiment in *Outside History*.'

In China in September the Institute of Poetry officially pronounced a river venerated for centuries by poets as *Poetry River*. The Qihe merits this title, said Zhang Tongwu, the Institute's president, at a ceremony of dedication, because it is widely recognised as the cradle of Chinese poetry. It is not a very long river – at 160 kilometres, in the Chinese context, it is hardly even a haiku of a river. It rises in Shanxi and flows into Henan province where it joins other rivers and makes its way to the Yellow Sea. From the eleventh to the first centuries BC it was poetry's own river, and 39 of the 305 verses of Confucius are said to describe the landscape of the Qihe, said Zhang. In northern Henan, in the prefecture city of Hebi, a three-kilometre wall inscribed with 1500 verses of early poetry about the river and the city has been built. Earlier in September in a visit to a Beijing university the president of China declared that classic poetry should be inculcated into the memories of students and transformed into part of the genetic structure of their native culture, a change of emphasis from the 'new broom' approach of earlier times.

The Chilean poet and anti-poet NICANOR PARRA ('there's enough poetry for everyone') celebrated his one hundredth birthday on 5 September. The president of Chile, Michelle Bachelet, visited him at his home where he has lived in relative seclusion for years. Throughout Latin America his survival and his poetry were celebrated with readings, and in Chile with song and dance. His poem 'What does an old man get from going to the gym' is characteristic of his self-deprecating poetry: 'Silly old man his mother tells him / you are just like your father / he didn't want to die either / God give you life to drive your car / God give you life to talk on the phone / God give you life to breathe / God give you life enough to bury your mother.' His first collection appeared in 1935.

Chilean President Bachelet was also called upon in August to present the Iberoamerican Neruda Poetry Prize to the Cuban poet REINA MARIA RODRIGUEZ at a ceremony in the Moneda Palace in Santiago. Bachelet noted that Rodriguez is the tenth recipient of the award and the youngest so far honoured with the $60,000 dollars and the promise of book publication. Parra won the prize in 2012.

The Iranian poet SIMIN BEHBAHANI, the *de facto* national poet of Iran, died in Tehran in August at the age of 87. She was a politically engaged and a 'subversive' poet, who published her first poem when she was fourteen. She was a master of the ghazal, bringing into the form a modern and contemporary idiom and reference. She adopted various strategies to circumvent the censors (not always successfully), her work energised by a struggle against inequality (she was awarded the Simone de Beauvoir prize in 2009) and for thematic openness. Her poetry is a kind of fever chart of the expectations and disappointments of her people in a turbulent century. She preferred to stay in Iran when many of her contemporaries chose exile. It is where she belonged, whatever the promise and prosperity of exile might have offered.

The First World War diaries of SIEGFRIED SASSOON were published online on 1 August, a substantial resource for general readers keen to engage the war close-up. Sassoon himself wanted to savour the extremes of experience, and when he did his reaction was unexpected and puzzling. 'My inner life is far more real than the hideous realism of this land, the war zone.' Cambridge University Library has digitised 4,100 pages of these diaries, which include stains from the material world in which they were written (mud, wax, cricket scores). John Wells, the archival librarian, noted how, 'unlike edited, printed transcriptions, the digitizations allow the viewer to form a sense of the physical documents, and to appreciate their unique nature as historical archives'. On screen one can come very close to the world in which the hand rested on the little page and the words followed the days' inexorable progress.

Material culture was the subject of a modest, successful appeal by the Wheal Martyn China Clay Museum in St Austell, Cornwall, to restore the 'shabby' desk where the blind Cornish poet JACK CLEMO (1916–94) wrote his poems. One anonymous donor provided £300; the additional money collected will go towards restoring his rickety bookcase.

NIALL CAMPBELL was awarded the £20,000 Edwin Morgan Prize for his first collection *Moontide* (Bloodaxe), reviewed by Neil Powell in this issue of *PN Review*.

Jamaican poet, essayist and novelist KEI MILLER was awarded the Forward Prize for Best Poetry Collection for *The Cartographer Tries to Map a Way to Zion* (Carcanet) at the Southbank Centre on 30 September. The chair of the judges, Jeremy Paxman, said: 'Kei is doing something you don't come across often: this is a beautifully voiced collection which struck us all with its boldness and wit. Many poets refer to multiple realities, different ways of observing the world. Kei doesn't just refer, he articulates them'. The shortlist included new collections by Colette Bryce, John Burnside, Louise Glück (also Carcanet) and Hugo Williams.

The Forward prize-giving event was dedicated to DANNIE ABSE, one of this year's judges and among the best-loved contemporary British poets, who died the weekend before the prize was announced, at 91. He contributed 'Nothing' to *Poetry Nation* 4, a poem already worrying at the theme of age. It opens: 'Amnesia. A keyhole. A glass eye. / In sleep, dreams between long blanks; / awake, blanks between brief dreams. / This is the cemetery side of fifty. / This is the taste of pure water. / This is the dread revealing nothing.' And in his last contribution, to *PN Review* 209, he wrote 'In Highgate Woods', which concludes: 'Old poets stay at home to become explorers; / the older they get, the smaller they get / and, relentlessly, the trees grow tall.' (The Welsh Academi director described him two years ago as 'at the top of the Welsh tree', which has become a rather tall one.) He was made a CBE in 2012, rather later than one might have expected for a figure so generous and so central to the 'scene', a physician poet, a Welshman, a Jew. His final collection, *Ask the Moon*, will be published next February.

Reports are circulating that the poet and activist TENZIN TSUNDUE was detained by police ahead of Chinese President Xi Jinping's visit to India. Tsundue, of Dharamshala in Himachal Pradesh, is associated with Friends of Tibet (India) and has been detained before for protesting against the Chinese occupation of Tibet. He was said to have been released when Jinping had concluded his visit.

James Sutherland-Smith writes:

MIODRAG PAVLOVIĆ, the last surviving member of the great Serbian modernist triumvirate of Ivan Lalić (1931–96), Vasko Popa (1922–91) and himself, died on 17 August this year. He was born in 1928 in Novi Sad, the second city of Serbia, and trained as a doctor, although he soon moved to working in literature, eventually becoming Director of the National

Theatre in Belgrade and a chief editor at the Yugoslav publishing house of Prosveta. In addition to Serbian he was fluent in English, French and German. In 1952 he published his first collection, *87 Poems*, a book which can be said to have inaugurated modernism in Serbian literature, with Popa's first collection appearing in 1953 and Lalić's in 1955. He also wrote short stories, novels and a number of important works in literary criticism. From his withdrawal from active work as a publisher he divided his time between his homes in Tuttlingen in Germany and in Belgrade. Miodrag Pavlović was an extremely prolific poet, but only a tiny fraction of his work has made its way into English in book and chapbook form. In comparison with Lalić and Popa he never reached a wide audience in the English-speaking world. Like many Serbian writers his fluency in a number of languages meant that he was also a distinguished translator and he mentioned to me when we first met that he had even translated Sir Geoffrey Hill's work. He was twice a nominee for the Nobel Prize in literature.

A selection of his poems, translated into English by Nenad Aleksić and myself, was in proof when news of his death reached me and will be published shortly by Salt. We completed the translations with Miodrag in the conference room at the British Council in Belgrade. Despite being eighty years old at the time, he went through our draft in great detail, pointing out inaccuracies and sometimes demanding from me 'a better word choice, please, James'. It was a humbling yet inspiring experience.

The Portuguese lawyer, politician, poet, novelist and translator VASCO GRAÇA MOURA died on 27 April this year. This interview, with Bernardo Pinto de Almeida, was one of the last interviews that Moura gave on the subject of his poetry.

Fifty years of published poetry: how have the poems changed?
Each poem is a new experiment with language and the energies that come out of it – a new way to relate word and world. The changes are to do with that: at first I was more open to avant-gardeism. But that never went very deep. Gradually I matured till the very obscurities of my poems were a kind of quest for clarity.

Tell me about constants and changes.
I gradually gave up techniques deriving from surrealism. I wanted more and more to combine two things: reawakening classical forms and metres and a diction that tends, as Montale said, towards prose – but rejects it.

What kind of a thing is a good poem? Which poem by someone else would you most like to have written?
A good poem comes to life by escaping definition. It takes its energy from our very being. Its verbal power goes on reverberating long after it has struck us. I should like to have written some of Camões' sonnets and Brodsky's 'Elegy for John Donne'.

You're not only a poet and novelist. You've earned international recognition for your lifelong work as a translator of poetry. Your translations include some major classics. How
has this affected your poetry? How has your own poetry helped the translator?
I only translated works that challenged me, that spoke to me personally. It was hand-to-hand combat with the source language and even more so with my own. There were moments of the great European literary traditions that I wanted to bring into Portuguese. So it was a kind of training in expressive form. And it left traces that germinated in my own work. Now and then you hear the echoes.

You have been critical of Pessoa and the space he occupies in the Portuguese literary scene. What other family trees do you recommend?
The line of Camões, obviously. The line of Césario Verde. And someone later than Pessoa: Vitorino Nemésio. And don't forget the major Brazilian names, especially Carlos Drummond de Andrade and João Cabral de Melo Neto.

What do you think of the new Portuguese poetry? What voices would you pick out?
There's a young poet, Tatiana Faia, you'll hear a lot more about. I recommend her latest book, *Lugano*. Another name to keep in mind is Margarida Vale de Gato, who wrote 'Mulher ao Mar'. There's a fascinating poetry being made in Portugal now that combines experiment with the great literary tradition.

Is there a poem you still want to write?
Yes. My best one yet.

Translated by Chris Miller with Ana Hudson

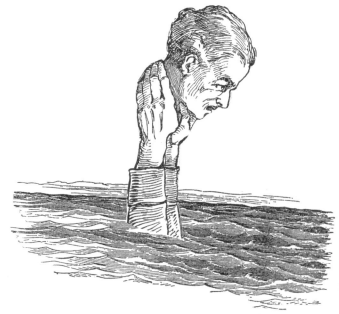

Augustin 2012

Back to Essex

Sir:

In my review in brief of James Canton's *Out of Essex* in the *TLS* (13 April 2013) I said that 'it largely skirts the wilder shores of psychobiography'. In this I was perhaps over-generous if Chris McCully's review (*PNR* 217) is true to the author's intentions. McCully speaks of 'pregnant mappings', of 'a mapping of intersecting memories', and in a paean to Essex sees the county as 'a flood-plain catching human tides', as both 'challenge and refuge'. Further, we are told that 'writers use Essex'. Well one would have thought that some do, and some don't.

For example, in the Edwardian period a number of prominent writers set up residence in the Home Counties: these include Henry James, Chesterton, Bennett, Shaw, Conrad, Kipling. Few made extensive imaginative use of their new locales, the major exception being Kipling, whose 'Puck of Pook's Hill' magics up layers of human history from the Sussex Downs. Canton cites Wells and his Mr Britling, but for the most part these writers wanted only a more or less 'rustic' retreat that was in relatively easy reach of London. Conrad at one point lived in the Essex village of Stratford-le-Hope, though Canton's researches fail to identify which house he occupied. But maybe this is something of a quixotic venture to begin with: what of significance would have been achieved had he succeeded?

Canton attempts to make connections with literary ghosts, and mostly fails, either because, like Shakespeare, they were never there in the first place, or simply because no traces remain of them. Could the tile he finds at Tilbury have once belonged to Defoe's former brickworks? Maybe. Maybe not. Is there some occult significance in the fact that one of his informants in his search for Defoe bears the surname Flanders, thus recalling Defoe's notorious Moll? Surely not, one would have thought.

Canton's findings, it must be said, are scarcely very tangible, and his connections often so contrived, or merely whimsical, that one must have doubts about the method and the purpose of the quest, and indeed the intellectual credentials of psychogeography in general. If the book, nonetheless, however much one might question its substance, has a certain charm, is well written, and offers some evocative descriptions of the Essex countryside, this is surely more despite, rather than because of, its guiding preconceptions.

ROGER CALDWELL
by email

Dermot Healy

Sir:

Dermot Healy used to tell a story of walking into Sligo town, late in 1995, and being stopped and congratulated by a woman who pulled over in her car to tell him that she always knew he had it in him. A bit bemused, he asked what it was he was being congratulated for: 'The Nobel', he was told. Healy grew used to being mistaken for Seamus Heaney and said he was occasionally, years later, still being asked to sign copies of the Derry poet's work.

In *PNR* 219 Healy is again the victim of a case of mistaken identity, when the obituary credits him with founding Beaver Row Press, in fact the work of Dermot Bolger, another Irish poet-novelist.

Healy is best known for a memoir, *The Bend for Home* (1996), and his novels *A Goat's Song* (which won the 1995 Encore Award), *Sudden Times* (1999) and *Long Time No See* (2011). He also wrote a clutch of plays and five books of poetry, including *The Ballyconnell Colours* (1995), *What the Hammer* (1998) and *The Reed Bed* (2001): his poems had the same rhythmic inventiveness as his prose and a quick, wry humour. Minute glosses on the natural world ('Praise be the hares on Oyster', begins 'Hares on Oyster Island', 'as they curl on the stone beach / And look across at the Rosses! // Do they take that shape to look good – / A soul looking toward heaven / But not ready to go yet?') as well as melancholy and sometimes comic exile's letters, like this reflection on Philip Larkin: 'Better be abrasive in Hull / than go shouting "Go fuck yourself!" // to no one in particular / on a windy peninsula.'

After many years moving between Dublin, London and Belfast, he settled in a house at the edge of the Atlantic in County Sligo, where he also founded and edited the notable literary journal *Force 10*. He was 66.

JOHN MCAULIFFE
by email

VAHNI CAPILDEO

Reading Dante's Inferno in Port of Spain

The 'rabbit-throwing riots' which occurred in 1696 in an area of Oxfordshire that nowadays falls within David Cameron's constituency are recorded as having involved some ordinary people. These included a blacksmith, a gardener, and the yeoman William Stock, named as an alleged leader in digging out the rabbits live and hurling them (possibly chopped up) at the better half of the wealthy couple whose recent enclosure of land to build a mansion on Eynsham Heath had impeded access to furze, bracken, firewood, and coney meat.

Any mention of 'ordinary people' naturally leads to thoughts of poetry. However, such an incident – perhaps a seventeenth-century commonplace; arguably unacceptable today, when it might be understood less as an expression from the heart of the folk than as symptomatic of deviancies fitter for prose (Lionel Shriver or the *Guardian*) – could shake one's faith in the universality of human emotion across place and time, had one's faith not already been cracked by poetry books with and without annotations, and by poetry reviewers who, ignoring biography, misattribute, for example, nationality, as did a good British poet-reviewer who reassigned a good (Canada-based) Caribbean poet-scholar to Jamaica, 789 kilometres distant from his native Bahamas.

What if a sceptic about universality re-reads a canonical text like Dante's *Inferno* in three places – Italy, England, and Trinidad – and finds it each time equally but differently arresting? Might aspects of those locations draw out, or hint at, the poem's quasi-inexhaustible richness? Hurrying over the Ponte Vecchio, noticing how people catch at each other with voice and gesture only to whirl away into their separate preoccupations, I became hypersensitised to the *Commedia*'s dramatic qualities. Walking back from work, I found Dante's descriptions (the note of crane-song; the longed-for return of soft weather; variations on a savage wood) inviting attention outside their context, phrases like found poems transplanted into fenland December where silhouetted holly and mahonia prickle against the moon.

Tonight in Port of Spain the sleeper whose spine, disintegrating like a palm tree in the north-east trade winds, compresses her nerves, which then jerk her limbs independent of her volition, screams in her sleep. Loud, wordless pain pierces the walls. In this house, I am reading. Correspondingly, the pain in the *Inferno* lights up, revealing the thirty-four cantos as a construction of intricate cruelties by someone emerged from civil conflict and familiar with bodily hurt.

It is easy to credit the historical Dante, or the poem's 'Dante', with compassion – wouldn't either or both the journeying poet guided by Virgil, and the exiled sufferer in Ravenna, have insight into, and kinship with, the inhabitants of a Hell they traverse and create? – easy to numb oneself to the massive currents of power in the writing. 'Dante' in the poem insists on his helplessness, overloaded, fainting dead away; clinging to, carried by, his paternal Roman. The author Dante has taken control of past and future, scrap by human scrap, and makes no bones about putting the impressed or impressionable, tamed or docile reader through, or into, hell.

'Dante' knows when he acquires a traumatic memory. He declares it: never again will he cross icy water without recalling the sight of human faces turned doglike (hopeless, persevering, pleading, struck down, stretch-mouthed, clammy-eyed?) by freezing cold ['mille visi cagnazzi / fatti per freddo' (Canto XXXII)]. Even a reader who has not felt such temperatures may, if properly traumatised in turn by incorporating Dante's words, share that image, find it summoned up, should s/he ford a winter river.

If the pain-pierced wall in Trinidad moves me to look towards the window to regain focus (on the sufferer or on the book), my eye is met by white-painted arabesques, the safety grille known as 'burglar proof', long ago grown up around houses in nice areas. This triggers a memory. A respected lawyer told a story. He happened to be present, he claimed, at an interrogation in an enclosed space with little equipment. He was, he said, proud of helping by coming up with ways to use the burglar proof. Now the wrought metal becomes Dantesque, no longer signifying protection: someone else's shaking and screaming have stuck to it.

'Tell me...'. 'Who are you?' Appeals from 'Dante' to the trapped souls echo throughout *Inferno*. When is he bewildered, when after information? Towards the end, 'Dante' shows little compunction about refusing the favour of his attention, or even offering violence, to them. He is 'out of place' in being alive. They are forever 'out of place', on the wrong side.

Reading in some other city, I might not have linked Dante's *Inferno* to Elaine Scarry's *The Body in Pain* (OUP, 1987 [1985]). In her chapter on torture and interrogation as an exercise of dominance that destroys the victim's world and ability to refer to that world, Scarry speculates: 'for the duration of this obscene and pathetic drama, it is not the pain but the regime that is incontestably real, not the pain but the regime that is total, not the pain but the regime that is able to eclipse all else, not the pain but the regime that is able to dissolve the world' (p. 56). Does the *Inferno* operate like 'the regime'? Can the reader escape collusion in a Tuscan-centric scheme of looped divine and political punishments; collaboration via the sustaining of extreme image-making? Does the *Inferno* as drama or as lyrical mosaic yield to the *Inferno* as the engineering of trauma?

It could be said that any good poem affects the reader like this: dis- and re-connecting associations, re-shaping 'language' and 'world'. Nonetheless, with poetry as with sensation: the amount and detail of it will change the quality and definition of what it is. Seldom so much, so furiously, so long as the *Inferno*.

For, just as in Scarry's interpretation of a torture scenario 'room' comes to mean isolation and exposure, not shelter or sharing; 'refrigerator', 'chair', become weapons, not objects; 'wall', too, becomes a site of wounding, not the extension of a domestic embrace; and, by implication, a survivor's future rehabilitation into ordinariness is at least temporarily nonsense, unimaginable – just as Eynsham Heath nearly meant 'enclosure', 'ownership', 'lack', not 'openness', 'freedom', 'plenty' – so, after the long trip through the *Inferno*, the world is coloured by the book: few steps will seem unthreatened by a precipice; no neighbour exempt; trees not innocent but hung with corpses, strange fruit, the whole environment branching into bloody speech.

The seven words in which Virgil, Dante, and reader exit hell and see the starry sky are the last vibration of a tongue about to try on silence. It would be too arduous to take *Purgatorio* as immediately following. In between there must slip a volume of non-writing where such painful reverberations are stilled, before the possibility of music can make sense.

PAUL ROSSITER

The Weather in Tokyo

There have long been English-language poets at work in Japan, mostly in Tokyo or in the Kansai area of western Japan. Some of these are Japanese writers who choose to use English, a tradition that goes back at least as far as Nishiwaki Junzaburō, whose first two collections, *Spectrum* (London, 1925) and *Poems Barbarous* (Tokyo, 1930), were written in English; a greater number of these writers, however, are long-term resident Anglophone poets, of whom the late Cid Corman is the most famous.

From at least the 1980s on, writers in Tokyo have been supported by a series of small presses, the earliest of which, TELS Press, was a cooperative operating under the aegis of the rather grandly named Tokyo English Literature Society – in fact, an informal writers' workshop which met once a month in a municipal building in the Shinjuku district of Tokyo. The society also had a journal, *Printed Matter*, which published work by workshop members and others; founded in 1977 as an A4 mimeographed bimonthly, it went through various incarnations, culminating in the early 1990s in a sleek, well-printed, well-designed quarterly, and then in two blockbuster 250-page, A4-sized annuals in 1998 and 1999. In due course, the magazine spawned Printed Matter Press, which published six volumes of poetry (including my own first book) between 1991 and 1999. The magazine ceased publication in 1999, but the press – now privately owned – still exists, occasionally publishing work mostly in a neo-beat or spoken-word style.

Another press operating from the 1980s and into the twenty-first century was Drew Stroud's Saru Press (*saru* means 'monkey' in Japanese). Stroud, who later took the Japanese name Ryu Makoto, was a poet and a translator from Spanish, and the press specialised in English writing from Japan, translations from Japanese – Shuntaro Tanikawa's *Naked* (1996), for instance – and translations from Spanish and Latin American poets; sadly, since 2007 Drew Stroud's illness has prevented any further Saru publications. Yet another press, Ahadada Press, founded in 1998 by Jesse Glass, and specialising mostly in experimental work, also now seems to be dormant, although the associated online magazine *Ekleksographia* continues to be accessible.

So, with TELS long gone, Saru and Ahadada silent, and Printed Matter almost quiescent and – insofar as it is active – focusing mostly on neo-beat writing, there seemed room for a new press publishing mainstream and modernist writing. The aim of Isobar Press, which I established last year, is a simple one: to make English-language writing from Japan more widely available. Some English-language poets living in Japan have been published in the UK – Peter Robinson was published by Carcanet during the period when he lived in Sendai, for example, and Gavin Bantock is published by Anvil – but when seen from elsewhere, Japan often seems a distant and peripheral place. In fact, there are – and have been – many fine writers here, working in a variety of styles ranging from relatively traditional to modernist to experimental. The problem is that not many of these writers have books easily available, and one aim of the press is to make Japan more visible as a location for contemporary writing. Another aim of the press is signalled by its name, Isobar Press: the meteorological metaphor ('a line on a weather map joining points of equal pressure') is intended to suggest that even though the writers (all of whom are geographically centred in Japan in some sense) are located in very different places on the stylistic map, they are all nevertheless operating at equivalently high levels of poetic pressure. In other words, the press aims to represent both the variety and the excellence of work being written in English in Japan.

Isobar has so far published eight books by seven writers (one Irish, two British, and four American). Stylistically these range from *Arc Tangent* by Eric Selland, which clearly originates from a strongly modernist location on the stylistic map, to Denis Doyle's *The Rhododendron Forest*, which is technically and aesthetically the most traditional of the Isobar books so far. The other books occupy a variety of positions between these poles of *haibun*-like modernist prose-poem on the one hand, and formal verse on the other. Andrew Fitzsimons's *What the Sky Arranges: Poems made from the* Tsurezuregusa *of Kenkō* is a series of witty verse variations on the fourteenth-century prose work by Kenkō usually known in English as *Essays in Idleness*; Fitzsimons's second volume, *A Fire in the Head*, consists of a sequence of haiku written in the aftermath of the earthquake and tsunami of 2011. *A Great Valley Under the Stars* by Royall Tyler, the first book of original poetry by the award-winning translator of *The Tale of Genji*, is a book-length modernist poem reflecting different facets of a younger self. *The Insomniac's Weather Report* by the Kobe resident Jessica Goodfellow is a collection of formally various and scientifically informed lyrics. *Whispers, Sympathies, & Apparitions* is a selection of surrealistic and psychologically acute prose-poems by David Silverstein, who lived in Tokyo in the 1980s and 1990s, and who very prematurely died here in 1992. The eighth publication is my own collection, *From the Japanese*.

There are, and have been, many other poets than these working in English while living in, or otherwise strongly connected with Japan, including not only native English speakers, but also native speakers of Japanese who choose to write directly in English, and fine translators into English of contemporary Japanese poetry. There is also a vibrant community of contemporary Japanese-language poets waiting to be translated. Most of these writers – including, it seems, all contemporary Japanese-language poets other than Shuntaro Tanikawa – are hardly visible, if visible at all, to a wider English-language readership. Future plans for Isobar thus include not only continuing to publish Japan-related Anglophone writing, but also publishing English writing by Japanese authors, and developing a list of modern and contemporary Japanese poetry in translation.

Isobar Press can be found at http://isobarpress.com

SAM ADAMS

Letter from Wales

John Edmunds, a friend of many years' standing, spent a day with us recently, breaking his journey back to London. Some will remember him as a regular BBC TV newsreader, and he has also been prominent in theatre, as an academic and, more recently, as a translator of Lorca, *Four Major Plays* (for the OUP World's Classics series), and *Four French Plays – Corneille, Molière, Racine* (for Penguin Classics). We hadn't seen him for some time and there was a lot to talk about. One of the tales he told us concerned the novelist Richard Llewellyn (1906–83), author of more than twenty novels, but remembered for only one, *How Green Was My Valley*, his debut in the genre. First published in 1939 and an immediate bestseller, it has never been out of print. It garnered a huge international readership, has been translated into thirty languages and frequently reprinted in several of them: by the 1970s the bulk of the author's income came from translations. Llewellyn had a military bearing, acquired by service as a captain in the Welsh Guards in World War II and six years in the pre-war army, mostly in India, and was a tweedily stylish dresser. Much of his life after the war was spent travelling to collect stories and local colour, but he occasionally returned to Wales, where he had spent part of his boyhood with grandparents living in St David's, Pembrokeshire, and found in the history of the South Wales coalfield and the Griffiths family of Gilfach Goch the theme and setting of an enduringly memorable book. Those of my acquaintance who met him found little to like in him, perhaps because they sensed his habitual dissimulation. He hid his formative years, growing up in London and apprenticeship in the hotel-keeping and catering trade, as he did his real name, Richard David Vivian Llewellyn Lloyd, under a smokescreen of pretension.

In the 1970s, he wrote to Sir Goronwy Daniel, principal of UCW Aberystwyth, to say that he was available to tutor students during the summer term. As 'creative writing' did not exist at the time, John Edmunds, who, not long before, had been appointed professor of the newly created bilingual drama department, was invited to make appropriate arrangements for Llewellyn's extended visit. This was well nigh impossible, for by the time he arrived teaching was almost over and the students were either revising for exams or sitting them. When the famous author turned up for sessions there were no students; and when a few of them were cajoled into appearing, he didn't arrive. A public lecture was scheduled and advertised and a small audience cornered. Perhaps the latter took Llewellyn by surprise, because he came unprepared and in ten minutes had finished all he had to say. With his customary gruff courtesy the principal thanked the guest speaker, who liked to live in style, but in later life could not be relied upon to pay his way, or indeed, deliver what he promised.

Within the last week I have re-read two courtroom episodes in *How Green Was My Valley*. At least that was my intention, but once the book lay open on the table before me I was drawn to other scenes, and was soon adding to layers of marginalia from previous readings. The grip it has on my imagination has scarcely lessened since I first picked it up many years ago. When I arrived at them, the courtroom scenes were a little disappointing. I thought perhaps they would convey a flavour of the trials of miners during the strike of 1910–11

(mentioned in my previous Letter, *PNR* 218). They do not, but one is a fictionalised version of the successful case Joseph Griffiths brought against coal owners and management when he was financially penalised for union activity. In the novel, Davy, the narrator's brother and a union firebrand, sues the company for paying him less than the agreed minimum wage. The company argues that his money reflects his incompetence in the workplace but, because he is able to present before the judge years of carefully preserved pay dockets showing he has regularly earned several times the amount of the claim, he wins the case. Davy has already planned to emigrate to New Zealand, knowing there will be no more work for him in the Valley – the actual fate of Joe Griffiths.

While not so melodramatically lit as the action of the novel by Llewellyn's often rhapsodic, biblically inflected prose, newspaper accounts of the trial of miners more than a century ago are in their own way fascinating. So they seem to me at least, and I offer that as explanation for my return to this theme. I have just discovered these primary resources, the raw material of history, which are now generally available at 'Welsh newspapers online', a free treasury of digitised information, courtesy of the National Library of Wales. The *Weekly Mail*, a forerunner of today's *Western Mail*, was one of the papers to cover events in Gilfach Goch on 29 November 1910, where 'violence and intimidation' against William Gould, an assistant manager of the Britannic Colliery, was witnessed by his police escort, and on 24 December in Pontypridd, where some at least of the perpetrators were brought to trial. In Gilfach, Gould had been on his way to the (steam) engine house, where a worker named Rees Jones was feeding the fires to keep the pumps going and prevent the pit from flooding, when he was approached by a large and hostile crowd. A police witness testified: 'Some of them shouted, "Kill the _____." and "Chuck him in the river."' Gould himself claimed a number of men attacked him, striking him about the head, forcing him to the ground and kicking him until he promised to leave the valley. 'We will see you don't come back', came from the crowd. The defence lawyer pointed out that, apart from a minor bump on his face, Gould bore no sign of injury, and extracted from the police the admission that there had been 'laughing and chaffing as well as booing' among the crowd, but there was no mitigation: on 20 December, in good time for Christmas, two of Gould's assailants were jailed and several more convicted with fines.

The same newspaper confirms the daily attendance outside the court of several thousand miners, adding that on 14 December over ten thousand had gathered at the Rocking Stone, a famous (and still existing) landmark on the common overlooking Pontypridd. A photograph of the mass meeting showing thousands in the universal miners' uniform of Dai-cap and white muffler accompanies the text. Noah Rees, a respected miners' leader, tried to dissuade them from besieging the court, arguing that aggression would be 'suicidal' in view of the large force of military and police stationed in the town. The reporter estimated about half the assembly heeded his appeal. The rest marched into town as they planned, but there was to be no dramatic rescue of the defendants, who were spirited away from the courtroom by a back door.

All that occurred more than a century ago: how can it matter now? Data published in a recent academic study show that in 2012, the average number of jobs per hundred residents in Great Britain is 67; in the former coalfields as a whole, it is 50; in the South Wales coalfield it stands at 41. Perhaps because the communities of the south Wales valleys still suffer in the aftermath of what was thoughtlessly, peremptorily removed, that old lump of history still sticks in the throat.

VIDYAN RAVINTHIRAN

Gamini Salgado Revisited

The Sri Lankan critic Gamini Salgado may well have been this country's first non-white Professor of English – joining Exeter University in 1977, after studying at Nottingham. He wrote on both Renaissance literature and D.H. Lawrence, a strong influence on the style of his sadly out-of-print memoir, *The True Paradise*. Constructed posthumously of gathered fragments by Salgado's widow, Fenella Copplestone, it was published by Carcanet in 1993 – an extract had previously appeared in this magazine – and includes as an appendix his inaugural lecture at Exeter on 'Shakespeare and Myself'. Here Salgado argues for clear writing in academic criticism, a challenge to postcolonial norms which has all the personal authority one could wish for, and which should be taken seriously. He also defends the practice of learning poems off by heart – a term he prefers to any other, for 'if we remember what we love, we can also learn to love by the effort of remembering [...] in our educational activity we have lost any sense of the connection between memory and love'.

The reminiscences of *The True Paradise* are unashamedly lyrical. It deserves to be reprinted, and to be widely read, for its historical importance – I'm thinking here of Salgado's unique academic achievement, and his record of one middle-class boy's Buddhist-Sinhala upbringing prior to Independence, and the civil war. But it's also wonderfully written. Here Salgado describes, of the local temple, the reclining statue which occupied 'the entire back wall and reached, at the shoulders, right up to the ceiling':

> The even, ochre-coloured stone folds of the sleeping Buddha's robe fell away towards the enormous feet like ribbed sea-sand. I could not cover the nail of the big toe with both my palms. The vermilion lips seemed strangely out of place in the gentle, candle-coloured face.

The lovely orchestration of this passage – which I'd quote, if I could, at greater length (though really I want to give you the whole page, chapter, the book itself) – reveals the author's total control of sound, syntax and tone. The *o* sound prominent in the first sentence is picked up by 'big *toe*', as the astonishment of the child-observer is reinserted thrillingly and livingly into what might become a static description; the long *a* sound of that gigantic 'nail' generates in the final sentence a rhyme-sound linking 'place' and 'face'. Salgado learned the trick of repetition, or refrain, from Lawrence, whose poem 'Reading a Letter', for example, features both 'earth-coloured life' and 'chalk-coloured tulips'. Salgado's peculiarly estranged perception (it is of course the author himself who will soon be, culturally and geographically, 'out of place'; he knows, too, he's discussing a Ceylonese sculpture in stylised English prose) is similarly nuanced by the shift from the Buddha's 'ochre-coloured' robe to his 'gentle, candle-coloured' visage. This adjective takes a changed inflection if we remember its precursor – the soft jostling of 'gentle' against 'candle' also contributes to its judged exquisiteness.

Although *The True Paradise* is unfinished, such repetitions are deliberate – these aren't hiccups to be edited out – and are, from the perspective of style, as remarkable as the narrative arcs which make of Salgado's memoir a work of art, instead of straight autobiography. In 'A Journey to School', he's arrested for squeezing onto the footboard of a crammed train, and when asked by the authorities for his name, provides that of James Joyce's Stephen Dedalus. A portrait of the artist as a young man: the way in which this chapter moves from lyrical excitement to humiliation to eventual triumph also recalls Joyce's semi-autobiographical novel. Salgado captures marvellously the intonations of Ceylonese English, and is alert throughout his memoir to different linguistic registers and how class and context are expressed through diction. The town crier deploys a 'kind of pompous pseudo-classical Sinhalese, rather like that used by monks in their sermons', which are – skipping ahead a few pages – 'delivered in a uniform sing-song drone which was inescapably soporific'; the white Registrar-General who arrives to certify the marriage of Salgado's parents speaks not 'the English read in Father's beloved books but a dry airless tongue, a language clipped, filed and orderly, a bald impersonal necessary language'. And on that train journey to school, 'a trousered and solar-topeed gentleman in the corner seat' takes the boy's bag, but is disappointed by the copy of *Portrait* it contains:

> 'Once upon a time and a very good time it was there was a moocow coming down along the road met a nicens little boy named baby tuckoo... I say, I say, what is all this nonsense, man? You're sure you are not bringing your baby brother's Beacon Infant Reader by mistake, hah?'

This 'Joyce James', the gentleman avers, must 'be American – English authors know how to write better than that. Not even a single comma or full stop anywhere that I can see. After all their own bloody language no?'

Joyce is of course an Irish writer, and this humorous anecdote makes a serious point. Salgado shares with Stephen Dedalus his politically nervous relationship with English, as well as his final move away from an aesthetic of suspicion and towards a liberated cosmopolitan freedom which claims that language as one's own. The young boy is amazed by the verbal gymnastics of his lawyer de Silva (hired with a couple of rupees he was meant to spend on biryani at a cricket match); 'a man who only a few minutes ago spoke in the English everybody used in Ceylon, sounding now like "Sheridan's Impeachment of Warren Hastings" in my father's *Gems of English Eloquence*':

> 'Your Honour, we have here a truly piteous case of oppression and harassment. Consider this young lad setting off at break of day with shining morning face, eager to arrive at his alma mater and there imbibe the invigorating waters of learning from the Pyrennean springs.'

The magistrate looked imploringly at Mr de Silva but he was too far gone for imploring looks.

> 'Education, Your Honour, is the inalienable right of every citizen of this resplendent isle. It is the cornerstone of our democratic system, the stepping stone on which each and every one of us rises from our dead self to fresh fields and pastures new.'

Colonial English is an aspirational, a power-perfumed, obsequious, corrupted language. Yet this hilarious passage turns de Silva – with his bonkers mélange of literary and classical allusion – into, really, a Wildean hero of style. The allusion to *As You Like It* – the 'schoolboy with his satchel / And shining morning face, creeping like snail / Unwillingly to school' – is particularly important, given Salgado's deep scholarly interest in Shakespeare, whose plays his parents used to read aloud to each other. Passages like this reveal the origins of his own fascination with not just the English language but *literary* English – impassioned, poetic, even over-the-top. His own lyricism accepts, and does something intelligently nuanced with, an impure inheritance. The 'true paradises' – Salgado's epigraph is from Proust – are those we have lost, and the style of this book acknowledges the author's distance from a homeland which has changed dramatically and which he knows he can only imperfectly remember. It must be restored to our bookshelves, not only for the unique sensibility it captures, and which will not come again, but also for the example it holds out to writers and critics of any background interested in the true, the personal connection between history and style.

FRANK KUPPNER

From a White Notebook (1)
(or: Notes Towards a Discussion of Everything)

1. Hmm. Listing actual *All-That-Is*es in terms of their inherent probabilities surely ought not to be *quite* so time-consuming?

2. Yes, well – what else is the actual universe *supposed* to be like?

3. At the very least, surely the entire Universe must be the cause of any *x*?

4. Still: if nothing existed, it would no doubt be inaccurate to *say* that nothing existed. (And certainly that *Nothing* existed! (But this is indeed much ado about next to nothing.))

5. Anyway, why isn't there *something else*, instead of either this or nothing?

6. Presumably that which just happened, could just have happened any way it liked? (Not that it *really did like* (or, indeed, *was* like) anything.)

7. Perhaps it all started (or most of it did, or nearly did) when two different sorts of Nothing clashed? (Well, why not? (Or combined?))

8. Nothing can teach us what God is.

9. Yes. Certain types of Nothing(ness) seem to be incommensurable too.

10. Still. 2) Nothing can teach us what God is.

11. Or perhaps the very concept of Nothing existing (and therefore of being something – anything) is itself already a contradiction-in-terms? (Or is this pretty much nothing too?)

12. But let's see. What is the difference between a non-existent cat and a non-existent dog? (And what do they have in common? (Their non-existence, perhaps?))

13. More broadly: what would differentiate a non-existent Universe from a non-existent anything else? (An ill-fitting wig, for instance.) (Or, indeed, from absolutely anything else at all? (A non-existent Universe is not a sort of Universe either, is it?))

14. A 'non-existent anything-at-all' is a contradiction-in-terms, is it not? Are we not at least sure of that? A non-existent *x* is not some sort of actual *x* – any more than it is some sort of actual *y*. (Where *x* and *y* are any two real things – presumably different things. A non-existent God is no more a sort of God than it is a sort of Dog. Or, indeed, Cat. The breed is immaterial. (As, indeed, technically speaking, is everything else. (In short, Anselm, a non-existent *x* is not really any sort of letter at all, is it?)))

15. Oh, for God's sake – the entire Universe has let me down, darling. Why should you be any different?

16. And yet in terms of *What Else* is one to discuss the Absolutely Everything?

17. But it doesn't really matter much whether you choose to call the Unknown: Pater, Father, Dad, Daddy, the Old Man or, indeed, *Pop*. It's *still* not your father.

18. And how can an utterly mysterious explanation be a true explanation anyway? (Indeed, how can it be an explanation at all?)

19. (Then again: how can anyone reasonably blame God for it? He only created it all.)

20. This God, it would seem, is a sort of Black Hole with an opinion on things like flattery and ethical banking.

21. That which is inaccessible to us could presumably be or have been or will be *absolutely anything*. No? (How can we *possibly* tell?)

22. Talking inappropriately about the Indescribable!

23. Show me first that it is at least actually possible. After all, it surely requires very little faith as such to disbelieve the impossible. (*Even less faith*, perhaps it would be safer to say.)

24. Actual things are the actual things. One would just like to know: Where, with God, is there ever the actual (*primum* or) *secundum quid*? Which is to say, the thing which is just God – God and nothing else at the same time besides? Not something else, identified (metaphorically, etc.) with God. (What, one might ask, is the *quidditas Dei*?)

But it seems there is no physical object which is also (part of) God and not something else material too. In other words, in physical reality (i.e. in all but conceptual reality) what can be called 'God' can always also primarily be identified as something else first. (And this something else, however astonishing, is just what it actually is.)

25. And how can *Everything* [meaning *absolutely everything* – all there is, including God, or whatever the term is] have a meaning in terms of something else? *Anything* else? (After all, by mere straightforward definition, unless I'm missing something, there is still no something else.) And what meaning then can it have in terms of itself? How can any utter totality genuinely justify or explain or give meaning to itself? (If *x* is significant, it is significant in terms of the less significant *y* and *z*. It can't just *be significant* in itself. (Can it?))

26. But, for all that, and whatever the truth of these great little matters might be, Life very soon floods out all at once and limitlessly in more directions than we had ever supposed could even exist. Over and far, far beyond the bounds which our narrow, theoreticising, inexperienced youthful anticipations had set for it. Yes, the complex but, for all that, ultimately neat canal system we had thought to investigate ever more authoritatively turns out in fact to be something more like an endless, featureless, planetless, absolutely never-heard-of-you, stop-at-nothing level ocean (within an ocean, within an ocean, within an ocean –

27. And no life, be it never so alert or well-informed, knows even 1% of 1% of 1% [etc. etc.] of what is or was happening around it. (Or, indeed, is even remotely aware of this. (Or indeed, for that matter, of what is going on *within* it. (Of what life itself involves. (My apologies if all this already seems as painfully self-evident to you as it sometimes does to me.))))

'Noctilucent' and Other Poems

Noctilucent

We cross the garden: slant sun, slack tide of shadow.
He is remembering woods below San Pietro, the ragged end of a war.
Soldier and red-cloaked shepherd on the road,
the old man stilling his dog, waiting in the white road.
He watches now: his stumble down, wading knee-deep
through tangled nets of dazzle, spills of shade,
to the soft chalk curve between the trees,
the red cloak burned in his eyes. His hand, unsure.

He says, *If a person walking raises his hand*
he sees the shadow of each finger doubled.

Trees slide down to lap us, attentive to our solitudes,
until the hollow dark is filled with memory of light –
fluorescence, phosphor glow, poppies' slow burn;
ghostlights to guide our double-going.

James Turrell's Deer Shelter Skyspace, *Yorkshire Sculpture Park*

Temple, lake, deer shelter triangulate arcadia's vanishing point.
Leaves skitter in the empty summerhouse; beyond the sliding water
shadows herd beneath the arches of the deer shelter.

*

Walk into a concrete silo open to the sky.
There's nothing to see here.
What does nothing look like?

Flying over the curve of the Painted Desert, air opening like water,
barrel-rolling over fathomless sky in Pyramid Lake; farm lights at night far-flung as stars.
At dawn, the hangar shining: a memory of sunlight on a wall.

*

7.30am: mussel shell; split of gold; skirl lifting and spilling,
1pm: ragged pennants; vapour swags; sting of rinsed shorelines,
5pm: damson stain; smoke feathers; ink.

That this is nothing – how do we live with this?
We stare like deer into the event of light.

In the jagged months

In the jagged months when you lost even lost
and knew it, you gave up arguments and grievance –
those intricate machines you had built for years,
their ratchets kept oiled and sharp to run sweet –
and broke glass. Your hand was a wrecking bar
smashing ice on a pond, you splintered yourself open
to haul down through a mulch of black leaves for what lay

in the sump of winter's slow bruising.
You had seen them, bent under four o'clock dark
throwing your box in the pond, the box that held your streets,
your tools, the white leaves of your books, your days of the Arno –
days when green branches swaying upside-down in a pool
rose like a promise through the pliant skin of water
which opened to your hand, and was whole again.

The years before

That time my grandmother went to the sixpenny hop
in the years before they became the years before
Tom Baxter and Rabbity Dixon played through the roiling night
of longways and hands across down the middle back again and
turn and *K-K-K-Katy* and *Haste to the Wedding*

      and oh how

Tom could play the birds out of the trees with that old concertina
pouncing and bucking high jinking over the honk and growl
of what moved in the forest at the edge of the tune
Rabbity sharp and quick as his traps to snare the beat
sending the tambourine's silver starlings whorling

      over and over

towards a room she walked into one afternoon
when Will ran into the kitchen *come down to the shop*
you must come and see this there's a man here says he's a
and there among boxes of collars and gloves resting palm to palm
the day quietly folding its hours away she shook hands with a lion tamer

      and heard again

all that wild blaze reeling and swooping
heel and toe stamp turn about and
Goodnight Ladies and oh *The Girl I Left Behind Me*
somewhere out in the forest rough music rising
in the year that was becoming the year before

Watching a nineteenth-century film in the twenty-first century

Adolphe, Mrs Whitely and Harriet wait in the garden
still in an angle of sunlight
that will never fall across the bay window
or slice the mottle of summer-weighted shade.

They take four steps to turn into the shadows
at the edge of their afternoon;
four steps wheeling past us – skirts swinging, coats flapping –
a breath's length away as we watch in their dark.

Their bodies are a shower of particle-scatter,
their footfall a trick of snapshooting time.
They flicker to the edge of the frame at twelve frames a second
for two seconds for ever
through a speckle and grain of sound too distant to reach us:
Adolphe counting their steps – and turn –

a neighbour's shout, a laugh, a road beyond the hedge spooling out, out
into the smash and roar of the world that's falling towards us.

Hushings

hushing: to silence; to wash out mineral deposits by releasing a torrent of water

Clough

Up on the tilt where the moor begins its slide into Lancashire
and the village shrinks back at the sour peat out past the turbines
we're trying to make sense of what isn't here:
a clean sweep of mountain wasted sheer into wind,
glaciers that snouted down from the north in a roar of rubble and sinkholes,
burst open, sluicing green meltwater, drifted off into hag fleece,
goits and headraces, limekilns, the yellow drench of their smoke.
There's a whole phantom moor in this washed-out clough
and we're feeling our way by echo location
towards a hurly of diggers and carters, stokers, women hefting picks.
Every winter the light falls more thickly, layer upon layer.
The hushings are deepening by one millimetre a year.

Ore

There are things we remember only because of their absence,
like a word I need for the light that blows in from the west
after rain, or the hollow house in a field of bleached grass
we walked to one hot afternoon – and now we've both lost the path back
you think I've imagined the moment we pushed open the door
onto summers of butterflies faded and heaped like old letters,
their dry sift over the floor, their tiny stir in the draught.
My father once told me a secret he'd learned as a child:
the exact spot on the pavement where, if you stood very still,
you could hear the river running beneath the street –
a trap opening onto something implacable that would always be waiting.
He remembered that all his life, but not where to stand.

HORATIO MORPURGO

More Than One View of Somewhere in Central Ukraine

When *Animal Farm* was distributed among Ukrainian refugees in 1947, the translation came with a specially written preface. Orwell wrote it for no payment within a fortnight of being asked. He told a friend that he regarded Ukrainian Displaced Persons as 'a godsent opportunity for breaking down the wall between Russia and the West'. He wrote more freely about the novel in that preface than he ever had before or ever did again.

'Russia and the West' are at odds once more and, together with the Grad rockets, wildly off-target talk about the 1930s and 1940s is flying in all directions. In the din of our own information wars, the trouble taken with that preface is worth recalling. The translator made only a couple of alterations. Orwell wrote 'I have never visited the Soviet Union'. His translator changed the phrase to 'I have never visited Russia' and in a letter explained why: 'about half of the prospective readers are Western Ukrainians, who were Polish citizens until 1939…'

He was gently pointing out that, for many Ukrainians in 1947, being from 'the Soviet Union' was very recent and a very sensitive issue. The same letter explains that the publishers, by contrast, were 'Soviet Ukrainians', meaning Ukrainians from the centre and east of the country. They were supporters of the October revolution disillusioned by Stalin's 'Bonapartism' and by 'Russian nationalistic exploitation of the Ukrainian people'. To such people, the translator went on, 'Britain's socialist effort' was deeply important.

Animal Farm was, then, originally part of that Europe-wide search for a new start. The story which we all think we know was intended as comment on recent and current events, and was 'eagerly read' as exactly that. The pigs and Mr Pilkington staring across the table at each other *was* the Teheran Conference of 1943, taking place even as Orwell put his story together. To re-read *Animal Farm* now is to be reminded of what writing about current affairs can be. It's a reminder we could surely use.

There were other reasons why Orwell was so eager to reach a Ukrainian audience. Manor Farm's revolutionary transformation into Animal Farm is, as every twelve-year-old once knew, an allegory of the Russian revolution. The 'Englishness' of the story's setting has tended to conceal, though, especially perhaps from twelve-year-olds, that it is more specifically a satire on agricultural collectivisation. That process was nowhere carried out with more cruelty than it had been in Soviet Ukraine. English literature's best known fable about revolution is connected by a kind of underground passage to the Ukrainian countryside.

The European landscape is riddled with a whole network of such tunnels, much of it sadly now fallen into disrepair. The time has been, not so long ago, when it connected up all the countries involved in this present dispute. One of Orwell's most famous essays was a reading of Tolstoy through two Shakespeare characters. His *Nineteen Eighty-Four* was, as he acknowledged, a response to Yevgeny Zamyatin's *We*, a novel which was, in turn, heavily influenced by Zamyatin's reading of H.G. Wells when he worked in Britain as a shipbuilder.

What much of the present shrilling about Ukraine announces, above all, is a world which has completely forgotten where those tunnels are, or doesn't even know, rather, that they are there at all. And yet it is a world which sounds to me uncannily like the telescreen and Two Minutes' Hate. Sentences and 'stories', pictures and captions become little more than opportunities for pressing certain well-worn buttons. Knowing one another's literature, by contrast, allowed and might surely still allow people of good will, in any country, to by-pass their ruling caste, to make oblique appeal to the consciousness of other peoples.

It is time to reopen some of those tunnels. Or to remind ourselves, at least, of their existence.

*

Of the world in which Joseph Conrad learnt to walk, very little now remains at Terekhove, in Central Ukraine. Acres of weed-grown concrete mark the site of the old collective. The large office block in the village, from which the farm was once administered, is now derelict, though part of its ground floor has been converted into a village shop. Teenagers hang about outside at the weekend and the effigy of a Soviet bruiser still presides over the scene. Conrad might have been consoled in some measure to find that he is not entirely forgotten. The small museum, crammed with editions in every conceivable language, is tended by an extravagantly well-read guardian.

Conrad's parents were living in Terekhove when their son was born but his actual birthplace was, according to the only surviving record, in the nearby town of Berdychiv. There is, though, a record of his arrival more revealing than any birth certificate. It is a poem written for the occasion by his father, in 1857, and it plunges us straight into young Jozef's personal drama as well as the history of this region.

To my son, in the 85th year of the Muscovite oppression, it reads, the 'Muscovite oppression' being a reference to Russia's seizure of this territory from Poland in 1772. *Baby son*, the poem goes on, *tell yourself / You are without land, without love, / Without country, without people, / While Poland – your mother is entombed.*

For their part in fomenting unrest in the Russian Empire, Conrad's parents were driven into exile and then into early graves. This circumstance surely goes some way to explain the growing boy's 'mysterious vocation' to a life in the British Merchant Navy and his determination to forge such a drastically new identity. The young scapegrace was a riddle to the uncle charged with his upbringing. When Conrad later wrote that it had been his aim to 'make Polish life enter English literature', he probably meant several things. One of the things that certainly entered English literature through him was a tragic view of what empires, all empires, do to people. The world he was born into in Berdychiv had supplied him with sobering early experience of this.

His relationship with Russia was and would remain a troubled one, though tempered, like Orwell's, by a profound regard for its writers. *Under Western Eyes*, shot through with a very Polish suspicion of the Russian state, is plainly also, among other things, a tribute to both *Crime and Punishment* and *The Devils*.

In 'Autocracy and War', written in 1905, Conrad compares the Russian and German imperialisms already then squaring up, as he saw it, for a fight that would be quite unlike anything seen before. In the new century, wars will be 'fought out differently', with 'the savage tooth and claw obstinacy of a struggle for survival. They will make us regret the time of dynastic ambitions, with their human absurdity moderated by prudence and even by shame, by the fear of personal responsibility and the regard paid to certain forms of conventional decency.' He saw what was coming as an age in which this new type of war would gain a hold over the public imagination as never before. In 'The Shadow-Line' (1915) he would allegorise Europe's new wasting sickness just as it took hold.

*

The baroque dome of Berdychiv's Carmelite monastery was hit by a shell in 1941 and the Germans converted its crypt into a prison for Jews. At the back of the building was an execution ground. A monument marks the site of a mass grave. Just across the road from that monastery's entrance was Yakti. Blocks of flats now occupy the site. This was the neighbourhood chosen to serve as the ghetto into which the town's Jewish population was driven shortly after the Germans arrived. Five mass graves just outside the town were filled in a single day with people who had been marched there from Yakti that morning. A monument, its inscription in Hebrew and Ukrainian, stands nearby on a grass plot above the river.

Jewish Berdychiv has, for what it is worth, a finer memorial than black granite will ever furnish. *The Family Mashber*, written in Yiddish through the 1930s and 1940s, will remind any English reader of *The Mayor of Casterbridge*. Any Russian is sure, and with better reason, to hear undertones of *The Brothers Karamazov*. It is in fact neither. Written by another native of the place, it was intended, rather, 'for the sake of historical clarity', as a lovingly detailed tribute to the community in which 'Der Nister', its author, had been raised.

Der Nister shows us respectable folk and their fine houses, religious enthusiasts in their hovels, the Polish gentry in their cups. All these he aims and eerily succeeds in bringing before the reader. The atmosphere is almost sociological: the town's market stallholders, its bar-owners and kitchen servants, doctors, dreamers and cobblers, its mentally ill, its hired thugs and government spies – each of these is minutely described.

There is no explicit mention of the looming catastrophe. It is, however, given to one of the novel's most troubled characters to dream one night that the whole town is lifted into the sky, turned upside down and shaken until all the furniture out of all the homes, all the goods out of all the shops, all the Torah scrolls out of all the synagogues and all the town's Jews lie burning in a great dusty heap below. Only the church tower is left as it was.

It may be objected that the literary culture I'm speaking of here is elitist or nostalgic. But one thing *The Family Mashber* abundantly does is show how people, even as they disagree, as they hustle and help and hinder one other, can meanwhile share the places where they live, the scene of their common story. That is hardly elitist and is certainly more than our telescreens know how to do. You might call it nostalgic but isn't that ability to cohabit just what we need to be relearning at the moment?

*

To the Red Army advancing in 1943, capturing Berdychiv was as crucial as it had been to the Wehrmacht two years earlier. As a railway hub it was 'the key to Lvov' (i.e. the west of Ukraine). Kiev, as one general put it, could 'breathe freely again' only once this town had been taken. Travelling with the Russians was a writer already well known for his reportage and fiction.

Though Vasily Grossman had written from the front line at Stalingrad, and would recast his experiences there in fictional form, it was the recapture of this provincial town which became, in a sense, the pivot round which his whole life turned. In the same year that Conrad was writing 'Autocracy and War', even as anti-Semitic pogroms raged across the Russian Empire, the year after Der Nister left Berdychiv to avoid conscription in the war against Japan, Grossman was born in the same town to a family of secular Jews.

An absentee father, precarious dependence on wealthy relations, resentment at the small town and its religiosity – all these left him unsentimental about the place. He satirised it in letters and articles he wrote in his twenties, though he remained in contact with his mother and it was a short story about the town which first brought him to public attention. Conrad had fled westwards, to make his home in a maritime empire. Der Nister headed north for the large Jewish communities around the Baltic. Grossman went east, to opportunities being afforded now to Jews as they never had been before, in the great cities of the newly created Soviet Union.

Returning in middle age, to the little place he had scorned, and to the certainty that his mother lay in one of those pits by the airfield, it was above all remorse that he felt. He would for the rest of his life reproach himself for not having done more to get her out. His personal involvement in the tragedy is not mentioned in 'The Murder of the Jews of Berdichev', which he wrote for *The Black Book of Russian Jewry*. But it was in transcribing what witnesses and survivors told him in his home town that he became the first writer to describe what we now call the Holocaust. He would before long, at Treblinka, be the first man to describe a death camp. His account was used as testimony at Nuremberg.

The limits of our ability to comprehend have their origins, Grossman would write, in psychological defence mechanisms. These mechanisms represent 'a positive characteristic of the human consciousness, since it protects people from modern torment and madness. This limitation is at the same time a malevolent characteristic of our consciousness, because it makes us thoughtless, permitting us to forget...' His mother's murder would haunt Grossman to the end.

The first scholarly study of what happened in Berdychiv in September 1941 appeared only in 2011, in *Die Dynamik des Tötens*, by a young German researcher, Michaela Christ. Her account makes clear that the 'complacency' Grossman reproached so bitterly in himself was shared by many in the town. From written documents and interviews, she has assembled a view of the situation there as it unfolded from 1939 onwards. How was it, she asks, that two thirds of the town's Jewish population stayed on even as the Germans advanced? There were, of course, many answers, the vast majority of which we will never know. The very young and very old had to be looked after. Not everyone had friends or relations they could rely on elsewhere.

But above all, what the Germans were about to do was simply inconceivable in advance, to a major novelist or anyone else. In their decision-making, people drew on what they knew, as we all continually do. Ukrainians, Russians and Jews alike assumed that this would be a pogrom like those of the past – frightening enough, to be sure, for those being targeted, but relatively brief and leaving essentially intact the many social continuities of a settlement where peoples had been co-habiting for centuries.

Even a veteran of Stalingrad was stunned by the malignity of what actually happened. Grossman would in due course arrive at conclusions about the Soviet state which made his books unpublishable there in his lifetime, ruined his career and finally destroyed his health. Its earlier commitment to Jewish emancipation soon faltered. Der Nister died in Siberia in 1950 having been denounced as a bourgeois reactionary. Grossman would argue that the Soviet Union, through its organised famines and purges and labour camps, had shared fully in the common civilisational collapse of Berdychiv and Treblinka. To which we might add the names Dresden and Hiroshima.

*

Another Russian writer struggling to comprehend what overtook his world in the twentieth century put it like this: 'Macbeth's self-justifications were feeble – and his conscience devoured him. Yes, even Iago was a little lamb, too. The imagination and spiritual strength of Shakespeare's evil-doers stopped short at a dozen corpses. Because they had no *ideology*. Thanks to *ideology*, the twentieth century was fated to experience evildoing on a scale calculated in the millions.'

Far from absolving his own country from this charge Alexandr Solzhenitsyn compared its efforts to engage with its past very unfavourably with West Germany's 86,000 convictions for war crimes. 'A country which has condemned evil 86,000 times from the rostrum of a court,' he wrote, 'and irrevocably condemned it in literature and among its young people year by year, step by step, is purged of it.'

Grossman did find a language to engage with this other than reportage, of which he was, incidentally, a master. In *Life and Fate* he attempted to reconstruct life in the ghetto from which his mother was led to her death. Through the thoughts and impressions of a female doctor trapped in the town, he reimagines the speed and confusion of the German arrival, the baffled procession of people suddenly now defined only by their ethnicity, carrying their allowance of possessions through the town under armed guard.

Men are taken 'to dig potatoes' and never return. The woman writes knowing this will be her last letter. Rumours circulate about pits being dug at the edge of town. Everyone *knows*. And yet they get their stoves fixed and their clothes and shoes mended in readiness for winter. They get their hair

cut, they set up schools. This hope they evince is 'something quite irrational and instinctive'. All of these varied activities are fed by a common source, 'the life instinct itself, blindly rebelling against the fact that we must all perish without trace'. 'Blind' because it could not, or would not, rather, see that a whole world of 'marriage customs, proverbial sayings and Sabbaths' was about to disappear. Even here, though, life *would* 'stir again', and she urges her son above all to *live*, be a part of that life to come.

The entire novel, to which this scene is so central, is dedicated to his mother. When the film-maker Fred Wiseman turned this chapter into a play, *La dernière lettre/ The Last Letter*, he set it on a blank stage, arguing that with minor changes it could be about Rwanda or Bosnia or Timor or anywhere else. He told an interviewer, with a rather glib universalism perhaps, that its essential contents were not tied to Ukraine or anywhere in particular.

*

Reportage, scholarship, fiction, drama, film – might all of these not help, now, in the search for a language that is not complicit in the violence? Journalism jabs its finger at 'them'. The piece I ended up writing earlier this year about Ukraine was more of the same. It might be described as 'reverse journalism'. Reverse journalism is language which jabs its finger, however justifiably, at other people jabbing theirs *and imagines it has thereby solved the problem*. The right words for this do not come so easily.

They do not necessarily come at all. Even in this provincial corner, a long way from the actual war zone, my bus to Berdychiv was continually stopping at road-blocks. On the day I went to see those burial mounds out by the airfield, I found myself in the midst of an artillery brigade exercising on the edge of town. My blank staring at five memorial plaques in succession was accompanied by the creaking and screeching of caterpillar tracks in the middle distance. This was May. It's a certainty those guns have since been deployed in the east.

The Carmelite monastery, its restored dome visible from far out in the surrounding countryside, was returned to the Catholic Church in 1991. Its crypt was used as a gym after the war but parishioners used it as their church while the building above them was slowly restored. The town has its selling points. Balzac married the love of his life here. Chopin studied nearby. Isadora Duncan danced in the theatre which is now the town's former cinema.

One part of the monastery complex houses a music school. Another outbuilding will soon be home to a new Joseph Conrad Museum, courtesy of a Polish foundation. Due to open earlier this year, this was deemed politically tricky and has been delayed.

The Ukrainian nun who has overseen that museum's installation opened the place up for me and a retired history teacher from the town was on hand to interpret. I was admiring its interactive touch-screen displays, the slide show and the short film, when a dreadful shrilling, a sudden clamouring broke out somewhere very close by.

I turned to find my hosts covered in embarrassment, engaged in panic-stricken struggles with a remote control. They had meant to cue the sound of ocean waves gently lapping but had hit the button for something else. The history teacher searched in vain for the word, then suddenly had it: 'Seagulls!'

Yet the sound had been, for a moment, quite unrecognisable, though I hear it all the time in my home town. It's a paradox to some, that a man regarded as one of the great writers about the sea first saw the light of day far inland, in a little town in central Ukraine. Perhaps the confusion is our own. Perhaps it comes of overplaying the tales of maritime adventure which his publisher required of him, while under-estimating both Conrad's significance as a political novelist and the role of his origins in that.

It was, he wrote, from an 'unconscious response to the still voice of the inexorable past' that the characters of his fiction were 'remotely derived'. Watching an empire destroy his parents determined Conrad's subsequent development as an artist and he understood this very well. The experience gave him his distinctive insight into his adopted country's imperial assault – one that was carried out largely by sea – upon Africa and Asia.

Heart of Darkness is, famously, the story of a search for Mr Kurtz. Kurtz is the agent of a European company. A charismatic, he has established a personality cult and a hellish mini-state on the Upper Congo, and is rumoured to be ill. The story is told by Marlow, the man sent to persuade him to return home. Kurtz himself collapses into megalomaniac ravings and dies on the steamboat as it carries him downstream. He is buried in 'a muddy hole' by the river.

But the image of Kurtz with which Marlow returns to Europe is a figure on a stretcher 'opening his mouth voraciously, as if to devour all the earth with all its mankind'. What has broken down in Kurtz, Marlow repeatedly reflects, is all restraint. Europe's future wars, Conrad felt sure, would be a delayed revisiting upon Europe of its shameless predations elsewhere, its abandonment of all restraint.

Heart of Darkness is perhaps now best known through its cinematic translation to American empire, namely to the Vietnam of Francis Ford Coppola's *Apocalypse Now*. In both versions the breakdown of restraint is close to the dark heart of the matter. As a theme, this recurs in writings about the wars and revolutions which Conrad already saw coming in 1905. In the Soviet Union the state 'liberated people from the chimaera of conscience', as Grossman would later put it. In Berdychiv as administered by Kommandeur Martin Besser of Polizeibattaillon 45, in Mr Kurtz's Congolese fiefdom, in all the ways these have been represented and translated, what are they, ultimately, other than studies in the breakdown of all restraint and the breakdown of human identity which follows?

*

Back in the village where young Jozef learnt to walk, a cuckoo is calling and the caretaker scythes round a school building in the weekend quiet. A small space near its front entrance is marked off by a low fence, as if it was once a memorial garden. It is tulip time in Ukraine: this little rectangle is ablaze with scarlet, but whom or what did these blooms celebrate in tulip-times gone by?

The former focus of the arrangement is still in place – it's a small granite plinth with its inscription very thoroughly scratched out. I could decipher nothing and the caretaker for his part could not recall. He could show me, though, an overgrown slope at the back of the building, where the obelisk which once stood atop it lay on its side.

Well, let it lie there, let it sink every year a little deeper into the leaf-mould, I thought, just where it was indecorously dumped. Let the caretaker not recall, let the splendid title remain illegible. Will the world really miss a few lines of Soviet or post-Soviet bombast? I even wondered if some wise educationalist might have deliberately set up this vacated plinth just where children will find it without too much difficulty.

Whatever it once celebrated, let this stump of a monument, in Joseph Conrad's first home, serve a chastened new purpose now. I move that it be re-dedicated to the memory of Europe's literary underground, to that network of tunnels which once connected up any little place with all the big questions. Cured of the telescreen, ever warier of its button-pressing, ever readier to entertain second thoughts, may we re-learn restraint in word and action.

LYNETTE ROBERTS

A Letter to the Dead

(A lost poem in memory of Dylan Thomas)

To you Dylan with my own voice I pay tribute
With as natural a grace as though you were near,
Remembering in a dark night, your hand in mine
When you told me to think of myself, to go abroad
And over the bounds with my poetry: to care not a fig
Pig or jig for anyone, for it was Rabelais all the way, or
Then drew out the lines, the sonorous images
Of my own work that pleased your heart and eye:
                    ...light birds sailing
          A ploughed field in wine
          Whose ribs expose grave treasures
          Inca's gilt-edged mine,
          Bats' skins sin-eyed woven
          The long-nosed god of rain...
So many years ago, the poem I would forget.
How many years was this?
Then followed the war, correspondence between us;
And you became best man at the 'Show'
Which turned out to be, not exactly happy but worthwhile,
And your head was flooded with the wedded words
Of pomp, fruit and carnal rectitude,
Caitlin patient, gentle, smiling at your side.
We have your signature to this, and photo in the Western Mail.
And we crossed the Estuary and visited or stayed at your domain,
Sending messages ahead with the ferryman, ringing his bell
To carry us on his back and row us in his cormorant boat,
While we, the lesser ones in the humble dwelling
Paying three and six a week to your four-storied house
Invited you, or unexpectedly found you both
Wandering in the neighbouring fields or lifting the iron gate.
Drinking and drinking, I have never done so much drinking,
And declared I would never do it again.
But you and he and they and she would insist,
And at it again, in order to discuss, listen,
Or conjure a word from you, and up with the glass again.
But what mattered: or what was remembered:
Cherished just then: the reading of those Anglo-Saxon poems
Which I gave you, 'the first time you had seen them' you said,
Riddles on our lives: the half written poem, the concentration
And discipline of your behaviour to your so eloquent a craft:
Or walking up to me, your mind tight with the unsprung words,
Was I the 'Bird woman' then? 'What bird is that?' you would say,
'And that? And that?' impetuously as they trilled and winged away
Sound and feather out of sight. It was on a cliff overlooking
Your Boathouse remember? Whimbrel, sandpiper and curlew I replied
And marveled that you did not know. '*I want to know about birds?*'
Was your repeated reply. Then rising out of that flowing Bay
Seven years later, the birds *yours*, were lifted on to the page,
Recreated, made new, with us for ever.
Then in a span of time ... not seeing ... in the years of grief,
Until my caravan pitched in the graveyard
Where your body now lies, stood for as long as Eternity,
Or so it seemed to me then. The spirits in it rising
Over my distress and stress of doom.

At such unexpected moments we met,
In ship's pub and sea pubs drinking, and at it again
If only to be alive with you, was there no end to this?
Drinking and drinking, for I hated the damn stuff,
Until the evil spell cast upon me drove us apart
I to another region away from the duck green forests
Darkened by cormorants. To the metropolis of London.
There already a legend, your name was spilled about in the air
And your voice cast over the waves, the ninth wave
Charged with Mabinogion magic, or heard from a box
Reverberating that atomic symphony of Cain.
This, then, was our last meeting in the wings
Behind the bare auditorium hall
Where you and Edith stood alone.
Then when I did turn up that second time,
It was to arrive too late, too late for life
At the Churchyard Gates, passing up, through the down-going
Dying faces, up to your ever living form. Alone
At the grave, dug so many feet deep, by the gravedigger
Known to us both, the Laugharne owl staring from the yew.
You staring. And O I must tell you he had a hard time picking
At those rocks. The stone face refused to yield
To give her young Bard so soon a bed.
I saw Louis in the shade as his tears fell.
And past them all as they gathered round the pub
This time I had no need to drink against my will
For your company was everywhere. Out on the cliff edge I walked
Overlooking the Bay, its mudsilt, greying water-dunes and birds
Quietly stopping at the Boathouse, thinking to call.
What distance, since the others did not remove us,
Holds us together? What bird or bind of word
Substance of sound or rhythmic flow?
Could you, if you wished, now cold as a stream,
Warm my keen pen as it wanders afar
Out into the crystal air to charge those hypocrites
Who would acknowledge you with the mockery of your own voice
Snatch at your images, instead of their own
The rhymesters and feathered curs.
                                        If the air above Dylan,
If the air above had ears, and could hear my request,
Would it caress your head, that for me, so personally
Brought a standstill to my heart. I would say Amen on this;
Or write Lynette to end the page. But continuous as the thought
I write for you Dylan evermore.

Lynette Roberts

[Dated 12 February 1954; Laugharne and Llanybri, Taf Carmarthen Bay]

Lynette Roberts and Dylan Thomas: Background to a Friendship

In the early hours of Saturday 8 April 1939 the British cruise liner *Hilary* ran aground in dense fog at Carmel Head, Anglesey. It had begun its voyage to Liverpool in Manaos, nine hundred miles up the Amazon River, collecting holidaymakers at various stops en route, including two young women writers returning to London from an extended stay on the Island of Madeira. The *Daily Mail* report on the following Monday had an especial interest in 'sun-tanned cruise girls' rudely awakened from their cabins, but it also highlighted the morale-boosting spirits of the two writers: in the third-class lounge, as the ship listed to port, Celia Buckmaster began playing the piano, while her friend Lynette Roberts sang along.[1] Amid the excitement of the occasion it may or may not have occurred to Roberts that this shipwreck, as she later styled it, was a kind of unexpected homecoming. For Lynette Roberts was of Welsh descent, albeit through several generations of familial expatriation in Australia and then Argentina, where Roberts spent the first fifteen years of her life.

Whether this grounding and the ensuing evacuation of the ship via the Holyhead lifeboat was symbolic or not, within a year Lynette Roberts had made a home in a small Welsh village in Carmarthenshire, following a marriage to Keidrych Rhys at which Dylan Thomas was best man. Thomas found the bridesmaid Celia Buckmaster every bit as attractive as the *Daily Mail* had earlier that year. Writing in an otherwise spitefully satiric mode to Vernon Watkins, Thomas was to comment of the wedding: 'I can tell you that it was distinguished mostly by the beauty of the female attendants, the brown suit of the best man, the savage displeasure of Keidrych's mother'.[2]

At the time of her holiday in 1939 Roberts was living the bohemian London life as a single woman, poet and self-employed florist under the name of Bruska, importing exotic flowers directly from the Scilly Isles to sell to wealthy clients. She probably met Keidrych Rhys, poet and editor of *Wales* magazine, at a Soho poetry reading in 1938, and through the auspices of Tambimuttu. At this point she was engaged to Merlin Minshall, an extraordinarily adventurous figure who raced cars across Europe and who was later to work for British Naval Intelligence. Indeed he is thought by some to have been the model for Fleming's James Bond, and Roberts stated that he also somewhat resembled Tarzan. He used to cook Chinese food for her, and was divorcing his wife, whom he introduced to Roberts. She threw her Tarzan lookalike over, however, when she met Rhys, and by summer 1939 she was accompanying Rhys to his Carmarthenshire family home, from where they went to Laugharne to ask Thomas to be best man at their wedding. They married in the early weeks of World War II on 4 October 1939 in the Church at Llansteffan. The best man's notable brown suit had been borrowed from the taller Vernon Watkins. Roberts noticed the inevitable result with her eye for detail:

> For the wedding I did not buy anything new. I carried wild flowers and gave Dylan a bunchful of wild flowers for his lapel. Vernon Watkins' trousers were draped around his shoes. Caitlin looked outstanding in pink with a rose pinned to her breast.[3]

The photograph of the wedding party, with overlong trousers clearly visible, was published in the *Weekly Mail and Cardiff Times* on 7 October 1939, and includes Keidrych Rhys, Lynette Roberts wearing an elaborate headdress, Dylan Thomas, and the novelist Kathleen Tomkinson (née Bellamy), another bridesmaid and a childhood friend of Roberts.

After a short honeymoon in Swansea Rhys and Roberts moved to a small cottage in Llanybri, a village on the other side of the Taf estuary from Laugharne, and began a period of ten years of turbulent and creative marriage, during which their geographical proximity to the Thomases, and shared interest in poetry and drink, sustained a sporadic friendship. Rhys and Roberts separated and divorced in 1949, following which Roberts briefly lived in a caravan in the Laugharne graveyard where Thomas was shortly to come to rest. When Thomas died in 1953 Roberts was about to publish her last book, *The Endeavour*, a kind of historical novel based on Captain Cook's first voyage to Australia, and drawing on her experience of sea voyages along similar routes, including her own shipwreck on the *Hilary*. *The Endeavour* was published by Peter Owen in 1954, and in February that year she finished the typescript of a long epistolary poem, an elegy for Dylan Thomas, which revisits her memories of their encounters during life, and her attendance at his Laugharne funeral in November 1953.

In the months and years following the untimely death of Dylan Thomas there were many memorials and elegiac tributes, including the Dylan Thomas Memorial Recital in February 1954 at the Festival Hall, with readings by, among others, Michael Hordern and Peggy Ashcroft; Stravinsky's *In Memoriam Dylan Thomas*; and many poems of remembrance by poets ranging from Edith Sitwell to Charles Olson.

There were several poets among the mourners at Thomas's funeral who subsequently wrote elegies. In his 'At the Wake of Dylan Thomas' George Barker clearly faced difficulties that were far from his alone, struggling to find an appropriate voice, and lapsing into occasional Celtic cliché:

> Is it you, Cymric, or I who am so cold?
> Was it a word and world America killed?

1 Anon., 'Girls Stage Cabaret as Ship Grounds', *Daily Mail*, 10 April 1939, p. 9.
2 Dylan Thomas to Vernon Watkins, letter postmarked 8 October 1939, in Dylan Thomas, *The Collected Letters*, ed. Paul Ferris (London: Dent, 2000), pp. 473–74.
3 Lynette Roberts, 'Notes for an Autobiography', in *Diaries, Letters and Recollections*, ed. Patrick McGuinness (Manchester: Carcanet, 2008), p. 210.

The wedding of Keidrych Rhys and Lynette Roberts at Llansteffan. The best man, Dylan Thomas, is standing to Lynette's left. Reproduced by permission of the National Library of Wales.

The brainstruck harp lies with its bright wings furled.[4]

John Ormond published his elegy for Thomas twenty years after the funeral, by which point he was reaching for fading signifiers of memory, attempting to capture the ghost of an image available to him through its rhyme with an artistic representation of physical type:

> You would stand in the corner, your glass raised,
> Your head flung back, a cigarette stuck
> To your lip like a white syllable, removed
> Only to quaff or cough or for the defiant
>
> Steeplejack raids into your tried thesaurus
> Of laughter; with that badly-drawn Rubens hand
> (Under the bookie's suit, your shirt-cuff
> To your knuckle) yet conduct the concert's
> Spendthrift conceits[5]

Louis MacNeice, whom Roberts saw 'in the shade as his tears fell', remembers Thomas in various Cantos of *Autumn Sequel*, and for him too the memory is sustained in part through vignettes of bar-room poses:

>   Debonair,
> He leant against the bar till his cigarette
> Became one stream of ash sustained in air
>
> Through which he puffed his talk.[6]

Canto XX describes MacNeice's affecting journey to Laugharne, the burial service, and the crowded bar later on. Moving away from the burial itself MacNeice remarks on the estuary and the birds, a focus also for Roberts's poem:

> His estuary spreads before us and its birds
> To which he gave renown reflect renown
>
> On him, their cries resolve into his words
>   (MacNeice, p. 413)

Edith Sitwell was on a ship to the USA when Thomas died, and she became directly involved in the events surrounding the aftermath of his death. She did not return for the funeral, but wrote an elegy to Thomas, characteristic of a certain kind of mythologising response to his early death, and at a late point in her career when she was perhaps at her most grandiosely mythopoeic:

> And he, who compressed the honey-red fire into holy
>   shapes,
> Stole frozen fire from gilded Parnassian hives,
>
> Was Abraham-haired as fleeces of wild stars
> That all night rage like foxes in the festival
> Of wheat[7]

Roberts's poem is distinctive in being a most personal and intimate account of fading yet persisting memories, with

4   George Barker, 'At the Wake of Dylan Thomas', in *Collected Poems* (London: Faber, 1987), p. 311.
5   John Ormond, 'Section from an Elegy (for Dylan Thomas)', in *Poetry Wales* 9:2 (Autumn 1973), p. 20.
6   Louis MacNeice, *Autumn Sequel*, Canto VIII, in *The Collected Poems*, ed. E.R. Dodds (London: Faber, 1966), p. 404.
7   Edith Sitwell, 'Elegy for Dylan Thomas', in *Collected Poems* (London: Macmillan, 1982), p. 423.

occasional gestures towards a shared local poetic and mythological language. This is in part owing to the direct address sustained by the epistolary form, but also because the poem is centred on vignettes of friendship rather than questions of redemption or reputation or significance, with only a brief swipe at the unnamed 'rhymesters and feathered curs' whom she perceives as appropriating Thomas for their own ends.

Some Notes on 'A Letter to the Dead'

Roberts's 'Notes for an Autobiography', written several years after the events they recollect, identify various visits and exchanges with Dylan Thomas before and subsequent to her wedding. The likely timing and sequence of some of these recollections is somewhat suspect, but the general shape of the anecdotes persists in her elegy. She recalls: 'I took some clothes down to Wales and went to spend the weekend with Dylan and Caitlin. I took for Dylan Everyman's Rabelais Vols 1 and 2 and another book the title of which I forget but it had a number of forms for writing poetry – circular, triangular, octangular, square and many other shapes' (p. 209). Both here and in the elegy Roberts is perhaps hinting at a possible influence on the genesis of Thomas's post-war collection *Deaths and Entrances*. In illustrating their mutual discussions of poetry on this occasion she incorporates some lines from her own poem 'Song of Praise' (from 'light birds sailing' to 'The long-nosed god of rain'). This was first published with the title 'To Keidrych Rhys' in October 1939 (the month of their wedding, or the 'Show', as she calls it in her poem) in *Wales* no. 10. The issue also included Thomas's story 'Just Like Little Dogs'. Her poem is a kind of travelogue of visual experiences, with the lines here evoking a remembered image from her early childhood holidays in Patagonia.

In 'A Carmarthenshire Diary' Roberts describes the local ferryman and fisherman John Roberts arriving with flatfish from the estuary, which he caught by feeling them with his feet on his crossings of the Taf. Her 'Notes for an Autobiography' describe taking

the pastoral way to Laugharne [...]. John Roberts in his Breton suit was soon seen untying his ferry. It was lying in the River Taf Estuary. He rowed over, his trousers rolled above his burnished knees. This was because the river was deep at the two sides. He took us on his back and dropped us into the boat. We rowed across the narrow stretch and we were in Laugharne. [...] Dylan and Caitlin were pleased to see us.

(p. 215)

It is a short walk from Llanybri, where Rhys and Roberts were renting the small cottage called Tygwyn for 3/6 a week, down to the crossing point, and to the pastoral mode of transportation across to Laugharne, where from July 1938 the Thomases were renting Sea View, a large four-storied house. With the journey back being dependent upon the tide, and so with hours to kill, the resulting drinking session, Roberts recalls, left them the next day with 'a Dylanesque problem – no money' (p. 215). Elsewhere in her diary she comments that John Roberts had nice legs.

Many of Lynette Roberts's poems take birds as their subject and theme, and her engagement with natural history is detailed and exacting. Her elegy describes an occasion

where she identified some of the estuary birds for Thomas as 'whimbrel, sandpiper and curlew', and a later handwritten note on the manuscript of the poem explains further that 'this was on your [Thomas's] birthday in October and the October poem was finished but for the last line'. She has in mind Thomas's 'Poem in October':

It was my thirtieth year to heaven
Woke to my hearing from harbour and neighbour wood
And the mussel pooled and the heron
Priested shore[8]

While the poem was finished during the summer of 1944, during a stay at Blaencwm in Carmarthenshire, Thomas makes it clear in a letter to Vernon Watkins that it is 'a Laugharne poem: the first place poem I've written'. Paul Ferris's footnote to the letter indicates that a version of the poem pre-dated Thomas's thirtieth birthday by some distance: 'Watkins said that the poem had been "contemplated" since 1941, and originally the first line read, "It was my twenty-seventh year to heaven"' (*Collected Letters*, p. 580). As a Laugharne poem it is likely that its inspiration derived from the earlier period when Thomas was living there (until 1941). 'Poem in October' was first published in February 1945, and was collected in *Deaths and Entrances* (1946). Roberts writes, 'Seven years later, the birds *yours*, were lifted on to the page', a timeline which might suggest that Thomas was working on the poem even earlier, in 1939. The wedding between Rhys and Roberts had taken place on 4 October that year, and according to a letter from Thomas to Glyn Jones on 27 October (the day of Thomas's twenty-fifth birthday) Keidrych Rhys was due to visit Thomas the day after. Whether Roberts accompanied Rhys on this occasion, and talked with Thomas about birds, remains a speculation.

Roberts moved into the caravan in Laugharne graveyard in 1949, the year that Dylan and Caitlin Thomas moved back to Laugharne and into the Boathouse, with their friendship reconvened 'in ship's pub and sea pubs drinking'. The subsequent shift of the elegy to London alludes to Thomas's broadcasting career: 'your voice cast over the waves, the ninth wave / Charged with Mabinogion magic'. The transformation of (air) waves to 'the ninth wave' is typical of Roberts's bringing together of the technological and mythological worlds. The 'ninth wave' reverberates with an echo from Tennyson's 'The Coming of Arthur':

          And then the two
Dropt to the cove, and watch'd the great sea fall,
Wave after wave, each mightier than the last,
Till last, a ninth one, gathering half the deep
And full of voices, slowly rose and plunged
Roaring, and all the wave was in a flame:
And down the wave and in the flame was borne
A naked babe, and rode to Merlin's feet,
Who stoopt and caught the babe, and cried 'The King!
Here is an heir for Uther!'[9]

But perhaps more immediate for Roberts is an echo

8 Dylan Thomas, *The Poems*, ed. Daniel Jones (London: Dent, 1990), p. 176.
9 Tennyson, 'The Coming of Arthur', in *The Works of Alfred Lord Tennyson* (London: Macmillan, 1891), p. 315.

out of the Welsh medieval bardic tradition. The text of 'Câd Goddeu' ('The Battle of the Trees'), from the Book of Taliesin, had been reassembled by Robert Graves and published in Rhys's *Wales* magazine, along with various articles on the subject which were to form the groundwork for *The White Goddess*. Graves considered the text to contain other poems, one of which he separated out and published alongside his version of 'Câd Goddeu' in the twenty-first birthday issue of *Wales*, under the title 'The Blodeuwedd of Gwion ap Gwreang', dedicated to Angharad Rhys (Rhys and Roberts's young daughter). The poem ends: 'Long and white are my fingers / As the ninth wave of the sea'.[10] Roberts had provided considerable help with Graves's work on Welsh mythology, and is acknowledged in the foreword to the first edition of *The White Goddess*. Blodeuwedd, a beautiful maiden formed from flower and tree blossoms, is metamorphosed into an owl in 'Math, Son of Mathonwy', the fourth branch of the Mabinogion, which may resonate with the 'Laugharne owl staring from the ycw' in the graveyard towards the close of Roberts's elegy.

Roberts describes a specific occasion in London for her final meeting with Thomas, at a concert performance of Humphrey Searle's setting to music of Edith Sitwell's poem 'The Shadow of Cain', for two speakers (on the night in question, Dylan Thomas and Edith Sitwell), male voice choir, and orchestra. This is the 'atomic symphony of Cain', an elegiac and apocalyptic response to the atomic bombs dropped on Japan, and the ensuing post-war nuclear age. It was performed at the Palace Theatre, London, on 16 November 1952, and a review by Neville Cardus for the *Guardian* exclaimed that 'it was a joy and a privilege to hear the English language spoken with Dr Sitwell's and Mr Thomas's intense feeling for the beauty of words'.[11] Sitwell was a champion of Thomas's work, writing in a review of *Deaths and Entrances*:

> I think of the martyred youth of the time – and remembering that in this world made hideous by the cruelty and greed of mankind there is still a young man who can give us a song of the heaven that this world could – can – be, I think, perhaps there is still hope for us.[12]

Roberts had also known Sitwell for many years, and they corresponded extensively from 1942 onwards. Sitwell wrote to Roberts from Sunset Boulevard in Hollywood in January 1954, sorrowful for the loss of Thomas: 'First there was Dylan's death, under appalling circumstances about which I will tell you when I see you'.[13] When Thomas died he was in the early stages of planning an opera with Stravinsky, a work which was to imagine the world following a cataclysmic atomic incident.

The final recollection of Roberts's poem centres on Thomas's funeral and burial at St Martin's Church, Laugharne, on 24 November 1953. She mentions one of her fellow mourners, Louis (MacNeice), and otherwise comes back to the subject of drinking. Thomas's childhood friend Daniel Jones, who is most prominent in the British Pathé news footage of the occasion, gives some sense of the atmosphere: 'The day was deteriorating, or improving, according to the way you look at it. Drinkers poured drink not only into themselves but over one another. [...] Someone suggested that a jar of pickled onions and a pint of bitter should be poured into Dylan's grave.'[14]

In this, Thomas's centenary year, it seems fitting that Roberts's quietly personal poetic remembrance of Thomas should finally come to light.

Editorial Note

The poem, to my knowledge, has never been published before. It exists as a typed manuscript held by the Harry Ransom Center, University of Texas at Austin, and the copy I have worked from, owned by Roberts, has additional handwritten emendations and marginal comments. Roberts also typed out a clean copy of the poem at a much later date, incorporating many of the handwritten emendations, and reworking whole passages. The text given here is a reconstruction of the earlier typed manuscript, ignoring the later emendations. The initial incarnation is surer of itself as a poem, and closer to the events it remembers. I have silently corrected obvious typographical errors in spelling and punctuation, and a couple of word and phrase orders are best-guess reconstructions from ambiguities in the manuscript itself.

Charles Mundye, August 2014

10 Robert Graves, 'Two Poems', *Wales*, 5:8–9 (December 1945), pp. 22–25 (p. 22).

11 Neville Cardus, 'The Story of Hiroshima in Music', *Manchester Guardian*, 18 November 1952, p. 5.

12 Edith Sitwell, 'A True Poet', *Our Time*, 3:9 (April 1946), p. 199.

13 Unpublished letter, Edith Sitwell to Lynette Roberts, 31 January 1954. The original manuscript is held in the Harry Ransom Center, University of Texas at Austin. Later in the same letter Sitwell reiterates a point she often made in their correspondence: 'You are the only young woman who can write. I have always said so, and I continue to say it.'

14 Daniel Jones, *My Friend Dylan Thomas* (London: Dent, 1977), p. 6.

'Daphne' and Other Poems

Daphne

Poet, that fear of staying put,
your legs and arms arrested, night-
mare style ('Her feet but now so swift
were anchored fast / in numb stiff
roots'); of, worst, the tongue
gone wooden in the mouth, its language
leafing, helpless, out, into a silent
spring; is yours, not mine. I
evade your grasp with his. I run
not out of utterance, but into it.

The quoted lines are from A.D. Melville's translation of the
Metamorphoses (Oxford University Press, 1986).

Heartwood

Within the least growth ring inscribed
within the other, greater rings,
their evidence of drought or plenty,
the living verge of the cambium,
the heartwood neither beats nor grows:
abiding, it's the memory of a stem.

Within me your heart beats; you grow.
Your blood won't mix with mine, although
we're part and parcel: you my living
verge – and I your memory?

Psyche

A candle and a window ope
at night to let him in? Nope.
I don't need a flame to know
my flame, in bed or out. He's no
matinee idol, no idol, no god,
no demon, no devil, no fly-by-night Broadway-
romance, no hero, no Clark
Kent: my dear, the dark
glass *is* the face. The same.
He's Love. By any other name.

Callisto

Before you were born I licked you into shape:
how is it now I am not capable
of recognizing you, nor you
me – nor, for that matter, I
she who, it seems, for paws
and claws with which to guard you, has
traded her lily hands, her golden
hair. Perhaps when you are older
we'll be able to pick out
the constellations: the hunter, the Great Bear.

Kerf

I dreamed you called your tools black terns:
the axehead diving on the kerf
where, already, concentric rings
are spreading. When you strike, what springs
apart? The poplar splitting like
it's never been unsplit; the lake,
no sooner cracked than closing
over, as if it's never been unwhole.

'Letter to an Elderly Poet' and Other Poems

Letter to an Elderly Poet

Better to be writing your will again,
To be feasting in the great hall by firelight
Playing the harp to your grandchildren.
What is that terrible cry at the end of the garden?
It has gone now.
Could have been birds. Wild geese perhaps.
Let your trembling hand draw an expressive line.
Consider the scuffs on the risers of the stairs,
The dent of the doorknob hitting the wall
Always at the same place. Unpurse your lips.
You are not writing prescriptions.
Nor falling downstairs in a foreign language.
Practise the smile of the Indian swami.
Relax, your rivals are dead.
At least you're not in a Mexican motel.
Hang up the picture of a Chinese sage
Sweeping things under an enormous rock.

Real Tennis

In the days when girls' names
Were postage stamps to unlikely countries
Persephone Blount was my blue Guadeloupe.
Her face in the college photo
A daisy in a graveyard.
The boater hovered like an aureole.
I followed her *au pas de loup*.
She played real tennis
(Not recognised by our tennis club,
Being played by Henry VIII
With a triangular racquet.)
Walking Deirdre round the Meadows, I gathered flowers
But threw them away, thinking of real tennis.
The tennis I played began to seem unreal.
So I changed religion.
If I was from an old Catholic family, with a real tennis racquet,
Would I be up to scratch?
Later, at an Elizabethan restaurant above the Chaplaincy
We ate marchpane together by candlelight
(With stuffed sows' wombs, as they also did Roman cookery)
And discussed the Neoplatonism of Professor Zvov.
Her accent was irresistible
But then so was Professor Zvov's
Especially when he said *Pico della Mirandola*.

The Road to Kraków (Empirical Sonnets)

– Are you an academic?
You dance like an academic.
I'm being hauled about like a sack of potatoes.
(She goes white and has to sit down in a different room.)
– It's like riding a donkey on Brighton beach.
– Do you go to Brighton a lot?
I've got so old my wife can only go out with me after dark.
Another cramped little poem in its little seat-belt.
So I go to this psychiatrist.
– I think things are funny which are not funny.
– You're not mad, she says. (I could tell she was hopeless.
I could see from the pictures she hung on her walls.
– I don't like walls hung with reproductions, I say.)
– They're originals, she says. (So it's worse.)

So I organise a getaway minibreak to Kraków.
My wife says – That's fine, I'll organise it:
Midweek senior citizen rail supersaver to Stettin
Via Łódź before 28th dep Luton 0330 in a group returning
In time for you to be back at work on Friday.
– But I wanted Kraków.
– You don't want Kraków. When you get to these places
All you do is drink coffee. You don't need to go all that way
To drink a cup of coffee. I'll buy you some coffee
And we can make it and drink it here. Why Kraków?
– I want to hear Polish girls talking Polish.
– Play Chopin. Shut your eyes and you're in Kraków.
– Yes! It's better than Kraków! (But I'd still like to see Kraków.)
– Why?

The Summerhouse

I've been reading a book about poetry.
It's complicated.
And mysterious designs on the cover.
You'd think she was writing about the origins of life
Looking down a spectroscope
To discover *élan vitale*
In a summerhouse before term starts.
The poets appear like children
Dressed in enormous overcoats,
And they all belong to different schools
And are trying to tease each other. My school
Had a canary yellow blazer, and our crest
Was a summerhouse. (A Doric temple
The size of a phone booth.) Other schools
Sported tigers, mailed fists, or griffons.
We brandished a summerhouse –
Symbol, Mr Rudge said, of effortless ease.
He was trying to produce a generation of small summerhouses
Some of which would revolve effortlessly,
Suggesting ill-defined juvenile longings.

'Late Hour' and Other Poems

Late Hour

We have found a new routine:
slightly earlier to bed, slightly less late talking
as we sink in this low-lying futon to dream.

The day slips off as easily as our clothes;
the heating makes a dull milk-shed moan
and something outside our hilltop flat grows and grows.

Is it night? A star's tincture? The sense
of what we will not know? Our world
shrinks to the width of the bedroom's lens.

Night thickens and the white wall,
a desert sphinx, a blank Buddha,
says nothing, a nothing, that is all.

October

a new quarantine,
days that hold before the clocks change,
the summer air chills to a setting coolness
like a dish removed from the oven.

The earth is preparing
to become its own walk-in larder,
the heat of life turned down daily
by half degrees.

Some burly blacksmith
has quenched the sun
in the cold sea of the sky,
the cherry flames, distant, intensify.

Is that the sun setting
beyond the hill, or a fire
flaring the crooks
of the black ash trees?

Owl

I shuffle between rooms because I can't sleep
and I think of the owl I listened to on Dartmoor
flitting between branches, climbing the clumpy valley,
invisible in darkness, announcing each move
with a sharp ker-wick that grew louder,
traversing the row of river-tied trees and me,
in the field's edge, risen to night and sharp-eared,
listening until it landed on the lame lopped holly,
now near and present as though
it had landed on my own right shoulder.

And, as I stoop in darkness between doorways,
wishing I was asleep, mind-mysterious,
head pitching like a hand-held lamp,
I wonder: what tree or branch was I vainly looking for?
The owl flew on with a silk-slow hush;
a cape sweep of unclasped wings.
And I knew I had been left by a creature
who knows the nights' hollows better than me:
can let go into the dimness, unperturbed,
can find in the black blindness what it needs to find.

Tomas Tranströmer: Schubert's Ghost

And deeper than did ever plummet sound
I'll drown my book

Raymond Carver's last poetry collection, published the year after his death, is elegantly, tantalisingly structured. *New Path to the Waterfall* (1989) is divided into six sections; a few lines of poetry or prose by Jaroslav Seifert, Charles Wright and Anton Chekhov among others preface each one. Taken at a glance these pieces serve mainly to introduce what follows, namely Carver's meditations on various themes and events in a life reaching its premature end. The second section starts with a short poem – it is most definitely a poem – by the Swedish poet Tomas Tranströmer. The poem is brief, a mere fifteen lines long, and is about the driver of a car who gets sleepy and pulls off the road to rest. Waking up, he experiences real difficulty remembering his name. This causes a wild panic. Eventually the name comes down 'the long staircase' to consciousness and his identity is restored. The poem ends on a chastened note – he will never be able to forget the 'fifteen-second battle' by the motorway.

The poem has a twofold meaning. It describes a physical reality that is existential, generalised. It also accepts the existence of a secondary realm that is contextualised by psychological and emotional states. A random act represents the point at which these two worlds intersect. This is not new and apologies if the analysis sounds like an evening class on Henry James in the Weimar Republic. What Tomas Tranströmer offers and what is new is a clear statement underpinning the poem that there is no division between the individual memory of an event (like the one experienced by the driver) and its impact. In a sense that is the function of the televisual gothic 'written into' the poem; it serves to emphasise the point that, stripped of its silences, a poem can be a kind of benign containment, one that introduces, and does not abandon us, to the cold places that lie in the shadow of our everyday experience.

***

Franz Schubert's *String Quintet in C* (1828) is characterised by its musical arrangement and by the scale and depth of its emotional range. Unconventional in its instrumentation, Schubert's only fully-fledged quintet is scored for two violins, one viola (instead of two) and two cellos (instead of one). The composer presumably wanted to exploit the versatility of the cello, either to produce a stronger bass line, add richness to the middle texture or indeed to lead the melody, as happens here. In any case the result of this new arrangement is that the scope and range of the piece is deepened and expanded and a large degree of orchestration becomes not only desirable but essential.

Richard Holmes' biography of Shelley ends a compelling analysis of *Prometheus Unbound* by concluding that the poem is devoid of optimism, that it points the way ahead to revolutionary social change but stops short of including it. Tomas

Tranströmer is similarly, though not terminally, disinclined. His poem 'Schubertiana'[1] offers no vantage point, no prospect across a river, no antiquity. Neither does it indulge the conceits of social consensus, preferring instead a language of the imagination that is entirely edenic, improvisational, aleatoric, and finally, compositional. We might think of *A Man in Armour*. Van Rijn was searching for irony that would be *approximate* to art. Tranströmer is similarly preoccupied and finds it so inaudibly we nearly miss it. The first step towards a remarkable conclusion is taken in slippers.

The last two paragraphs demonstrate the difficulty of our task as readers, even with a poem as seemingly 'untrammelled' as 'Schubertiana'. Perhaps that's the reason. Rothko would have understood this; is it really the case that not only the exhibits in the museum are dead but the visitors too? We have been here before, with Brodsky – silence before the noise. Modern poetry seems divided between those who throw stones and those who are hit. Sensibility as armour is not enough.

***

I

In the evening darkness in a place outside New York, an
outlook point where one single glance will
encompass the homes of eight million people.
The giant city over there is a long shimmering drift, a
spiral galaxy seen from the side.

The poem dwells on its origins long enough to take them in. The 'glance' that fixes New York is intriguing. Is it *la mirada*? The exegetic *coup d'oeil* that divines a subtext (of slavery) in Masefield's *Cargoes*? We might even flick back through and, after several attempts, find Carver's unheroic 'Crow'. But that urban prospect is important. Provisionally we know where we are; the full extent of our field of vision is revealed in a trice; city, population and the eye on which the image is literally written.

We have already alluded to the poem's relativity, different from Brodsky's, different entirely from that of Szymborska. For the reader, historical relativity in its most obvious form is provided by the title; one hundred and fifty years separate the quintet and the poem. That might be enough for some, but it's a finer relative sense we need, one in which the relationship between the reader and the poem's teleological drives isn't surrendered to complexity, and which allows us to envision the poem, warm to its strangeness, shift our feet to its music.

Tranströmer tries on the slippers again, this time with a heavier foot, in lines 4–5. The city as a 'shimmering drift' is concentrated into the image of the 'spiral galaxy'. With the previous detail of 'eight million people' the suggestion is of volume and extent, the smoky, sideways drift of a cosmic print. The line break to 'seen from the side' is crucial. It carries huge significance, but is pushed out. This is because it establishes an unexpected perspective, the horizontal. Typically Tranströmer frames these four words in a minor key, draws our attention towards the poem's real subjects, which are meaning and propinquity, the relativity of music to a musical poem. How Tranströmer achieves this is *our* subject.

II

In the forgetfulness of my body
And everything it touches
I remember you…[2]

A brief word about structure.

A thrown stone skims across the water. It's a good one, glides on and on, once, twice, three times, gaining momentum, accelerating, sending out small ripples each time it skips off the surface. Quite suddenly it stops, tucks under the placid water and sinks. How many was that? Six? Seven? You lose count. What made it soar that time and not the others? You try again; it goes under in two…

…each time it hits, it peals, and each pealing goes down and down, tolls to the core of the Earth. Poetry starts with the returning echo.

We should avoid fetishising, but fetishism in poetry is just poor reading, born of the desire to strike a posture. We might look again at the music analogy as a way of taking us further.

It is a truism that chamber music is essentially an intimate conversation between the constituent instruments. One leads, cajoles the others into following, recedes and is replaced in the arrangement by another. As is the case with Schubert's quintet that arrangement can be symphonic. Tranströmer would have been very aware of this. His earlier poem 'C Major' (1962) is latent with semantic (though not structural) possibility, ending with the image of a 'trembling compass', which is the point at which the poem both reaches its tangible extreme and suggests an expanse into which it can't (or won't) go. Fifteen years later, 'Schubertiana', relativised, horizontalised, attempts to take the further step by the use of an arrangement of the text – five sections, five musical instruments – to create a kind of universal poetic 'space suit' that allows for scaling the heights as well as the depths. The poem succeeds structurally because it inhabits that further space beyond tangible extremes, suggests musicality, and, when scrutinised in the light of day, betrays no messenger, melts away.

III

The endless expanses of the human brain are crumpled
     to the size of a fist.

The second section follows a pattern that is very similar to the first. Great concentration produces concentrated images, in this case a swallow returning from Southern Africa to nest in the same barn as it had done the previous year, that combine reason and intuition in a narrative style that also has elements of revelation. Having been assured 'without statistics' at the end of the first section that Schubert was being played somewhere in the city, we are at the end of the second

plausible onlookers as the composer works 'on the wonderful centipedes of his manuscript'.

But why the pugnacious 'fist'? In terms of a contrast in size, the condensed image works. Perhaps we shouldn't underestimate a more personal aspect to the symbolism. One of the most powerful themes in Tranströmer's poetry has been terror. It is not stretching things to say that some of his poems are Goya-esque; they foreground terror and the grotesque in ways that are extremely affecting. This might be the key, that in keeping with the poem's structural audacity the image reconnects with a particular aesthetic tradition while at the same time functioning as counterpoint to a vertiginous poetic conceit. This might seem rather 'concentrated' as an explanation, but what it means is that Tranströmer is rather closer to a Germanic tradition that places the 'self' at the centre of its tradition rather than at the margins, preferring a poetry of fuller human engagement to the manifestos of poetic activism.

IV

The string quintet is playing. I walk home through
     warm forests with the ground springy under me,
curl up like an embryo, fall asleep, roll weightless into
     the future, suddenly feel that the plants have
     thoughts.

Part 3 is by some way the shortest section and contains all the ingredients of a Tranströmer poem: a childlike, pristine sensibility, precisely weighted imagery and phrase-making, and a very real sense of unexplored naturalistic depth. The tone of the quatrain – we can reasonably call it a quatrain – is sweeter, lighter. The vocabulary is diaphanous, highly personal; the 'I' of the poem is circumscribed by musical facticity. The use of the forest imagery suggests an internal shift towards a more psychological realm and from there to a world of dreams.

The last two images are crucial to our understanding of the poem and of Tranströmer's poetry more generally. The use of 'roll weightless' and 'suddenly feel' place the self at the heart of the search for meaning. There is also a sense in which they function unevenly, concessively, as signifiers of a deeper level of cultural discussion that is embedded in the poem. The terms of this discussion are basically as follows; advances in the field of the 'human sciences' (politics, economics, sociology, psychology and so on) have enriched and expanded our sense of ourselves certainly in the last two hundred years, from the way in which we function individually to our interactions at an institutional and societal level. According to this view, 'culture' is what we might call a process within which these new modalities are processed, refined and transformed, albeit at a laggard pace. This is to say the least a contentious view of cultural history that reduces it to the level of its means of production. You can almost hear the clanking of chains in the Bastille. As radical as this outlook is – and 'Schubertiana', written at a time when the Scandinavian social democratic model had transformed the quality of life of Nordic people within a generation, shares much of this radicalism – Tranströmer's 'method' is both more contained and, arguably, more challenging still. In a style that is reminiscent of Szymborska, it engineers a relationship that mixes self-interrogation on the part of the reader with the promise of enhanced aesthetic enjoyment. In other words, in order for us to believe that the poem has meaning Tranströmer asks us to believe that it does not. We have gone beyond terror, beyond relativity, into a *demi-monde* of dark comedy, theatre and good faith.

There's no doubting the legitimacy of such a leap, but it does mean the poem runs the risk of breaking on its own subtlety. If we were being hypercritical (and trite) we might say that the poet wants to have his cake and eat it. However, the beauty of 'Schubertiana' – the beauty of Tranströmer's *oeuvre* – is that with enormous subtlety, as well as great courage and honesty, it embraces modernity in all its aspects without diminishing the force of the 'fly scribble' on the page.

V

So much we have to trust, simply to live through our daily day without sinking through the earth!

The integrity of the poem derives entirely from the fact that it accepts its limitations. Written in the late 1970s, 'Schubertiana' is very much a poem of its time: it emerges from a distinct Swedish tradition (of nature poetry) to become (even more) manifestly internationalist in outlook; is written against a backdrop of social experiment that involves political, economic, legal and welfare advances and which imagines the universalisation of those advances ('in the evening darkness outside New York…'); and draws inspiration from forms of idealism that are predicated on the existence of 'public space'. Now, nearly four decades later, that idealism is still there, if more thinly spread.

A sense of righteousness shouldn't cloud the lens. 'Schubertiana' is a poem shaped by meaning. Whereas social change since the late 1970s has been radical and in many cases ruinous, it has been as nothing compared to the advances in our systemic knowledge that have been hard earned over the last two centuries, sometimes in tragic circumstances. Such has been the extent and quality of that change, it is a process that is unlikely to be repeated. It is against that backdrop that the poem *earns* its meaning, and it is that backdrop that largely explains the forward momentum of the piece as a whole. Arguably it is to this end that we read the word 'trust' four times in this section and 'trustingly' once. It also explains Tranströmer's commitment to the singular thrust that poetry can provide when he describes with great astuteness the wonderfully tactile metaphor of fingers feeling along a handrail that knows its own way in the dark.

VI

The long melody that remains itself in all its
transformations, sometimes glittering and pliant,
    sometimes
rugged and strong, snail-track and steel wire.
The perpetual humming that follows us – now –
up
the depths.

Feeling its way along the handrail in the dark, 'Schubertiana' confronts a reality in which the simple fact of keeping going is regarded as heroic. It might not be the 1970s after all.

Thus far the poem, for all its difficulty, has followed a traditional pattern, building up narrative detail towards a point at which the individual section is poised for musical uplift. In the last section that convention is subverted.

It begins with a scene in which two people are seated rather uncomfortably at a piano. They are described as looking 'a little ridiculous', like two coachmen on a rickety coach; their attempts at playing are untutored, absurdly inept. In the next line the focus shifts to those unexalted individuals (presumably in the general populace) whose lives are (badly) shaped by the choices they make. We're struggling at this point. It's only when a sudden further shift occurs that takes us back to the music that we see something of the reversal that has happened.

The last section works from back to front. In this instance music, to be more precise a notion of musical accompaniment, serves a distributive function; it guarantees thematic coherence, controls the shape and direction of the section and formalises a spatial awareness on which the poem's success ultimately relies. As a denouement it is remarkable and something of a *tour de force*. It includes a development of the notion of horizontality that was outlined earlier and works in three crucial ways.

By reversing a convention, Tranströmer adds significantly to the structural complexity of the poem; it provides a contrast with the previous sections and acts as a foil for the poem's revelatory conclusion.

He updates the idea of poetry as an *agora* by accepting a level of complexity in the philosophy of a free exchange with rules. Musicality, the 'perpetual humming that follows us', is used in no way negatively, rather it records in metaphorical form a nuanced understanding of the implications of social 'improvement'. This is the foundation myth of 'Schubertiana'. Placed at the poem's end, it functions retrospectively; without it the poem would be just so many particular solutions to so many particular problems. This way, its attraction is double-edged; it offers a prospect that is based on universal appeal.

The poem ends with a simple metaphor that Tranströmer delivers with trademark matter-of-factness: that where it matters our everyday lives are sustained by a human music that talks back to us from the past and from the future.

Notes
1 'Schubertiana', the poem discussed in this essay, is taken from the collection *The Truth-Barrier* (1978), which can be found in *Tomas Tranströmer, New Collected Poems*, translation by Robin Fulton, Bloodaxe, 1987.
2 From 'The Forgetfulness of My Body', by Jules Supervielle, included in John Ashbery, *Collected French Translations: Poetry*, Carcanet, 2014.

Epigrams

Translated by Brent Southgate

IX.38

Despite the speed and danger of your juggling,
Agathinus, you can't get that shield to fall.
It follows you against your will – returning
Through the air to sit on foot, or back, or hair,
Or fingertip. The stage may be slippery
With perfume and a gusty wind may tear
At the canvas overhead, but those boyish limbs
Keep steady as the shield tours calmly round them.
Even if you wished to blunder, something would stop you:
It would take your utmost skill to get that shield to fall.

V.34

Into your care, my dear dead parents,
I commend this darling girl, the little Erotion,
Lest she be frightened of the dark shades
And the monstrous jaws of Cerberus the hound.
She would have just passed her sixth winter,
Had she been granted only six more days.
Between you, venerable carers, may she happily play,
Prattling to you about me with that lisp of hers.
And Earth, rest lightly on this infant, who
Was never any weight on you.

X.40

Being constantly told my girl was sweet on a nancy-boy,
I surprised them. He was not a nancy-boy.

XI.21

How slack is Lydia? – well, just imagine
An equestrian statue's oversize bronze arse;
Think perhaps of a rhythmic gymnast's hoop,
Threaded untouched at every pass;
Think of an old shoe, soaked in muddy water;
An awning, sagging as the winds grow calm;
Think of a consumptive bum-boy's bracelet
Too big and dangling on his feeble arm;
Think of the ugly gape of a pelican,
Or baggy breeches of some vagabond.

That fishpond in which they say I fucked her –
I don't know, I think I fucked the pond.

XI.107

You give me back my book well-thumbed,
As if you'd diligently read it through.
And you have, of course. I do believe that,
I know it, I'm delighted, it's true!
I've diligently read your own five books
Just the same way as you.

V.78

If eating at home is starting to get you down,
Toranius, you can always starve with me.
I can give you an entrée, if that's your sort of thing –
There's cheap Cappadocian lettuce, a pungent leek
Or two, and under some chopped eggs you'll find one
Pickled tunny-fish playing hide-and-seek.
For mains, served on a black plate, you'll get green
Cabbage – mind your fingers, it's hot –
Straight from my freezing garden, a dear
Little sausage squashing the white polenta, and a streak
Of red bacon with some pale beans.
Then, if you want a second course, it's raisins,
Pears that could easily pass for Syrian,
And those finest productions of learned Naples,
Chestnuts slow-cooked in steam.
The wine? You'll make it into a good one when you drink,
And if Bacchus prompts the usual peckishness,
I can rescue you with some noble olives,
Boiled chickpeas, and warm lupin seeds.
It's a modest little dinner – can't deny it – but think
Of the advantages! No pretence required from you,
None from me, you can just recline there in peace
Wearing your own face, your host not being one who reads
Some damned thick volume afterwards.
Nor will you get much other post-match entertainment –
No naughty ladies from Cadiz moving their sexy bottoms
In well-taught wriggles – that sort of itch goes nowhere.
Instead, you'll get my little slave boy Condylus
Playing something on his flute, something not too, too
Serious but not lacking in polish either.
This is the meal, such as it is. I've invited Claudia.
Who would you like to bring with you?

XII.31

This grove, these fountains, the interwoven shade
Of trellised vines, the irrigation channel,
The rose-garden rivalling Paestum's that blooms twice,
The kitchen herbs that stay green all winter,
All these tame eels swimming in their tank
And white birds cooing in their dovecote
Are my honoured Marcella's gift to me, returning
To my native Spain after thirty-five long years:
The gift of a little kingdom and a home.
I could say, if the lovely Nausicaa should offer
Her palace gardens, 'I prefer my own.'

PROPERTIUS

Three Sketches of Cynthia
Translated by Patrick Worsnip

Cynthia's Birthday

I wondered why the Muses smiled
standing beside my bed at the blush of sunrise:
to celebrate the birthday of my girl,
clapping three times to bring her luck.
I want a cloudless day, the winds at standstill,
waves pattering safely on the shore.
No one's to grieve today,
Niobe's rock will dry her tears,
halcyons cease lugubrious cries,
the nightingale refrain from mourning.

You, darling, favoured by your birth-signs,
rise, pray to gods for just rewards,
wash off sleep with pure spring water,
style your bright hair between your fingers.
Slip on that dress that first caught my eye,
keep a garland round your head.
Ask that your beauty lasts forever
and your power to rule me never fails.

When incense drifts from flower-decked altars,
and propitious flames burn through the house,
think of nightfall, the time for feasting, drinking,
saffron pot-pourris that tease your nostrils.
The flute-playing fades into dancing,
risqué talk stirs your appetites,
amorous tiffs hold sleep at bay,
the street outside echoes to the noise.

We'll throw dice to decide which of us
is smacked the harder by Cupid's wing.
Then when enough cups have been downed,
Venus conducts the night-time rituals
we'll observe in our bedroom:
your birthday's climax.

Cynthia at Play

You drink slowly but steadily:
late nights can't stop you.
Your hand's not tired enough to drop those dice.
You're not listening to me,
just letting me prattle on,
as the stars fade.

Death tracked grape fermenting from the start,
the ruin of good water! Icarius
learned the bitter smell of the vine
(those Athenian farmers were right to throttle him).
Centaur Eurytion died of wine,
and the Cyclops – the strong vintage.
Liquor destroys looks,
corrupts youth,
makes a girl unable to tell one lover from another…

But to you it does nothing, damn it!
Drink on – you're beautiful,
wine won't hurt you.
Your garlands droop into your glass,
you read my poems aloud in a high voice…
Oh, soak the table some more with spilt Falernian,
let it fizz softly in that gilded cup.

Cynthia Awoken

On Naxos, Ariadne
comatose on the empty sand
while Theseus' ship dwindles into nothing;
Andromeda gorging on her first sleep,
free now from the unforgiving rock;
a Thracian maenad, danced out,
tumbled on the grass beside the river.

Cynthia, head on outsplayed fingers
and breathing quietly, could be one of these
as I stumble in, the worse for drink,
and the servants' torches gutter. It is late.
Not yet incapable, I weave
towards the couch her body lightly imprints;
Eros and Bacchus – neither to be denied –
fill me with their respective fires: just tuck
your arm, they order, gently beneath her frame,
press lips to lips, take sword in hand and…

Can't do it. Daren't disturb her rest.
She can be savage. I know her tongue's lash.
Instead I hover, gawping like Argus
at the horns that sprang from Io.
And, Cynthia, I put my garland on your brow,
amuse myself arranging your stray hair,
balance apples furtively on your cleavage,
only to see my largesse roll away:
sleeper's ingratitude!
Your every sigh,
every slight tremor has me terrified;
it means bad dreams trouble your head
– someone taking you by force…

The moon marching past the shutter slats,
the busy moon, its light lingering too long,
opens her eyes. She speaks, propped on one elbow:
'Back home to bed with me? She turned you out, then?
How nasty of her! So, where was it,
the place you spent the night you'd promised me?
Look at you, fit for nothing and the stars set.
You bastard! I'd like you to pass
a few nights the way you expect of me.
I tried to stay awake with needlework,
playing snatches of music as I drooped.
Just the occasional complaint, sitting alone,
that you were *quite* so long in that woman's arms.
That was my last thought as I lay back crying,
before sleep nudged me with its soothing wings.'

Note
In modern times, the Latin love poet Propertius has generally had a bad press by comparison with Catullus, who wrote about a generation before him in first-century BC Rome. The Romantics found Propertius lacking in 'sincerity'; literary critics thought he dropped the ball on making personal emotions a subject of serious poetry; he has been variously faulted for including too much Greek mythology, for becoming a propagandist for the emperor Augustus, and for having a male chauvinist attitude towards women. All this has impacted on English versions of his work, where the form adopted depends heavily on the translator's reading of the poet. From the eighteenth century, the Latin 'elegiac couplet' used by Propertius was typically rendered into heroic couplets, which do not reproduce his variety and subtlety, and distort his tone of voice. In 1919 there was a breakthrough when Ezra Pound began to publish his *Homage to Sextus Propertius*, a loose translation of some of the poems. This both reinterpreted the poet to stress his irony and employed a Poundian free verse radically different from anything that had appeared before. But the *Homage* is only a fragmentary account of Propertius and did not succeed in establishing him as a major player in Latin poetry (which I believe he was). He continues to be seen as a writer who, somehow, failed to fulfil his potential. He has been translated several more times, but nothing like as often as the more immediately accessible Catullus. The version I am working on seeks to highlight his psychological acuity, particularly in the many poems he wrote about a woman he calls Cynthia, as well as his formal experimentalism and frequent undertone of humour. It would be folly to pose as another Pound, or to try to 'complete' his work, and I have made no attempt to do either – every translator has to find his or her own voice. But the *Homage* has been a constant inspiration.

THE POLAR MUSE

THE
POLAR MUSEUM
SCOTT POLAR RESEARCH INSTITUTE

LUCY HAMILTON   REDELL OLSEN

SARAH HOWE   ANDREA PORTER

ROD MENGHAM   LUCY SHEERMAN

DREW MILNE   REBECCA WATTS

INTRODUCTION

This supplement is a first for both The Polar Museum and *PN Review*, the record of an innovative project exploring the connections between the writing process, curation and objects in museums. *The Polar Muse* invited eight Cambridge-based poets to select an object from The Polar Museum's permanent display and to use it as the basis for a new work. The resulting poems were installed on the glass of the display cases, in front of the items which inspired them, on 23 September; they are presented here in *PN Review* as a set.

Through *The Polar Muse*, we wanted to reflect on how the museum visitor's relationship with material is facilitated, how it is mediated. Looking itself becomes a complicated issue in a museum context, even at the simplest level: how do we look at museum objects? How *should* we look at museum objects? How much do we actually learn as we look? What role does language play in the process? The poems form both a visual and linguistic layer between the visitor and the objects, constituting an interruption which will invite audiences to reflect critically on their own engagement with museum artefacts and the kinds of engagement a museum can offer.

We were also keen for this to be an opportunity for the poets to capitalise on the full resources of the Museum, which so often lie dormant: the reserve collection, the catalogue information and, at The Scott Polar Research Institute, the complementary presence of a comprehensive archive and library, as well as the expert knowledge of staff. We were delighted to find that everyone involved plunged in; delighted, too, to discover that, in many cases, this involved uncovering the story behind, or buried within, an object.

Sometimes this meant searching out a lost voice, as in Andrea Porter's meticulously imagined and moving triptych on three Inuit women, 'Inua', based on a small ivory bird, a barrel organ and a comb from William Edward Parry's Arctic expedition, 1821-23. For Sarah Howe, inspired by Captain Scott's camera, it meant conjuring up the plosive, fussy talk of Herbert Ponting teaching Scott the art of photography, hopping between the lyrical and the imperative. Lucy Sheerman has woven language from remote sensing specialist Dr Gareth Rees' own field journals into her compositions, giving voice to the more contemporary project of mapping lichen in the Arctic.

p.t.o.

THE POLAR MUSEUM, Scott Polar Research Institute, Lensfield Road, Cambridge CB2 1ER is open Tuesday-Saturday, 10am-4pm (closed Bank Holiday Saturdays, open Bank Holiday Mondays).

On 4 November, from 6-7.30pm, the poets will be present at a public reading and discussion. Admission free, all welcome.

The poems, along with blog posts on the writing process and recordings of the poems read aloud by the poets, are also available online at: www.spri.cam.ac.uk/museum/polarpoetry/

A preoccupation with the language left over from Polar expeditions, the troves of journals and letters kept in the Institute's archive, has informed a number of the works. Rebecca Watts has spun an intoxicating dream of greater comfort out of Apsley Cherry-Garrard's accounts of sleeping in Antarctica, centred on Captain Oates' sleeping bag; Rod Mengham explores the 'wind-fed rumours' of slips of paper scattered by balloon across the Arctic, sent out in search of Sir John Franklin, who, in search of the North West Passage in 1847, disappeared with his crew and two ships. Lucy Hamilton's 'The Diarists' brings the journal entries and last letters of members of Captain Scott's last expedition into contact with the concerns of a present-day diarist, 'amplifying the past in small stages', while the two parts of Redell Olsen's 'Whiteout Film for Snow Goggles' even begin to incorporate the forms of the objects themselves into their language, mimicking the narrow slits of Inuit-style goggles and aping crystalline structures with small stanzas and snowflake asterisks.

For 'Reindeer Lichen', Drew Milne chose the only object on display in the Museum without a caption – a small piece of reindeer lichen. In doing so, he exposed a moment of curatorial absenteeism, revealing hierarchies that can, or perhaps must, emerge, despite the best of intentions, when arranging objects for display – an irony, considering the fact that this lichen was mistakenly called reindeer moss for many years and overlooked by early explorers. Was it a case, in Milne's words, of curators becoming 'blinded by prospects of relics' more showy?

The poems perform wonderfully as installations: they will remain in place until 20 December 2014. However, the enduring success of the project is in the quality of the works themselves, gathered and presented here, where the voices of their objects will resonate long after the glass at The Polar Museum is clear again.

Heather Lane and Joseph Minden,
Scott Polar Research Institute, August 2014

LUCY HAMILTON

from THE DIARISTS

Pictures & Frames

The British
Antarctic
Expedition
1910-1913

The Diarist is writing a century after the Expeditions. She is not eminent but is resolute, delving deep, excavating through layers of memory and silted-up grief. Unlike the men, she has achieved a venerable store of years. She is trying to form a greater picture, framing the two explorers in parallel as they set off in the same year, same century. She wants to shift her obsession to theirs just as *Pennel 'swung' the ship for compass adjustmen*t — to absorb herself in their joys & trials until the bitter end, so her pain becomes theirs and so their acceptance and grace — *I ought not to complain, but it is hard to be philosophic* — becoming hers, might deepen into ... no, not closure — into a kind of forgiveness.

The British
New Guinea
Expedition
1910-1912

Letters & Diaries

୧୫ ୨୦
2 daughters
2 sons
1 sister
1 brother (deceased)
doctor/nurse
dentist
cleaner
gardener
୧୫ ୨୦

She will call them Capt. S. & Dr. S. she thinks, making a list, wryly noting the absurdity of her (Tesco) inventory alongside theirs as she fixes her stick & bag on the scooter that's like a sledge without huskies, thinking her cleaner will carry in the goods like a Sherpa. She too has a team — daughters & sons & grandchildren, a nurse bandaging the ulcerous leg in the comfort of ... oh to think of the frost-bite in that tent, to contemplate the swamps, the malaria & beri-beri — but where to start, how to sort & sift & record? She must re-read the diaries & letters, make lists, keep a journal of scraps & fragments — piecemeal as her strength & sight allow, positioning the magnifying-glass to bring it all closer, within reach, amplifying the past in small stages.

୧୫ ୨୦
apples /veges
Cornflakes
rice /Bully-beef
flour-for-
chapattis
dried peas
eggs
୧୫ ୨୦

Ice & Tears

The Last Letters

My Father, Sandy

Here is a man who knows he is going to die. *The boy will be your comfort I had looked forward to helping you to bring him up but* ~~he~~ *it is a satisfaction to feel that he is safe with you...* and the Diarist flicks to his photograph, envisaging the bitten lips, those final moments in the stricken tent with his two surviving companions. Dr. S. on the other hand, snatched away in a collision between a psychotic — *noun recorded 1910* — and a Cambridge fellow, opening his door to disorder, triggering the end. She leans over the magnifying-glass, moved almost to tears by the sloping letters she can barely discern, needing the typescript to read *I wasn't a very good husband but I hope I shall be a good memory certainly the end is nothing for you to be ashamed of.*

Glaciers & Robins

Dante was right when he placed the circles of ice below the circles of fire.
Apsley Cherry-Garrard, *The Worst Journey in the World*

The terrifying ice-cliffs are always changing, writes the Diarist, *constantly repelling and attracting.* How did they survive the long winter? Did they quarrel? Yes sir, damn you sir. This morning, sitting outside on her scooter, she'd begun to pull ivy from the primroses when the robin arrived like a spirit into her tiny world — so close she could see its black eye. She glances at the image: *I hate the way we seem so small in the menacing vastness, pulled down to unspeakable depths.* Those who'd returned like young Cherry-Garrard were never the same. Yes, and then suddenly her scooter had shifted, tilted, and was rolling down the bank towards the stream. And there she was, inches from the water, ridiculous, grappling for her phone as the image of poor Cherry flashed into her mind, swinging in his harness above the dark void.

SARAH HOWE

THE INSTRUCTION OF CAPTAIN SCOTT

See now
      is the plateholder
quite snug? The light
      is not our only
challenge. Take off
      a glove then brush
your naked hand
      too near the lens
and instantly a scrim
      of frost descends
no mere rubbing can
      remove. Recall
a brass knob will burn
      unwary fingertips
like red-hot iron. Still
      cold is quickly
mastered; light less so. First
      insert the amber
filter: take the groove-
      etched rim, like this.
For unless viewed through
      a honey jar's warm
this ice strafed moon-
      scape will tend
inexorably to blue. Only
      now draw out
the slide. Texture, man!
      D'you see it? That
play of bright white
      ridge, its shadowed
underside too coy
      almost to catch. Don't
release the shutter –
      yet. Today the snow
seems practically
      transparent, no?
Patience, Captain.
      The true photographer
will in his very dreams
      calculate exposures.
One perfect morning I
      waited two whole hours
for a trio of cavorting
      penguins to exactly
echo the mountainside
      behind. Have you
checked the lens cap?
      Nothing is forgotten?
The men were donning
      their skins with a yawn
when at last I flung off
      my ice-fringed cloth
that long-hunched gloom
      like Jonah
spat out, a prophet, to the light.

Blocked in by ice, the crew of Erebus watch. A strange balloon, passing from east to west, climbs and falls on a high current of air. Even the sharpest eye does not detect the length of charred twine in its lee.

This burning fuse, having released a whole flight of slips of paper, carries on in aerial dumb show. The last slip given to the winds was lost to sight weeks before.

The balloon carried nothing but language: denoting provisions left on Beechey Island; or Spring parties, searching by sledge, directed to Jones's Sound and the north shore of Melville Island. The weight of each word in this English passage was heavier than Greenland gneiss.

It provisioned only ideas. Some are strewn in the Barren Grounds, in wastes not seen for a year, printed in reverse on fossil-bearing rocks, their message unvaried, to promise or threaten results that would alternate from reader to reader.

Each word led to a pinpoint in wilderness, to a pixel of time that shrinks in reading, then lengthens to say, 'come back'. But space and time are glacial now. And there is no trace to be found, no reading the caves and arches of ice.

The poetics of fire balloons are reversible. On the recto side, it is 'not one word is wasted'; on the verso, the terrible waste of its four word ballast:
'Read The Other Side'.

For years, they tried reading the Other Side. They fired off rockets, the balloons flocked over tundra, from Hudson Bay to Alaska. They dispersed their paper credit. But only occasional Inuit picked up the wind-fed rumours, and forwarded them; passing them round and round, turning them over and over.

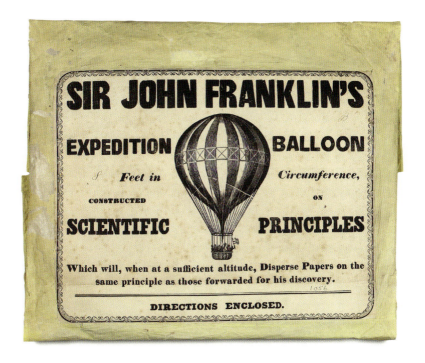

REDELL OLSEN

i. WHITEOUT FILM FOR SNOW-GOGGLES

"When I became snow-blind it was cloudy so it is not only sunlight
on the ice that can make you snow blind"

Roald Amundsen.

Look through these   ——   ——
Possible vision remains. One can never be sure of surroundings,
of distinguishing sky from brash, sewing all day, fixing up
expedition gear, embroidering *Rimed Needle Crystal* on hatbands
of *Discovery*. There may be prickly sensations of grit to eyes.
Violet rays lurk in shadows and take on diffuse shapes. Remain
alert in dull light. It is difficult to pick out unevenness of ice,
inequalities of the ground until he, as there is rarely a she
in this set-up, is right on them. No apologies for the discomfort.
No jokes in petticoats. The lens is filmic and laminated between
two pieces of glass. It is composed of countless flat crystals
arranged parallel to each other, lines slit to filter out vibrations.
Polarized at the edge of empty field myopia, tabloids to dissolve
tears. There is no focus for infinity or even for halo phenomena
recorded with more frequency than ever before. A Mid-Winter Day
Tree for June 21st 2014, from feathers, flags, anything else left
lying around; books, tins of food, post-it notes, biscuits, children's
clothes, plastic bags, junk mail. All that is broken and undone.
Explorers looking into the distance often struggled to focus
ahead and had to accommodate a near point. Dogs rather than
human endeavours are neatly caught on film. Sometimes things
slit open in a specular light to be reflected as if from a shiny
non-metallic surface, determined by the glare of closeness
beyond glass, or held as relics in a case. Letters preparatory
to a possible end, written with a lack of envelopes. Refocus
your camera, blacken your face. In case of frost, Scott chose
leather or wood. Glasses of light green or amber colour
abandoned in favour of a slit that restricts sight in all directions.
A photographic still taken cooling his head in the snow,
turned upside down shows, if it weren't for that curious sledge,
how arms might hold the earth up as a white but manageable
balloon, how feet might float in mid-air as mock heroic gest.

"Time after time in the diaries you find crystals—crystals; crystals…"

Apsley Cherry-Garrard,
The Worst Journey in the World

violet rays   halo
stellar crystal   rimed particle

                          *

corona   fog
scroll   graupel

                          *

prismatic sunrise   frost smoke
ice pellet   capped column

                          *

fog bow   willy waas
spatial dendrite   star

                          *

earth shadows   cloud
rimed needle crystal   depth hoar

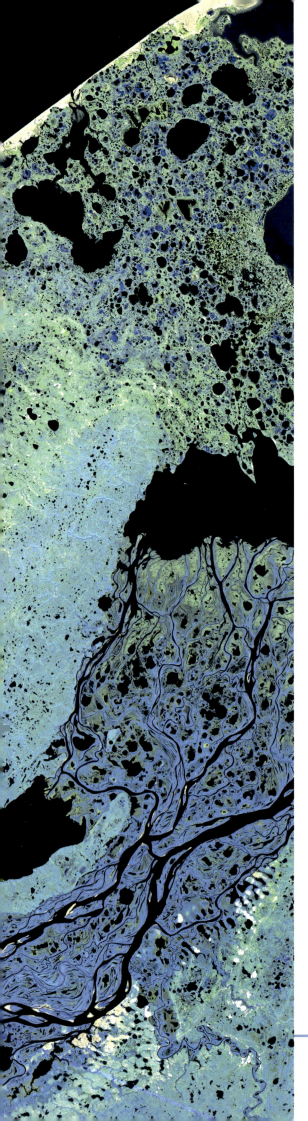

LUCY SHEERMAN

EXTRAPOLATED OBSERVATIONS
AT THE SCOTT POLAR MUSEUM

713647, 5787693 (30N)

14:32   24/5/14   13°c   523nm
                               12500 lux overcast

10mm   Daisy petal white, shaded, half-unfurled, bleeds into violet; green leaf fragment; tiny silver hairs; drowned in the yellow of stamens and pollen, drops of rain

10cm   Black fly, red eyes, translucent wings, takes flight; flowers, predominantly yellow; rain soaked leaves in sunlight, decaying, sombre green; (suspense of loss!); slick gleam effect

100cm   Crouched woman casts green shade; silver of raindrops; moss, grass, green in sunlight, restricted field; black patches of absence, shade-grey; brown leaf; discarded wrapper, maroon

10m   Pavement, pewter, rain-slicked; box hedge green; 2 faces tilted at clouds, (blank reflection); grassed area, mainly green; yellow road markings; car, dynamic red; sandstone wall

100m   Purple-black slate roof, gleaming, approx. 50%; people, shadows on lamp green lawn; pitch black street; vehicles, silver of light on paintwork; tree canopies, jade green

1km   Urban tract, clustered greys, (recognition slips up); black, red, verdigris roofs; green lawns/parks; metal curve of river; bird flocks, grey, scattered; shine of traffic threads

10km   White cloudscape; glimpse of leaden city; silver river, diverse green fields, charcoal grey roads, etc; water expanse, sky-blue; purple of shadow cast across the scene

100km   Pearl-white cloud; green, brown, golden arable landscape; towns, villages, bluish; glut of data, (colour not allocated); smoke-grey roads, railways; silver-blue trajectory of river & coastline

LUCY SHEERMAN

SOME MERGING AND SIMPLIFICATION OF THE GROUND COVER CLASSES

As scientists we do not choose to categorise things as beautiful, but we may have our private thoughts.
(Gareth Rees)

#1   Some of the information has been corrupted, rendering whole swathes of the territory indecipherable. The pixels have therefore been classified as no data, cloud, cloud shadow, water or bog. They define absence. Impossible to scale up from lived perspective to abstract, viewed from miles above our heads. The sublime rhapsody of flight gives the potential for serious misinterpretation. We might try reading meaning into emptiness.

#2   Satellite arcing across territory. Distributes impersonal snapshots which must be aligned to the GPS-derived location of the field data. How is this haze obscuring the view? We want to describe what was there but it has proved to be of unusable quality with a very poor signal to noise ratio.

#3   Perhaps we are wondering what all the different shades of green and brown and blue might mean? A fantasy of landscape, inhabited by degrees of colour, texture, heat and scent. Is it dense willow or birch scrub? All such speculation calls for field-based validation. Muddied fingers stroke the underside of these narrow silver leaves. What kinds of things must be discarded? It may pain us to do so but we must rely on spectral discrimination in the optical band.

#4   For the purposes of this extrapolation the names of particular categories of plant life are not significant. Nevertheless we have made detailed botanical descriptions. Absorbed in the precision of the field notebook, we look up towards the cloud which extends over our heads as far as the eye can see. We will find that colour has a way of deceiving us. That haze might be milky blue or mauve or opalescent. We should only trust wavelengths as true measurements of visible and non visible colour.

#5   We must tense ourselves against the grazing, nomadic patterns of irrelevance. Concerned only with mapping what general vegetation can be recorded here. We can resist such detail. The tiny flies alighting on every clause, sub-clause and pulse point snapped between the pages of this book. Still life made literal. The swarming discomfort of the scene moves once again into the mind's eye. We are satisfied by language's absence from such distortions.

#6   We might assert that all manner of vegetation thrives in this lush greenness even while we observe specifically 'arctic' limitations to the landscape. The classifications presented here suffer from the disadvantages of limited ground truth. We are poised between the intimate record of place and the impersonal distortions of scale. And thus, we are thrust once again into the actual. The stench of the bog, the whine of mosquitoes.

#7   Lichens, so adaptable and widespread are vulnerable to the relentless tread of metaphor. Their brittle leaves disintegrating under that inexorable pressure. We observed a large area, roughly circular and 100 – 150 m across which is entirely bare of vegetation. Not just a lack, it is a symbol of loss. The delicate submarine shapes receding into memory.

#8   We are on our hands and knees again, analysing the ground. Taking precise measurements with ruler and lens we can identify Stereocaulon, or snow lichen, it is common enough but impossible to include in a description except in the most general way. It may be possible to demonstrate that this tiny square of ground has altered over time but it is probably not meaningful to interpret any apparent differences between the spatial trends. Looking up to take our bearings, beyond us Lichen Ridge, we experience that ephemeral moment of recognition: bare ground and lichen tundra (these are difficult to separate). Detached from terrestrial constraint we begin to inhabit a landscape defined by this small window onto phenology which is purely abstract.

She gives him an ivory bird

It nests in the palm of her hand,
this small thing, this magic
that draws birds to the trap,
the flesh to the pot,
a token to carry into the world of the dead.
It dreams of salt water and cold winds,
each season carved
into the twitch of the heart.
The needle in its skull
shivers between here and the north.
Note the illusion of possession,
it has already flown,
only the bone of it left, a pale mark
in strange air.

She gives him her world

Mime the winding motion and she will come,
she will bend her head to the sound and hum
the silence from somewhere deep in her throat.
Concentrate and you can almost peel each note
from the air and feel her frost-smoked breath
on the back of your neck. She was never left behind.

Map maker, interpreter, wise woman, voice,
as their hunger devours her she marks
the endless ways salt water can meet the land.
The great bear has always given her the north,
the compass she boxes for them again and again
never shows her the stars, the purposes of dark.

Listen. . . She can still recite thirty-two ways to lose
yourself in ice. She will trace them with her finger
on your back in return for bread-dust or beads.

She barters with spirits older than words and prayer.
They tumble around the keel and squeeze the hull
in their jaws, creak the timbers to speak of themselves.
The sea woman gives her food and light and heat.
The womenless men also speak to spirits of finding,
the search for anything requires the price of belief.

She watches their forge, studies the gifts of fire,
the slow beating out of the double-edged sword;
planes, pay, Jim Beam, children ripped from families,
young sons dying too soon, their face to the wall.
She stares into the bellowed blaze,
and unbinds her hair for loss, for what will come.

She's here now and singing out there,
somewhere on that stretched white edge,
ice weeping through her fingers.

EMPEROR PENGUIN
(THE POLAR MUSEUM, CAMBRIDGE)

She gives him a comb

You crack open her carapace
of hide and fur and skin,
choose a knife, hunt for a vein,
clutch the cup to catch the flow.
You haul her up from the deep
with a thin rope of her blood.
At night you will take the comb,
trace each scored line and ridge
with those same finger tips
that felt for a pulse.
You will fall into dreams of red ivory
drifting through black waves.
It dreams of itself, of how to belong.
Blood   is blood   is blood

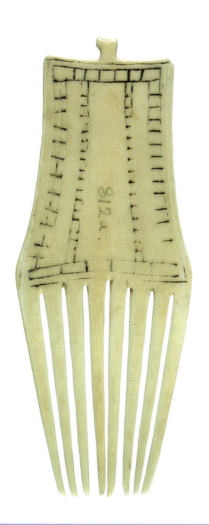

This afterlife
is inaccurate: everything here is dry.

I try to make
a true impression, but the chick

I've been given
refuses to play the part, persists with its leaning

as if it could
imagine anything beyond our destiny.

Before I was seized
my throat was an open channel,

my beak
a conduit for the sea. It is not shame

that forces
my head to hang: it is the inured act

I've grown too stiff
to shake off. Chick – even like this

you look hungry.
There is no escape. Turn in and face up.

ANTARCTICA

Heaven   is a sweet dream   Tinned peaches and syrup   sweeter
Awake   listening   in the dark   frenzy of canvas   wind   slapping
like so many frozen hands   Body   a quaker   Muscles crying
sugar   Tired   as a dog   but colder   *Colder*
Language   is a beggar   Hope   another.

Land of the South   pure   and Beauty   enough   to transfix or unfix
to turn a man's eyes blue   and Hope   they say   is a blue-eyed look
God   sender of daylight   scatterer of the terrors of the dark   planter
of strenuous prayers in the heart   Heart   keeper of the flesh   Heartbeat
a song   a step   a prayer   *Heave*
what a man must do   for God   for glory   for mercy.

Bird   like a snowflake like God   glittering   in a blue sky   lucent as an angel's wing
        Gift   given freely   with both hands   This Earth   is a good place
to live in   Die   as everything must   Numb   as a mass
of ice   frozen reindeer bag   coffin   crevasse   A good warm sleep
        a wish.   *Great God!*   *this is an awful place*

Give   take   Take   give   Keep temper   don't speak   God is
grace   Returning   a certain numbed pleasure   biscuit   talk
        write   rest   *sleep*   Comfort   of the Almighty's making
Peace   in the satisfaction of faith   *drifting*   eyes open
        All   that the Lord has given   taken away.   Blessed

Note: Some of the words in this poem are taken from the accounts of the 1910–1913 British Antarctic Expedition (Terra Nova) and Cherry-Garrard's 1922 retrospective The Worst Journey in the World.

REINDEER LICHEN

some for trophies some to flag
in canvas imperial some to lie
blinded by prospects of relics
scarce quick to a lichen trail
subsisting through the poo-jok
welcome to anthropogenic gases
our polluting breath one cloud
after another sung oft & aloft
tracers to cap data in cuilkuq
and beyond this arctic haze by
any other misnomer would smell
as rank in source signature of
Eurasian air the name spelling
car lungs into the troposphere
and albedo as the polar scalps
warm to softly falling sulphur
& carbons settling on cladonia
rangiferina misnamed cryptogam
or reindeer moss but still led
through by radionuclides taken
in along so-called food chains
what price pristine now & ever
wilds spent to a chemical sink
the sheet like flows so turbid
so given over to written scree

BIOGRAPHIES

LUCY HAMILTON

Hearing Eye published Lucy Hamilton's pamphlet *Sonnets for my Mother* in 2009, from which several poems have been translated into Arabic. She teaches creative writing, and workshops include Riddles & Kennings for a community project sponsored by the Department of Anglo-Saxon, Norse and Celtic, University of Cambridge. She is co-MC for Oxfam Poetry Cambridge and co-editor of *Long Poem Magazine*. Her collection of prose poems *Stalker* (Shearsman, 2012) was shortlisted for the Forward Felix Dennis Prize for Best First Collection. Prose poems from her second collection-in-progress have appeared in *Shearsman Review*, *PN Review* and *Tears in the Fence*.

SARAH HOWE

Sarah Howe's work has been anthologised in *The Salt Book of Younger Poets* (Salt, 2011), *Dear World & Everyone in It: New Poetry in the UK* (Bloodaxe, 2013) and *Ten: The New Wave* (Bloodaxe, 2014). Her pamphlet, *A Certain Chinese Encyclopedia*, won an Eric Gregory award in 2010. She is currently a member of Spread the Word's *The Complete Works II*, a national development programme for Black and Asian poets. She is working on her first collection of poems, *Loop of Jade*, forthcoming from Chatto & Windus in 2015.

ROD MENGHAM

Rod Mengham's most recent publications are *Paris by Helen* (Oystercatcher, 2014), the pamphlet *The Understory* (corrupt press, 2014) and *STILL moving* (Veer, 2014), which records, in the form of text and stills, film collaborations with Marc Atkins. Previous publications include *Bell Book* (Wide Range Chapbooks, 2012) and *Unsung: New and Selected Poems* (Salt, 2001). Mengham has also translated modern Polish poetry into English, most recently *Speedometry* by Andrzej Sosnowski (Contraband Books), as well as co-editing and introducing *Altered State: the New Polish Poetry* (Arc Publications, 2003).

DREW MILNE

Drew Milne's books of poetry include: *equipollence* (2012), *the view from Royston cave* (2012), *Burnt Laconics Bloom* (2013), and, with John Kinsella, *Reactor Red Shoes* (2013), *Sheet Mettle* (Alfred David Editions, 1994), *Bench Marks* (Alfred David Editions, 1998), *The Damage: new and selected poems* (Salt, 2001), *Mars Disarmed* (The Figures, 2002), and *Go Figure* (Salt, 2003). His work is also featured in collections and anthologies, notably *Conductors of Chaos* edited by Iain Sinclair (Picador, 1996) and *Anthology of Twentieth-Century British and Irish Poetry* edited by Keith Tuma (Oxford University Press, 2001). He edits the occasional journal *Parataxis: modernism and modern writing* and the poetry imprint Parataxis Editions.

REDELL OLSEN

Redell Olsen's work combines printed text with live performance and film, coupling poetic with academic and curatorial practice. Her most recent publication is *Film Poems* (Los Angeles: Les Figues, 2014), which brings together a number of recent works for film and performance. Other books of poetry include *Punk Faun: A Bar Rock Pastel* (Oakland, CA: Subpress, 2012), *Secure Portable Space* (Hastings: Reality Street, 2004) and *Book of the Fur* (Cambridge: Rem Press, 2000).

ANDREA PORTER

Andrea Porter's debut full collection, *A Season of Small Insanities*, was published by Salt in 2009. Prior to this she had two pamphlets published by Flarestack (*Bubble*) and Apothecary Press (*Kiss*). Porter's latest book, *The House of the Deaf Man* (Gatehouse Press), is a collaboration with the artist Tom de Freston. She collaborated with the dramatist Fraser Grace to produce a version of *Bubble* that was broadcast as a radio play on BBC Radio 4 and helps run CB1 Poetry in Cambridge.

LUCY SHEERMAN

Lucy Sheerman worked at the Arts Council for twelve years where she specialised in supporting the development of writers and new writing. Publications include *rarefied: falling without landing* (Oystercatcher Press) and the fan fiction project *Fragments salvaged from her diary: a correspondence with Rebecca* (Long Poem Magazine 10). Her writing has also appeared in *Archive of the Now*, *Infinite Difference: Other Poetries by UK Women Poets* (Shearsman), *Junction Box*, *PN Review* and *Poetry Wales*. Menagerie commissioned and produced her short play *What Did It Feel Like To Go To The Moon?*, which was a collaboration with the Apollo 15 astronaut and poet Al Worden.

REBECCA WATTS

Rebecca Watts is a poet, freelance editor and librarian based in Cambridge. Her poems have appeared in *PN Review*, *The North*, *Die Gazette* and *The Journal of Modern Wisdom*. A selection of her work is forthcoming in Carcanet's *New Poetries VI* (2015).

IMAGES

Supported using public funding by

ARAM SAROYAN

Notes on Being My Own Bibliographer

1

In 1943, the year I was born, Edmund Wilson wrote 'Thoughts on Being Bibliographed', an essay in which he noted that his own generation's enthusiasm for modernism had not extended to a new generation of literary academics, who preferred to compile a bibliography of Wilson's writing – when he was still in his forties – rather than write their own essays or stories. By the time I attended high school in the late 1950s and early 1960s, modernism, no doubt partly owing to the efforts of the intervening generation, had achieved such pre-eminence in our assigned texts – and in our young minds – that it was virtually all we knew: James Joyce to e.e. cummings to F. Scott Fitzgerald to Hemingway to Gertrude Stein's maxim 'A rose is a rose is a rose'. As the son of William Saroyan, a writer who had been part of the last wave of American modernists, I knew the example very close at hand.

Ironically, with modernism so firmly entrenched, the official culture of America wasn't very welcoming to the next wave of literary artists. When the Beat Generation erupted during my high-school years they were treated derisively in media that now included the television series *The Life and Loves of Dobie Gillis* with its 'Beatnik', Maynard G. Krebs, supposedly a satiric version of Allen Ginsberg.

And so, not long after that, when I began myself as a writer, I hadn't much sense of continuing in a family line, of taking my place in a viable profession practised by my father before me. Rather I was fascinated by what certain writers – the Beat Generation and the Angry Young Men in England prominently among them – were telling me about experience that I couldn't find anywhere else. Reading and writing, then, represented a kind of subterranean passage out of a powerful but largely vacuous public culture to deeper resources that I hoped would guide, inform and facilitate my life. I began not as a 'professional', but as a spiritual and emotional prospector in search of some kind of experiential bedrock. Meanwhile I worked in a Manhattan bookstore and then, in the fall of 1964, now a serial college drop-out, started a little magazine called *Lines* with a small inheritance.

I had no real expectation of a 'career' as a writer, and those I got to know in New York who were also writing seemed more or less to share this sense of indeterminacy. While the Beats had achieved notoriety in the larger culture, none of them seemed to be much better off for it – none of them, for example, had achieved through writing the economic level that my father had achieved.

Which left the adventure of writing itself – and then the advent of what we refer to today as the sixties, which began well after the decade itself and extended well beyond it. Since that onset coincided with my stewardship of *Lines* (1964–65), the adventure expanded fortuitously. As a poet I was soon caught up in a variety of aesthetic strains that achieved currency in New York including the Beats, Black Mountain poetry, minimalism, Pop art, concrete poetry and the no-holds-barred exfoliations of the second-generation poets of the New York School.

While uncertain about the larger questions of my life – relationship, career – I knew instinctively that as a poet there was now wind in my sails and by the evidence of the bibliography worked as copiously as most of my peers. In a matter of a few years, it seemed I was one of a small number of minimalists in poetry, though I wouldn't have put it that way myself. More to the point, it was exhilarating to be caught up in something I wasn't entirely certain about, but was at the same time fascinated by. 'Our doubt *is* our passion,' Henry James instructed.

2

'The poet thinks with his poem, in that lies the thought, and therein is the profundity' – so wrote William Carlos Williams as quoted to me at 20 by Robert Creeley in one of a series of letters that comprised a tutorial that has proven to be a lifelong resource. What occurred next was an unforeseen fast-forward: in the early summer of 1967, I met my future wife, Gailyn McClanahan, and Random House asked me to put together a book of my poems. That summer, the fabled Summer of Love, now sharing an apartment with Gailyn on River Street in Cambridge, I was charged with 'understanding' in a more literal way the 'thinking' I'd been doing in the poems themselves.

For all its suddenness, the mandate to make a book was not untimely since my involvement with minimalism had by now all but run its course. The question was what it amounted to: short poems for the most part, of a wide variety of forms, including one-word poems. What occupied me immediately was a concern to avoid trivialising work I thought might be perceived as a novelty item, merely clever or funny, when I thought the best of it went beyond that.

As I sorted the work out, two manuscripts evolved simultaneously, both moving from short minimalist pieces to even shorter ones and finally to instant, one-word poems. The scheme of both books embodied my now conscious recognition that there was a *physiological* difference between a short poem and a one-word poem: the short poem, that is, involved a reading process – thus a beginning, middle and end – while a one-word poem was a de facto instantaneous object. If a word was altered for a particular effect – as, for instance, the one-word poem *lighght* – that was only another aspect of the central fact that the event of the poem happened instantaneously.

When I met with the designers of the art department at Random House I realised immediately that there was only mild, perfunctory interest on their part in figuring out a way to present the work. If I'd been worried about a too-gimmicky presentation at the hands of a commercial publisher, those fears were now banished, but the ball was in my court.

The books that Random House published in two

successive years, *Aram Saroyan* (1968) and *Pages* (1969), are minimalist solutions to the problems I perceived. I eschewed any engagement with novel or larger or smaller typefaces and relied on my own typewriter font in facsimile printed, in the first book, on typing-paper-size pages. I also made the decision to run each poem on a right-hand page, leaving the left-hand page blank in the interests of showcasing the sculptural aspect of each work to the fullest possible extent.

It was about a year after both books had been published that it dawned on me with chilling clarity that the right-hand-page-only decision had the opposite of the intended effect: that instead it tended to prompt the reader to turn the page, indeed, created a kind of narrative momentum.

3

A new phase began in late summer of 1972 with our arrival in Bolinas, Gailyn and I now the parents of a one-and-a-half-year-old daughter. A small town with many poet friends already residents, the place was so welcoming as I was about to turn 29 that it seemed to kick-start me into the next chapter of my writing life. No longer a minimalist, after a series of longer poems, I wrote *The Street: An Autobiographical Novel* (Bookstore Press, 1974) and began reviewing mostly poetry books for the *New York Times Book Review*, the *Village Voice* and the *Nation*. Thanks in large part to my friendship with our Bolinas neighbour Donald Allen, the editor of the benchmark post-war anthology *The New American Poetry 1945–1960*, I was able to undertake a biography of the poet Lew Welch, who in 1971 at the age of 44 had disappeared with his pistol into the foothills of the Sierra Nevada, never to be seen again. (He had been living in a trailer on Gary Snyder's property). Welch's literary executor and publisher, Don graciously shared the poet's correspondence and other writings with me as I began to work on the book.

Genesis Angels: The Saga of Lew Welch and the Beat Generation, published by William Morrow in 1979, was attacked in major reviews in *Esquire* and the *New York Times Book Review* by writers of an age *between* the Beats and my own generation. Schooled in literary modernism, as we had been, they were too old, it seemed, to take the Beats at face value, and seemed offended that a younger writer, undeterred by the public hazing these writers still attracted, would address their lives and work with perfect seriousness, not to say veneration. But for me the interest of Beat writing from the beginning had involved the challenge implicit in it to our public culture, and so the derision was, from that perspective, a kind of validation. Still, these were the first major reviews of my career and they knocked me out of the box.

Did I really want to be the target of such *ad hominem* attacks? Should I not try my hand at screenwriting instead? 'Life is what happens to you while you're busy making other plans,' John Lennon sang. After working on film scripts, one of which had been optioned, I got a phone call from my sister Lucy, informing me that our father, from whom we were both estranged, was dying of cancer. So the 1980s began for me, a decade during which I published four books: *Last Rites: The Death of William Saroyan* (Morrow, 1982), comprising a journal kept over the course of three weeks preceding my father's death; *William Saroyan* (Harcourt Brace Jovanovich, 1983), an illustrated literary biography; *Trio: Oona Chaplin/ Carol Matthau/ Gloria Vanderbilt – Portrait of an Intimate*

Friendship (Linden/Simon & Schuster, 1985); and a novel, *The Romantic* (McGraw Hill, 1988). Encompassing multiple prose genres, these books represented an all-stops-out effort to achieve a literary and economic safe landing, with predictably mixed results. The economic safe landing didn't occur, and I began to search out a second career, eventually finding work in public relations. At the same time, I'd learned enough about the craft of writing to take up teaching, in addition to continuing to write as time permitted.

By now I knew that the adversarial reality experienced by the Beat Generation was also an inheritance of my own sixties generation, even as the Beats were gradually being absorbed into the canon.

4

Oddly enough, a small but vital income stream during these years was provided by the Special Collections librarians at American universities interested in acquiring my generation's literary papers. Beginning with my *Lines* archives I would sell my papers on an annual or biennial basis. And by the mid-seventies I'd begun to checklist the papers and correspondence I accumulated each year to facilitate these sales. It was around this time too that I started keeping a more careful record of each year's publications, and thus became my own bibliographer.

Checklisting the year's papers was also a worthwhile habit because it identified work soon to be removed from my own environs that otherwise might have been discarded, lost, forgotten or purposefully destroyed. Later on, if I wanted a look at a piece from years ago I could contact the Special Collections library where it remained intact.

In effect, while the public culture was prone to unpredictable mood swings about my writing – very good or very bad reviews, and not a great deal in between – academia provided a steady albeit modest remuneration for my efforts and also comprised a de facto filing system. With the advent of word processors in the late eighties, it became possible to selectively transfer any and all writing I needed to a computer smaller than a single file drawer. As a result of that option, I could make, for instance, a file encompassing all the poems I'd written during our twelve-year sojourn (1972–84) in Bolinas, which then spurred me to assemble *Day and Night: Bolinas Poems* (Black Sparrow, 1998), a book going back 26 years and including poems that otherwise would have been irretrievable.

Edmund Wilson, no doubt aided and abetted by his bibliography, had modelled similar decade-spanning compilations in his books *Classics and Commercials* and *The Shores of Light*, among others. But almost all of Wilson's pieces were originally written for mainstream American magazines, and therefore easily retrievable; whereas a great deal of my work had been published in fugitive little magazines that might only have managed an issue or two before expiring. The fact that this work remained available, courtesy of Special Collections, either in manuscript or in magazines, was crucial.

5

In the mid-1990s, when I first learned how to get online, I was surprised and heartened to discover that the poems in both my early Random House books, long out of print, were available on the web at Kenneth Goldsmith's pioneering online archive Ubuweb.com. And in a few years via this reincarnation on the internet the work achieved greater currency than ever before.

Then in 2005 I was invited by James Hoff, an editor at the time at Ugly Duckling Presse, to work with him in assembling a complete collection of the minimal work. Thus four decades after their original publication I had the opportunity to redress design errors I'd made formatting those early books, a long-wished-for opportunity. The design that would best facilitate a relaxed, unhurried apprehending of the poems, I thought now, would be one that embraced all of the bells and whistles of traditional book design, including a standard typeface, page numbers, author and title headers, standardised height levels for text and, when applicable, titles – and of course the use of both left- and right-hand pages. The published book, *Complete Minimal Poems*, fulfilled these criteria, and the fact that it was warmly received seemed to confirm my notions of the changes that needed to be made.

BENJAMIN FONDANE

Interlude: Visionary Anger, *from* Exodus
Translated by Andrew Rubens and Henry King

I

And I said to my vision: 'So what is Exodus?
What is Babylon? What is Jerusalem?
If there is not, in the world and under the world, a river,
that runs, unseen, beneath the appearance of peace,
if no one worries about the innumerable leaves
of the forest,
if human cries fall to the ground
like chestnuts, as the wind wills,
without disturbing the peace of Angels,
what then is Exodus?
If there is really no eternal thing
– what is it then?'
And I was abruptly thrown into the countryside of France.

II

From the Somme to the Loire
misfortune fell upon our weapons and the Meuse cried:
'Flee!'
And suddenly we were fleeing like the russet rain
of autumn, gurgling in the hollow gutters
of the roads,
coming from Arras, coming from Amiens,
coming from Reims, coming from Lille,
from Tourcoing, from Rouen,
in a heavy storm of supply-trucks and vans,
sleeping on horses like bronze kings
– a flash of weary anger in our eye...

III

Howl, Door!
Cry out, unconquered Reason!
Fire is hurling forth,
it burns all along the roads, it turns us
to shadows,
we have lost everything, we have lost everything
all we have left is the road, the night
and this shadow, which instead of destroying
the flame brings forth.

IV

What are we going to do if the rivers
one after another should leave us?
Oh God, oh God, what will we do?

The Meuse gave us the slip, the bitch,
and the Somme's been carried off...
If all the rivers should leave us
what will we do?

Sweet Marne, so canny, so pretty,
why did you stay in your bed?
Oh Seine, this is insanity,
Oh God!

There's still the Loire, she's waiting,
she's waiting for us for certain,
naked between her banks
– isn't that so, dear Loire?

But if she were to leave us too,
what would bread and milk be worth,
supposing there's any left on earth?

If she, if she left too...
Oh God, oh God, what will we do?

V

I have counted you all
yesterday's civilians, accountants, shopkeepers, peasants
and factory workers and tramps whose nests
are under the bridges of Notre-Dame
and sacristy beadles and dependants
of the State, all Frenchmen from France, with clear eyes,
or from Congo, from deepest Algeria, from Annam
with palm-trees floating in their gaze
and Frenchmen come from Caribbean islands,
French according to the rights of man,
sons of the barricade and of the guillotine,
sans-culottes, incorruptible foreheads, free,
and Czechs, and Poles, and Slovaks
and Jews from all the ghettos of the world,
who loved this earth and its shadows and its rivers,
who have sown this earth with their death
and who have become French by right of death.

[VI]

VII

We were leaving Paris behind us. Ah! If ever
I forget thee, Jerusalem… From that moment
you were a city no more, but an old piece of the Host
bread of flesh and blood
that stayed put, but which we were carrying
with us – in captivity, insult,
in anguish, offence and vomiting.
Sweet river, O Siloam!
O Seine! and you, Paris, wailing wall
reserved for a later date
when Assyria, swollen like a huge bladder
will burst apart!

Only Jews on this earth, Lord! who have doubtless
forgotten you, stiff-necked and strong-headed. Yes,
and yet we were crying out to You. Do You remember
the goat, back then, that the strong hand of Aaron
fell upon and chased into the desert, laden
with our uncleanness? Now I am Aaron.
I go down on my knees and I sob and cry
in a language I have forgotten, but which
I remember in the impassioned evenings of Your Anger:
'Adonai Eloheinu, Adonai Eḥad!'

VIII

Adonai Eloheinu, Adonai Eḥad!
Have pity, have pity on the land of France!
How beautiful it is! Just as You created it
from nothing, by Your wise and loving hands,
with its fine vineyards, its cathedrals and
its workhorses and its lucid men!
Have pity, have pity, Lord,
on this France that I knew from books,
pure, which now sickens me, dirtied and bloodied,
stomach open in the immaculate centre of the ode
– *Adonai Eloheinu, Adonai Eḥad!*
You know that when all is calm
on earth and in the heavens
we will have forgotten You. You know, from now,
that merely the secret memory of my prayer
will fill me with shame. I will be angry with You, do You see,
for having listened. I will be angry with myself, too
for having said it. I have, as You well know, other gods
than You, secret, perfidious gods!
But here, on the road, in disaster and in
chaos, there is no other God. You alone!
Terrible, Igneous, Merciful, Unique!

Note
This interlude, comprising in full 18 numbered sections, interrupts Benjamin Fondane's long poem *Exodus*, reflecting the Nazis' 1940 invasion of France and the subsequent displacement of the French population. Fondane, a Jew who moved from his native Romania to Paris in 1924 and took French citizenship, was later deported to Auschwitz and killed. Further extracts from the present translation of *Exodus* will appear in a selection of Fondane's work to be published as part of the NYRB Poets series in 2015.

ANDRÉ NAFFIS-SAHELY

'The Whole Shadow of Man': Alessandro Spina's Libyan Epic

Three months after Alessandro Spina's death in July 2013, Ilario Bertoletti, his Italian editor, published a memoir in which he described his first near-encounter with the notoriously reclusive writer: 'It was June, 1993. The bell rang in the late afternoon; moments later, a colleague entered my office: "A gentleman dropped by. He looked like an Arab prince, tall and handsome. He left a history of the Maronites for you."' The editor made some enquiries and discovered that Spina had been quietly publishing a number of novels and short stories since the early 1960s which charted the history of Libya from 1911, when Italy had invaded the sleepy Ottoman province, all the way to 1966, when petrodollars sparked an economic boom, exacerbating the corruption and nepotism that eventually paved the way for Muammar Gaddafi's coup d'état in 1969. It took Bertoletti, who runs an independent imprint based in Brescia, fifteen years to persuade Spina to let him reissue his books, or rather to assemble them into a 1250-page omnibus edition entitled *I confini dell'ombra: in terra d'oltremare/The Confines of the Shadow: In Lands Overseas* (Morcelliana, 2007), a cycle comprising six novels, a novella and four collections of stories, which Spina, who'd only settled on a definitive structure and title in 2003, summarised thus:

The sequence of novels and short stories takes as its subject the Italian experience in Cyrenaica. *The Young Maronite* (1971) discusses the 1911 war prompted by Giolitti, *Omar's Wedding* (1973) narrates the ensuing truce and the attempt by the two peoples to strike a compromise before the rise of Fascism. *The Nocturnal Visitor* (1979) chronicles the end of the twenty-year Libyan resistance; *Officers' Tales* (1967) focuses on the triumph of colonialism – albeit this having been achieved when the end of Italian hegemony already loomed in sight and the Second World War appeared inevitable – and *The Psychological Comedy* (1992), which ends with Italy's retreat from Libya and the fleeing of settlers. *Entry into Babylon* (1976) concentrates on Libyan independence in 1951, *Cairo Nights* (1986) illustrates the early years of the Senussi Monarchy and the looming spectre of Pan-Arab nationalism, while *The Shore of the Lesser Life* (1997) examines the profound social and political changes that occurred when large oil and gas deposits were discovered in the mid 1960s. Each text can be read independently or as part of the sequence. Either mode of reading will produce different – but equally legitimate – impressions.

A year later, *The Confines of the Shadow* was unanimously awarded the Premio Bagutta, Italy's highest literary accolade. It was an impressive achievement, especially for an author who'd insisted on publishing his books in limited editions with tiny outfits, all of which had fallen out of print by the early 1990s. However, the Bagutta nod only caused a faint ripple: a single radio interview, a handful of glowing reviews and a conference in his honour, which he didn't attend.

Lacking the 'hook' of a persona – the back flap doesn't even feature a photograph of the author – the book receded into obscurity. Spina remains little known even in Italy, where he spent the last thirty years of his life, despite the fact that *The Confines of the Shadow* belongs alongside panoptic masterpieces such as *Buddenbrooks*, *The Man Without Qualities* and *The Cairo Trilogy*.

Spina died two weeks before I concluded an agreement with a London publisher to translate the entirety of *The Confines of the Shadow*. Denied the privilege of meeting him, I was faced with a conundrum: the translation of such a monumental opus in the immediate wake of the author's death meant that any afterword I produced would have to deal with the life, of which I knew next to nothing, save that 'Alessandro Spina' was a *nom de plume* adopted in 1955 when Alberto Moravia published his first story, 'L'ufficiale'/'The Officer' in *Nuovi Argomenti*. Sporting an English reticence and safely ensconced behind his pseudonym, Spina had spent half a century eluding the limelight, refusing invitations to make public appearances or to concede interviews. Consequently, I realised any clues would have to be culled from the work itself. I therefore retreated to the books, sleuthing through *The Confines of the Shadow*, a 300-page *Diary* Spina kept while composing that epic, as well as three volumes of brilliant essays, and thanks to quasi-involuntary slips on Spina's part, I slowly began to assemble a narrative.

Alessandro Spina, né Basili Shafik Khouzam, was born in Benghazi on 8 October 1927 into a family of Maronites from Aleppo. His father, a wealthy textile magnate, had left his native Syria aged 17 to make his fortune and arrived in Benghazi, the capital of Cyrenaica – then a quiet city of twenty thousand Turks and Arabs ringed by Bedouin encampments – a few weeks after Italy and the Ottoman Empire signed the Treaty of Ouchy. Ratified in October 1912, the Treaty brought 360 years of Turkish rule and 13 months of war to a close and formalised Italy's possession of Tripolitania and Cyrenaica. A late-comer to the scramble for Africa, acquiring Eritrea and Somalia in the late 1880s, barely a couple of decades after it had been cobbled out of squabbling fiefdoms, Italy had long sought to lay its hands on the *quarta sponda*, or 'fourth shore'. After all, the Libyan coast – the last remaining African territory of the Ottoman Empire, which, as Baron Eversley put it, had grown used to having 'provinces torn from it periodically, like leaves from an artichoke' – lay only 300 miles south of Sicily. With trouble brewing in the Balkans and sensing the sick man of Europe was on his knees, the Italians seized their chance. Knowing they would only have to contend with a crippled navy and a handful of ill-equipped battalions, they delivered an ultimatum in September 1911, their soldiers disembarked in October, and by November, the Italian tricolour could be seen flying from every major city on the Libyan littoral.

Nevertheless, what was expected to be a pushover instead turned into a 20-year insurgency that was only quelled when the fascists took power in Rome and Mussolini, in a quest to solve Italy's emigration problem, dispatched one of his most ruthless generals, the hated Rodolfo Graziani (1882–1955), to bring the *quarta sponda* to heel and 'make room' for colonists. Genocide ensued: a third of Libya's population was killed, tens of thousands interned in concentration camps, a 300-kilometre barbed wire fence was erected on the Egyptian border to block rebels receiving supplies and reinforcements, and the leader of the resistance, a venerable Qur'anic teacher named Omar Mukhtar (1858–1931), was hunted down and unceremoniously hanged: a chilling story elegantly depicted in *Lion of the Desert* (1981), in which Oliver Reed and Anthony Quinn respectively portrayed Graziani and Mukhtar, and which was banned from Italian screens for several years.

In 1939, when Spina was twelve years old, Italy officially annexed Libya, by which time Italian settlers constituted 13 per cent of the population and over a third of the inhabitants of Tripoli and Benghazi, the epicentres of Italian power. At the outbreak of World War II, Spina's father dispatched his son to Italy, where he would remain until 1954. Initially leading a peripatetic existence that saw him alternate between Busto Arsizio and the spa town of Salsomaggiore, Spina and his mother eventually settled in Milan, where he became a devotee of opera: as luck would have it, the hotel where they lodged, the Marino on Piazza della Scala, was directly opposite the Teatro. While in Milan, Spina, by then fluent in Arabic, English, French and Italian, studied under Mario Marcazzan, penned a thesis on Moravia and began drafting his first stories. They were lush tapestries of history, fiction and autobiography featuring a cosmopolitan array of characters: Italian officers, Senussi rebels, Ottoman bureaucrats, chirpy grand dames, Maltese fishermen, aristocrats, servants and slaves. Spina nevertheless described each caste with the same finesse, empathy and intimacy – partly thanks to his immaculate fusion of Eastern narrative quaintness and the passion for encapsulating an entire way of life that informs much nineteenth-century European fiction, thereby distinguishing sentiment from sentimentality.

There is perhaps no better example of this balancing act than 'Il forte di Régima'/'The Fort at Régima', one of the early stories, set in the mid-1930s, in which a Captain Valentini is ordered south of Benghazi to take command of a garrison stationed in an old Ottoman fortress that 'recalled the castles built in Greece by knights who had joined the Fourth Crusade'. Valentini is glad to leave the city and its tiresome peacetime parades behind, but as he's driven to his new posting, his mind is suddenly flooded with the names of famous Crusaders who had 'conquered Constantinople, made and unmade Emperors, carved the vast Empire into fiefs, and run to and fro vainly fighting to ensure the survival of a system, which owing to its lack of roots in the country, was never destined to survive.

Employing only 500 words, Spina slices across 700 years, showing the inanity of the concept of conquest, as well as the existential vacuum it inevitably leaves in its wake: 'As he weltered about in his armoured vehicle, it seemed cruel to the Captain to be forced to undergo the same rigmarole after so many centuries had passed.' Our technological genius may be growing, Spina implies, but so is our historical ignorance. It's no coincidence that Spina collected these sketches under the title of *Officers' Tales*. His men-at-arms perfectly typify his concept of the 'shadow': their minds are haunted by the maddening darkness of the colonial enterprise, which still adumbrates our supposedly post-colonial times. More than

a metaphor intertwining his novels, Spina's shadow can be interpreted as an allegory of how the Italian presence in Libya was both *visible* by dint of its brutality and yet *incorporeal* because it sought only to rule, never integrate. Ultimately, the shadow is also life itself, amorphous and mysterious. Mysterious because history has seen us repeatedly fail to envision what lies beyond what we can see, past the horizon of our ephemeral lives and experiences.

At the end of World War II, Italy relinquished its claim to Libya, which was then administered by the British until 1951, when the country became independent under King Idris I. Aged 26 and with the ink still fresh on his degree, Spina returned to Benghazi in August 1953 to help run his ageing father's factory. Although typically working twelve-hour days, he would somehow find the time to write, locking himself in his father's office, whose windows looked out onto the fourteenth-century *fondouk*. Throughout his life, Spina firmly believed he'd acquired his discipline not *despite* being an industrialist, but *because* of it, in the same way Tolstoy refused to leave Yasnaya Polyana so as to stay among his people and chief source of inspiration. In his spare time, Spina would pick up the copy of *Le Temps retrouvé* he always kept by his side, or send letters to friends, which often featured pearls encapsulating the transformations his country was traversing:

A young scion of the royal family – 'of the highest pedigree' as Hofmannsthal might have said – the grandson of the old king who'd been deposed by the current monarch, has died in a car accident. Having come to convey his condolences, one of the King's cousins also suffered a crash on his way home to his desert encampment, an accident that took the lives of his mother, wife and son (he remains in intensive care at the hospital). I went to convey my own condolences. The Prince is very handsome, around sixty years old. He's extremely tall, his skin's a milky white and he sports a little aristocratic goatee. Eventually, the talk turned to the accident. The old man (his medieval view of the world still unmarred) remarked: 'Are automobiles meant as vehicles for this world or the next?'

(26 July 1963)

During the first decade of Libyan independence, Spina completed his first collection of stories, published a novel based on his days in Milan, *Tempo e Corruzione/Time and Decay* (Garzanti, 1962), and worked on a translation of the *Storia della citta di Rame/The City of Brass* (Scheiwiller, 1963), a tale excerpted from the *One Thousand and One Nights*. However, it was only in 1964 that Spina truly hit his stride and began writing the first volumes that make up *The Confines of the Shadow*. From 1964 to 1975, arguably his most productive decade, Spina produced *Il giovane maronita/The Young Maronite* (1964–69), *Le nozze di Omar/Omar's Wedding* (1970–72), *Il visitatore notturno/The Nocturnal Visitor* (1972) and *Ingresso a Babele/Entry into Babylon* (1973–75), which, while occasionally featuring such diverse locales as Milan, Paris or Cairo, are chiefly set in Benghazi, the kilometre zero of *The Confines of the Shadow*.

The Young Maronite, the first act of the Cyrenaican saga, opens in November 1912. The new Italian Conquistadors have barricaded themselves inside Benghazi and nervously look on as the Libyans muster their strength in the desert and begin their gallant guerrilla war against the usurpers.

Meanwhile, Émile Chébas, a young, savvy merchant from Cairo based on Spina's father, arrives in town with a meagre cargo. Émile nonetheless lands on his feet thanks to a chance encounter with Hajji Semereth Effendi, one of the city's wealthiest men and a former Ottoman grandee, who takes Émile under his wing and helps set him up, even loaning him one of his servants, Abdelkarim. Although technically the chief protagonist, it isn't until later in the book that Émile fully emerges from Semereth's, well, shadow. Spina's portrait of Semereth is immediately ensnaring:

In Istanbul, [Semereth] had occupied several public positions that prophesied a stellar career, but after a plot had been uncovered, the shadow of conspiracy had settled on him and prompted his fall. He had withdrawn to that obscure provincial backwater and been quickly forgotten. [...] He was very tall and his face was frightening. A gunpowder charge had exploded close to him during a military campaign and he had been left forever disfigured. His hair had been reduced to a few tow-coloured clumps of locks. A bad smell emanated from the wrinkles on his skull. He had an inbred seriousness and exuded an authority that made anyone who talked to him bashful and hesitant. It was like a spell that separated him from everyone else, but he was a victim of it, rather than its conscious master, as others instead assumed.

The first section deals with Semereth's unrequited love for Zulfa, the youngest of his four wives, who later betrays him with Ferdinando, an orphan raised in his household. Although Semereth tries his utmost to shield the lovers from blood-baying relatives, tradition ultimately makes an honour killing inevitable: the old politician is forced to watch while Ferdinando is stabbed and Zulfa is drowned. Unbeknownst to Semereth, his family tragedy is being quietly observed by two Italian officers, who, adrift in a violently hostile land – having arrived assuming they would be welcomed as liberators – grasp onto what they can to try to make sense of their new surroundings. Of all the cast members, it's once again the officers who attempt a systemic understanding of the alien world around them, but perhaps unsurprisingly, the results are never positive. Here is Captain Romanino's take on Italy's African venture during a soirée in Milan, where he is on leave:

Just as a language is only useful in the area in which it is spoken and is pointless outside of it, so it goes with Europe's *liberal* moral values, which don't extend anywhere south of the Mediterranean. As soon as one reaches the other coast, one is ordered to do the exact opposite prescribed by God's commandments: kill, steal, blaspheme... Once the Turkish garrison was defeated and a few key locations on the coast were occupied, we found a vast, obscure country stretching out before us, into which we're afraid to venture. Therefore we cloistered ourselves in the cities awaiting daylight. Instead, the night is getting deeper, darker, deadlier, and teeming with demons.

Although Spina's initial instalments of *The Confines of the Shadow* attracted some notice in the mid-1970s, with several of them, including *The Young Maronite*, making the shortlists for the Strega and Campiello prizes, his presence in Libya began to grow increasingly tenuous, especially

once his father's factory was nationalised in 1978. The years following Gaddafi's coup had seen the despot deforeignise Libya, a process he began in 1970 with the expulsion of thousands of Jewish and Italian colonists. Thus, at the age of 50, Spina witnessed the Italo-Arab-Ottoman universe he'd been born into flit away into nothingness. While this did not impair his work, it certainly impacted on its publication. Case in point: although Spina had penned *The Nocturnal Visitor* over the course of a few months in early 1972, he delayed its publication until 1979 to avoid scrutiny during the turbulent early years of Gaddafi's rule when dissidents – including a number of Spina's friends – were routinely rounded up and imprisoned. In between his novels, Spina had also composed *The Fall of the Monarchy*, a history in the style of de Tocqueville that analyses the events leading to Gaddafi's coup, which, as per Spina's wishes, will only appear posthumously. Circulated in samizdat among a select group of acquaintances, the book attracted the attentions of the security services, and when Spina left Libya for good in 1980, he was forced to smuggle the manuscript out in the French consul's briefcase. Safely removed from the reach of Gaddafi's men, Spina sojourned in Paris, and finally retired to a seventeenth-century villa in Padergnone, in the heart of Lombard wine country, where he consecrated his *buen retiro* to completing *The Confines of the Shadow*, his privacy as jealously guarded as ever.

Like Joseph Roth, another inveterate chronicler of a crumbled empire, Spina had from a young age set himself to resurrecting his lost world on paper, thus ensuring its survival in our collective consciousness. While historical novels habitually focus on the rise and fall of specific castes, very few of them (Roth's *The Radetzky March* being a notable example) ever capture the confused excitement that makes the very earth those characters tread tremble with unregulated passions. As Chateaubriand once put it: 'In a society which is dissolving and reforming, the struggle of two geniuses, the clash between past and future, and the mixture of old customs and new, form a transitory amalgam which does not leave a moment for boredom.' It is exactly these fleeting junctures in time that infuse Spina's sophisticated prose with such an unbridled sense of adventure. Besides being the 'right' person for such a job, Spina also found himself in the right place at the right time: a Christian Arab born during the apogee of colonial power, who then consolidated his Western education with his intimate knowledge of Libyans and Middle Eastern customs and history to produce the only multi-generational epic about the European experience in North Africa.

Yet despite winning such diverse admirers as Claudio Magris, his closest confrère, Giorgio Bassani and Roberto Calasso, Spina occasionally professed surprise at the utter indifference prompted by his work, or rather his subject. Towards the end of his *Diary*, he recalls a run-in with the poet Vittorio Sereni at the premiere of a play in the early 1980s and being introduced to Sereni's wife: 'Darling, this is Alessandro Spina, who is trying to make Italians feel guilty about their colonial crimes, all to no avail of course.' Not that he hadn't been warned. When Spina had sought Moravia's advice about his project in 1960, Moravia had counselled him against it, saying no one in Italy would be interested due to their sheer nescience of the country's colonial past. Twenty-first-century readers might do well to heed Solzhenitsyn's warning that 'a people which no longer remembers has lost its history and its soul'. Still, one must chuckle when one can: during the Libyan civil war in 2011, Spina was often approached by journalists on the hunt for soundbites, requests that Spina invariably declined; nevertheless, I've little doubt the coincidence of the civil war being declared officially over 100 years to the day after the Italians conquered his beloved Benghazi would have made him smile.

Note

The English translation of Alessandro Spina's *The Confines of the Shadow: In Lands Overseas* will be published by Darf Books in three volumes, the first of which – comprising *The Young Maronite*, *Omar's Wedding* and *The Nocturnal Visitor* – will be issued in early 2015. Darf Books have also commissioned an Arabic translation of the epic. Spina's works are available in the original Italian from Morcelliana, as well as in French: *Juin 1940* (Cahiers de L'Herne, 2009), translated by Michel Balzamo, and *Triptyque lybien* (L'Âge d'Homme, 2013), translated by Gérard Genot.

JAMES McGRATH

Two Poems

There's Nothing to Forgive

Your mate's in love. He forgets he said he'd meet you
from school on his Friday off. You wait by the bins
and stare at spare pebbles on the green-grey pavement,
not the shrinking crowd of coats and paper paintings.

You wait till the playground's turned the size of the sky
and there's only Lent, who's in your class, and her mum,
who helps on school trips. They walk over, holding hands.
You tread on chewing gum. You've never played with Lent

but 'You're Lent's friend', her mum calls. 'Is your mummy late?'
You say you're waiting for your mate. He's got a car.
Lent's mum bends down. 'Is your mummy poorly again?'
Your mum's just at your gran's. Your mate's driving you there.

Lent stares like a doll, but you're not going to cry.
'We're having sausage omelettes for tea,' her mum winks.
'You come home with Lent and me.' And Lent smiles at you,
so kindly, you nearly do cry. You can't answer.

'We'll phone your mum, and I'll explain about – your mate.'
Lent's mum holds out her spare, gloved hand, but behind her
halts a bike you know, and your granddad, grey with sweat.
'Gran was mithering. She said you'd still be here.'

Lent's mum smiles. 'Is this your mate?' Yes. This is your mate.
He trembles from his bike, and you all walk slowly
in the chain-ticked silence. But an engine moans loud –
it's your mate's red Mini, all clean, slowing towards you.

Your granddad rides away as you open the door
to a thrown-out *'Sorry'*, but Lent's mum grabs your arm.
'Wait! Is this man your mate?' You pause. No. He's your dad.
Mr Broad strides over, smoking. You shrink into the car

then wave to spare gloved hands. You breathe in after-shave
and overtake your granddad, fast. Your mate's in love.
He's told your mum he's never felt this bad before.
He reads the Bible. He forgets what mates are for.

Up the lanes, the engine begs to hide the silence.
Your mate ignores the farmyard where his father worked.
But as the bend arrives towards your gran's house,
and he stops the car, and you have to sleeve your eyes,

your mate forgets he's in love.

Names Bizath

My name is probably McGrath,
said like a verb on a guitath

but still I half-avoid both names
until a shyness kind of shames.

Sometimes I take my name afath
to move the posts and raise the bath.

It rarely works. My tongue just aims
away the sounds of national claims.

My name is probably McGrath.
That's why I leave the sound ajath.

'Souvenir' and Other Poems

Souvenir

It is irresponsible to dally
  with the horrible cliché of souls.
  But when I think of you, the flower

of the world is opened like a relapse
  and what I would call a soul begins
  to make a feeling like singing in

a strained and sincere voice. When the flower
  of the world's opening, it seems things
  perceptible are still: it opens

in them. Rows of shophouses in Georgetown,
  remembered walking with you in a
  sun too recent to be hot but rich

and generous in light, as though the stores
  were giving it out in bright pastel
  or a rot-freckled white. Pink brick, clear

beneath cracked stucco by the sea. The whole
  town, still waking in the sea's coolness,
  riddled with sinkholes of fresh coffee.

When it opens, these perceptible things
  seem still only because their rocket
  boosters have hit burnout and detached.

Moving at their greatest speed they appear
  to stop. The flower of the world, in
  opening, revives the soul like this.

Of the colours observable in muscovy glass

Our search after the true cause of colours.
– Micrographia, Robert Hooke

Slit it down and you divide the spars
and faces of colourlessness like
        possible geometries
        if moments in water took

the sweetened hook and rose, circling as
components of mobiles, dimensions
        of caught, frozen currents primed
        for measurement. These layers

of muscovy glass, mineral used
sometimes in windows or against fires,
        shave off with fluid's ease when
        plied with any tool from the

wide-eyed workshop of minutiae,
each paring transparent as the last
        and translucent to the point
        of final falling apart.

So, imagine now the quiet awe
when the cut which takes the latest flake
        a hair's breadth from sight and close
        to its disintegration

suddenly reveals colour, azure,
peach, grass-green, shifting under the thumb,
        nervous like a nakedness
        discovered and aurora

of clarity's opened core: colour
known from liquids, the surface of oil
        of turpentine; glare of snails;
        the film which trails behind sticks

stirred through gum arabic, pitch, rosin;
waters, glutinous with alcohol,
        flushed out from the pores of steel,
        running with their bright ribbons.

The endless divisibility
of the glass colours the horizon
        of sight and then defeats our
        instruments. If there could be

a thinner face of this mineral,
our tools couldn't slice it from the lump,
        our best lens could not claim it
        back from dissolving in light.

Mass

Often, voices warm the cold
 throat of the chapel: their warmth seems small,
  too quickly glasslike. Smoke mocks
the heat that made it, low in the air. Colours
cool in the wood. The architecture remains.

Imagine, high and vague past
 the aromatic haze, a row of
  twelve martini glasses split
along their central line and then switched places
so the curves are clinking back to back. What that

is, is a drinks party I
 have imagined and can't get in to.
  They only look like fluting
of avian bones, flushes of a peacock's
tail done in stone, rush strokes in cement, so on.

The weak incense, the voices,
 and the light's pooling in colours: all
  these fall short of synthesis
with the masonry, of making grandeur that
includes me. I need a canopy that takes

me to the sky humanly,
 which moves from me to edifice by
  song that warms into the walls,
doesn't slacken and grow cold like blossom. My
roof was built to bear the most vulnerable and

the invulnerable but fails
 the delicate, even though I built
  it and it is intricate,
is nothing but a made-up thing. Stained lances
strafe the tiles. If I sang my voice would diffuse.

You've bathed so many faces
 in a human beauty echoing,
  but evacuate the thrum,
leaving behind the greater face of silence
unrevised, the fanning of your untouched vault.

A Celebration of Eavan Boland

EDITED BY JODY ALLEN RANDOLPH AND MICHAEL SCHMIDT

JODY ALLEN RANDOLPH

Introduction

Two aspects of this special supplement on Eavan Boland's work seem especially worth noting. The first is self-evident. It is the achievement of Eavan Boland as poet, essayist and maker of a critique that has reshaped Irish literature and is influencing a global conversation about women poets emerging from resistant traditions. The second aspect is more general and less visible. It is the changing conversation about poetry in our time: the ways in which 'an apparently monolithic poetic past', as Boland described it in *A Journey With Two Maps*, has become a conversation that readers can 'join and change'. I have followed both Boland's work and this evolving conversation for the best part of thirty years, from Carcanet's publication of *The Journey* to its release this month of her eleventh volume of poems, *A Woman Without a Country*. Illuminating exchanges over those years with Michael Schmidt about this singular progress led to our collaboration on this special supplement.

The growth and achievement of Boland's poetry over five decades is by now a well-known story. This special supplement tracks the consistency of her themes and ambitions at both ends of this spectrum. It includes her most recent and best work – the title sequence of her upcoming volume *A Woman Without a Country*, as well as an essay by the same title in which she challenges us to rethink not the contemporary poem but the moral responsibility of the reader. But it also looks back at Boland's beginnings as a poet. In an essay on her debut volume, *New Territory* (1967), Irish poet Medbh McGuckian portrays a twenty-two-year-old Boland already 'passionately concerned with the problems of Irish history – "The dour line of North and South"' – but also 'addressing, with more arrogance than mere confidence, even with aggression, in stanzas of classical, mandarin, impersonal perfection [...] on their own Petrarchan ground, such sonneteers as Yeats and Shakespeare'. The American poet and critic Sandra M. Gilbert describes the middle and later Boland, writing her poems from the 'suburbs of modernism', from domestic interiors that were 'not just literal but truly symbolic spaces, spaces only apparently outside history that constituted an alternative architecture in which women, writing in rooms of our own, began to reimagine and revise the supposed centers of literature itself'.

Several contributors here have sought to define this progress: 'At the heart of her work,' as Mark Doty describes in this issue, 'is a bold act of claiming poetic legacy'. The journey that began as a struggle to find her place within the tradition of Irish poetry resulted, as Thomas McCarthy

explains, in 'a singular, visual leap of conscience, away from [the] curators of national narrative, into a new studio'. Over time and as her prose critique developed, as Elline Lipkin points out, this critique became 'part of a genre of necessary books through which one generation speaks to another'.

The second aspect of this special supplement – the changing conversation about poetry – also serves as a conduit between generations. While it is less visible it is nonetheless important. It is the clear sign that over the past two decades technology and travel have advanced and clarified the poetic conversation: have changed, deepened and enriched it so that it leaps across boundaries, barriers, generations, nations and aesthetics with an ease that would once have seemed impossible.

It is not that the poetic conversation didn't exist before. It did, but inevitably in compartmentalised and even provincial modes. Not so long ago a poet in North Carolina could not have been expected to know what a poet in Tuam in the west of Ireland was thinking until a fair amount of time had passed, if ever. Yet Gabrielle Calvocoressi and Joan McBreen can record their impressions here of Boland's influence at the time they discovered it, in different generations and separate hemispheres, and yet do it simultaneously. While at the same time Jee Leong Koh, from yet a younger generation of poets, adds his voice to the conversation, noting 'the great help Eavan Boland gives me, a gay Singaporean poet, in resisting and re-envisioning a patriarchal and colonial literary heritage'. *PN Review*, with its innovative and early commitment to digitisation, has been a leader in this widening and changing conversation, and so it seems especially appropriate that another example of it occurs in these pages.

The different readings of Boland's work provided by this supplement are also a reflection of a conversation that is growing more inclusive. One that allows a performance poet such as Máighréad Medbh to open her essay with 'I have always been affected by Eavan Boland, though we probably appear to be opposites'. The Irish poet Rita Ann Higgins from her vantage point in the west of Ireland explores the sense of dislocation that comes with the theme of exile in Boland's work, while at the same time the American poet and novelist Sapphire writes from New York City on the location of home, and the dangerous underside of the domestic, in which a poem becomes a place, 'a rock of fire, our own Island, our tongue'.

Boland's poetry, her essays and interviews have built a

portrait over time of a signature sense of how ethics and aesthetics connect. Here the poet and critic Linda Gregerson takes an instructive look at the formal relation between these two aspects in her essay on Boland's poem 'Quarantine'. The same issue is probed from a different angle in an interview by Caribbean poet Shara McCallum, in discussions of how ethics and aesthetics can separate in contemporary poetry. Confirming their relation in Boland's work Paula Meehan, the current Ireland Professor of Poetry, notes in her discussion of the poem 'Making Money' that 'Boland speaks, out of a profound moral sensibility, of what it is to be human, in the present moment, in language that is pure lyric'.

While some contributors take a wider view of the poet's context and development others look more closely at the text. Theo Dorgan provides the linguistic and historical context of Boland's poem 'Irish Poetry', where 'out of the word-music of Irish the bird flies up, up and out into Eavan's imagination, and out of the poem into ours'. Colm Tóibín follows Boland's love poems from their roots in both classical and Irish myth to the times and places 'when myths collide', and Yusef Komunyakaa highlights Boland's repositioning of overheard stories into a maternal creation myth in 'The Oral Tradition' where 'the folkloric is stripped down naked in a merciless light, and the reader can't help but see and

know the inner workings of history'. Another look at text is Tara Bergin's examination of Boland's narrative skills in weaving a story, while David C. Ward looks at both the text and context of Boland's famine poems as 'history poems that recover silenced voices, re-map the past and indict the political economy of oppression'. But even as Boland evokes silenced voices, as Lorna Goodison points out in her essay on 'Making Money', 'hers is a poetic voice that is both ancient and modern, one that speaks for people who had no voice but who need to have their story told clearly while keeping the mystery at the heart of it'.

While this special supplement pays tribute to one particular poet, the varied and eloquent voices here also make available a richer, wider, more global conversation about poetry than we have experienced in the past. One that can, as we've seen, encompass broad and even oppositional themes: domesticity and danger, home and exile, ethics and aesthetics. And one in which we as readers and writers can measure 'our contradictory responsibilities,' as Mark Doty puts it, 'to honour the unspeakable and to say what one can'. These have been exemplary themes in Boland's poetry over many years. They also reflect some of the widest and most challenging discussions in poetry today – challenges that, while they change our sense of poetry's past, can only strengthen its future.

EAVAN BOLAND

A Woman Without a Country

This sequence is dedicated to those who lost a country, not by history or inheritance, but through a series of questions to which they could find no answer.

Sea Change

What did he leave me, my grandfather,
Who lost his life in a spring tempest
At the Chaussée des Pierres Noires
At the edge of Biscay?

With his roof of half-seen stars
His salty walls rising high and higher
To the last inch of the horizon
He built nothing that I could live in.

His door of cresting water,
His low skies skidding on the waves
His seaman's windows giving on
Iridescent plankton never amounted to home,

And no one lay at night
Seeing these unfold in their minds with
That instinct of amendment history allows
Instead of memory.

I was born in a place, or so it seemed,
Where every inch of ground
Was a new fever or a field soaked
To its grassy roots with remembered hatreds.

Where even if I turned to legerdemain
To bring land and ocean together,
Saying *water-meadow* to myself for instance,
The distances remained.

A spring night in Dublin.
Neap tide on the Irish sea.
To the north of here in the Garden of Remembrance
The dead are defined by their relation to land.

When he looked over the ship's rail at midnight
Into his ocean garden
All he saw was oxygen unfrocking phosphorus
Lacing the sea with greens.

Lesson 1

My grandmother lived outside history. And she died there. A thirty-one-year-old woman, with five daughters, facing death in a hospital far from her home – I doubt that anything around her mattered then. Yet in her lifetime Ireland had gone from oppression to upheaval. And she had existed at the edge of it. Did she find her nation? And does it matter?

Art of Empire

If no one in my family ever spoke of it,
if no one handed down
what it was to be born to power
and married in a poor country.

If no one wanted to remember
the noise of the redcoats cantering
in lanes bleached with apple flowers
on an April morning.

If no one ever mentioned how a woman was,
what she did,
what she never did again,
when she lived in a dying Empire.

If what was not said was never seen
If what was never seen could not be known
think of this as the only way
an empire could recede –

taking its laws, its horses and its lordly all,
leaving a single art to be learned,
and one that required
neither a silversmith nor a glassblower

but a woman skilled in the sort of silence
that lets her stitch shadow flowers
into linen with pastel silks
who never looks up

to remark on or remember why it is
the bird in her blackwork is warning her:
not a word not a word
not a word not a word.

Lesson 2

The death certificate I have is simply a copy of page 539 in the Registrar's book for the year 1909. Legally, she died in the district of the South Dublin Union. Officially, her death was registered there. In the margin, it is numbered 453. Name and Place of Death. Certified Cause of Death.

Studio Portrait 1897

She stands
on a fraction of paperboard.

Holds still
without shifting. She is

fifty years away from
the worst famine in Europe,

thirty years
behind the new nation.

O sepia,
O stateless image-making.

Where is the source of her silence?

Not history, our old villain,
you say,

but a muttering under black cloth:
those words

she listened to just a minute since
as the shutter fell.

And obeyed:
Keep still quite still not move not stir not once.

Lesson 3

I wonder whether she turned in some corridor, looked up from some moment of play and heard the whispers and gossip. Did she hear in some muttered conversation the future of an armed struggle, the music of anger, the willingness to die? I doubt it. If she looked up at all I believe she was listening for her life. And what was I listening for?

The Long Evenings of their Leavetakings

My mother was married by the water.
She wore a grey coat and a winter rose.

She said her vows beside a cold seam of the Irish coast.

She said her vows near the shore where
the emigrants set down their consonantal *n*:

on afternoo*n*, on the e*n*d of everything, at the start of *ever.*

Yellow vestments took in light
A chalice hid underneath its veil.

Her hands were full of calla and cold-weather lilies.

The mail packet dropped anchor.
A black-headed gull swerved across the harbour.

Icy promises rose beside a cross-hatch of ocean and horizon.

I am waiting for the words of the service. I am waiting for
keep thee only and *all my earthly.*

All I hear is an afternoon's worth of *never.*

Lesson 4

I have come to accept that the story of Irish history is
not her story. The monster rallies, the oil-lit rooms, the
flushed faces of orators and the pale ones of assassins
have no place in it. Inasmuch as her adult life had a
landscape it was made of the water her husband sailed
and not the fractured, much-claimed piece of earth she
was born to.

I Think of Her

as if she had been made to drown
against the rigours
of squalls and wings.

As if her eyes were blinded twice,
first by a knife and then by salt
singing in the rigging.

As if she dove and rose with the bowsprit
her shoulders washed by phosphor,
her torso bare.

As if she had been made out of elm. *Ulmus*:
narrow-leafed coarse-barked,
uneven canopy

of my courtship evenings
strolling Herbert Road with
my husband-to-be: as if she were doomed

to weep the harsh weather
of the Irish Sea out of carved eyes.
One loss promising another.

Lesson 5

She was not a heroine. She was not Ireland or Hibernia.
She was not stamped, as a rubbed-away mark, on silver
or gold: a compromised regal figure on a dish or the
handle of a spoon. Her hair was not swept or tied back,
like on the prow of a ship. Her flesh was flesh. Not wood
or ink or marble.

Anonymity

In the museum, an exhibition:
Women from Ancient Cultures.
Figures in glass cases, brightly lit.

Opposite, on the wall, explanations:
This was the wife of a king in
A valley rinsed by a wealth-bringing river.

This was a servant: see the flesh-tones,
The beads. She was clothed in
An opulent fashion only when she died.

Reader, be here. Go from room to room.
Note the substances
Used to transpose rigid stances,

Seized-up faces and the final
Splendour of grave-clothes into these
Sign-makers in fluorescent light.

Powerless queens; stock-still, enslaved
Girls at the entryway to anonymity.
Women without a country

Assembled from the treasures of a country:
A finger of silver. A mineral breast.
An ear poured out in bronze.

Lesson 6

A century on, I lift my head, I look up. The issue
between an artist and a nation is not a faith, but a self.
The issue between an artist and a truth is not a self, but
an image. In an unrecorded existence she was neither
and both. What troubled me was not whether she had
included her country in her short life. But whether that
country had included her.

A Woman Without a Country

As dawn breaks he enters
A room with the odour of acid.
He lays the copper plate on the table.
And reaches for the shaft of the burin.
Dublin wakes to horses and rain.
Street hawkers call.
All the news is famine and famine.
The flat graver, the round graver,
The angle tint tool wait for him.
He bends to his work and begins.
He starts with the head, cutting in
To the line of the cheek, finding
The slope of the skull, incising
The shape of a face that becomes
A foundry of shadows, rendering –
With a deeper cut into copper –
The whole woman as a skeleton,
The rags of her skirt, her wrist
In a bony line forever
                          severing
Her body from its native air until
She is ready for the page,
For the street vendor, for
A new inventory which now
To loss and to laissez-faire adds
The odour of acid and the little,
Pitiless tragedy of being imagined.
He puts his tools away,
One by one; lays them out carefully
On the deal table. His work done.

A Woman Without a Country: A Detail

I

It was winter. I was a student in the National Library, waiting for my call number. The library was a Dublin institution, managing its circular lending room with Victorian grace and delay. You found your book by searching through heavy catalogues. You scribbled its number in pencil on lined paper and handed it in. And waited.

I was starting out as a poet. I was beginning to publish poems here and there. Almost all my reading had been in the poetry of the Irish Revival. Especially Yeats. Sometimes only Yeats. Now I was beginning to see the gaps in my knowledge, especially of contemporary poetry.

My catalogue searches were not yet targeted to individual poets. The books whose numbers I pencilled in were chosen for survey rather than specificity. Most likely the poem I stumbled on was in an anthology and not a single volume. It was called 'Pike' by the British poet, Ted Hughes.

It wasn't long. Eleven stanzas of four lines. In the first four, the pike – a fish I'd never seen – was described: its eerie grin, its gold-green stripes, its killer jaws. Later I would find it was a fish that could be found in Irish rivers, the Lee, the Barrow, the Erne. For now it only existed on the page.

In the second stanza the pike changes again. It becomes a creature of 'submarine delicacy and horror'. In the third it holds quite still, 'hung in an amber cavern of weeds'. In the fourth stanza the ferocity of nature, together with the poet's purpose, emerge together: 'A life subdued to its instrument; / The gills kneading quietly, and the pectorals'.

The fish, the pond, the twilight are elaborately staged. By the time the poem finishes, the speaker is afraid to cast in the darkness, 'with the hair frozen on my head'. But just at that moment I became distracted, brought to a halt where the poem shifts from pike to place.

It happens in the eighth stanza. The speaker describes 'a pond I fished'. He remembers its gloom; how the tench and lilies had outlasted the stones and structures of those who built the surroundings. How deep it was, how cold:

Stilled legendary depth:
It was as deep as England.

I remember my hand on the page, not ready to turn it. I remember the energy and surprise of the words: *as deep as England.* When I looked up the words kept their power, marching out from this single statement into distances of riddle and wonder. Outside in the winter dark, past the wooden doors and steep, grand steps of the library the city of Dublin unfolded through surfaces of history, colony, survival. It unfolded west and east into the Irish Sea, to the very edges of the island. My island.

But here came the meaning together with the riddle. Even supposing that I found a cold, deep water late at night, could I write similar words? Could I have made a phrase in which so large a claim lay under such a slight felicity? Could I have said that anything was *as deep as Ireland?*

No, I decided, I could not. Some ghostly resistance seemed to stand between me and the very idea. In order to write those words, you had to be confident of that unit of measurement. You had to have some ownership of the phrase. I had neither. I closed the book, handed it in over the counter, packed my book bag and went home.

II

A simple question. Why have so few women, in the history of poetry, been citizen-poets? Why have so few set up their poems with country, nation, nationhood, placing themselves at the centre of those themes? 'Words are women, deeds are men', writes George Herbert. And so it would appear.

Nor is the answer easy. In seventeenth-century America, Anne Bradstreet wrote with a sharp awareness of the social texture of the Massachusetts Colony. She was the daughter of one of its Governors, the wife of another. She managed an artful balance of devotion and assertion. But never with a reference to the nation-making going on all around her.

In nineteenth-century Britain Elizabeth Barrett Browning wrote the superb, scathing 'Mother and Poet'. She also declared in a letter 'I am of those weak women who reverence strong men'. It is hard to put the two modes together. But for her, as for many women poets of that time, a sense of nation seemed out of reach. Perhaps even out of mind.

There was no encouragement off the page either. Sir Samuel Evans in the House of Parliament in Britain in 1906 remarked that 'all the public duties of citizenship ought to be imposed upon man and man alone'. In the same debate, the Speaker of the House of Commons – the issue was women's suffrage – said he was 'too fond' of women 'to drag them into the political arena and to ask them to undertake responsibilities, duties, and obligations which they did not understand and which they did not care for'.

Did not understand. Did not care for. The terms prompt a counter-question. Why should women want to be citizen-poets? Setting aside the parliamentary language, there is an obvious reason. From Wordsworth's yearning address to Milton – 'England hath need of thee' – to Allen Ginsberg's fond invitation to Walt Whitman to stroll 'the lost America of love' to Yeats's trenchant 'Out of Ireland have we come', there is a rich, confirming tradition of national reference in male poetry. More importantly, within that tradition it's clear that male poets in England, Ireland and America are not just drawing on words and names when they refer to their countries. They are also pulling up a deeply sunk reference-hoard of power, nation and poetry.

Here is Whitman again, from 'The Preface to Leaves of Grass': 'The American poets are to enclose old and new for America is the race of races'. And now Philip Larkin: 'And that will be England gone, / The shadows, the meadows, the lanes, / The guildhalls, the carved choirs'. Or Shelley in a high temper in his poem 'England 1819', writing of 'An old, mad, blind, despised, and dying King; / Princes, the dregs of their dull race'. Even when the national reference is one of dissent, with Langston Hughes writing 'America never was America to me', there is a circuit of recognition provided just by giving the local habitation a name.

There is also an obvious ease and confidence in these comments. As there was in Ted Hughes's lines on the monastery lake. They show how national reference in poetry can amount to a language of shared values, almost to a *lingua franca*. Not to be able to speak it amounts to losing access to a dominant poetic dialect.

Nor is the dialect itself at fault. There is something musical and consoling even now in reading these gestures towards rootedness. Something heart-lifting in the evocations of country and context. 'And did those feet in ancient time / Walk upon England's mountains green?' Blake's question domesticates the wondrous to the local. The far-fetched to the near at hand. The improbable lends a shine to the available.

And yet it's hard to find the equivalent in women poets of the eighteenth and nineteenth centuries. Towards the end of the twentieth century activist writers such as Audre Lorde and Adrienne Rich and Denise Levertov were changing the picture. But further back in time, while there are occasional mentions, there is hardly any focus. There are national balladeers, such as Speranza in Ireland, or regional writers such as Rebecca Hammond Lard or self-styled laureates such as Julia Ward Howe. But they reflect the male paradigm: they don't amend it.

As a drama of contrast, we can take the years between 1850 and 1870 when Walt Whitman and Emily Dickinson confronted different realities in a similar time-frame. 'I hear America singing, the varied carols I hear' writes Whitman. Not so Dickinson. A single gesture towards nationhood in her work is compelling but also irrelevant. 'I've seen him from an ample nation choose one', she wrote in one of her strongest poems. But the nation referred to is not earthly. It is a region of chill and powerful speculation. It is not America.

The contrasts accumulate. While Tennyson wrote 'The Charge of the Light Brigade' and Robert Browning 'The Lost Leader', Christina Rossetti was either released or reduced – depending on your point of view – to writing poems about departures, flowers, prayers. Inevitably, these absences and silences prompt an aesthetic speculation: was it possible that the national references in male canonical poems had built a virtual, shadowy realm: a kingdom of entitlement and ownership in which there was no place for a woman poet's imagining?

The more I wrote poetry, the more I read those women poets from past centuries with a deep pleasure and instruction: Dickinson's cryptic lightning. Rossetti's management of a stanza, Bradstreet's bold, deceptive tone. But I was also troubled. When I looked at a particular poem, my mind would turn to the poet who wrote it. There with her book in my hand – with all the advantage of hindsight – I would be distracted trying to summon the wars, treaties, large events and small decisions that once governed her life. Weren't those the years of the gold rush, I would ask myself? Wasn't that beautiful lyric about determinism written in the same year as the Women's Property Act? After a while, however much I liked the poem, what was beyond it – what was unavailable to it – fell like a shadow across the lines. Sometimes when I put the book down, its author seemed to me a woman without a country.

III

Nadia Anjuman was born in 1980 in Herat, the largest city in western Afghanistan. A city so ancient that Ptolemy recorded it on a map. So prosperous that Herodotus claimed it could feed Central Asia. In the Baba mountains, part of the Hindu Kush system, the river Hari rises and flows south of the city. Herat lies on the great trade routes of the Middle East. Its roads are a gateway to Iran; in a different direction they lead towards Turkmenistan. This is an intersection, a meeting point, a crossroads of history and cultures.

Over the centuries, Herat became a centre of literary culture. When Robert Byron, a somewhat irascible traveller, came on Herat in 1933 he wrote lyrically about first catching sight of the city: 'This was the pure essence of green, insoluble, the colour of life itself. The sun was warm, the larks were singing up above. Behind us rose the misty Alpine blue of the wooded Elburze. In front, the glowing verdure stretched out to the rim of the earth.'

Among its most confident possessions, Herat holds the shrine of Jami, the fifteenth-century Sufi master. Like other Sufi poets, Jami wrote of the search for knowledge, gained through mystical union. 'Without a veil your countenance cannot be seen,' he wrote, 'Without a veil your eyes cannot be seen.'

His words were almost certainly intended as a figure for how the mind apprehends truth. Nevertheless, five centuries later, they throw a shadow of irony. Of all cities, Herat should have been the most sustaining for a contemporary Afghan poet. And in fact Nadia Anjuman began to write there, as a young woman, at the beginning of the twenty-first century.

She first comes into view as a member of the celebrated sewing circles of Herat. In these a Professor at the University, Muhammad Ali Rahyab, taught women literature in secret. She appears in a *New York Times* article called 'Afghan Poets Revive a Literary Tradition' written by Amy Waldman in December 2001: 'Swathed in black, she curled up like a cat in her professor's study, black eyes peering from an elfin face. She is 20 years old and has written 60 or 70 poems. As the first person in her family to love words, she has had to fight, like a number of Professor Rahyab's students, for her family's cooperation. She has fought, too, to stave off marriage, fearing it will limit her freedom to write. "I think I've been quite successful," she said. She writes mostly about women's lives, "because we have suffered a lot."'

Anjuman published her first book of poems – *Gul-e-dodi* ('Dark Red Flower') – in Herat in early 2005. She died on 4 November of that year at the age of 25, the victim of an apparent honour killing. Her husband of fifteen months, Farid Ahmad Majid Mia, a lecturer in philology at the university, was arrested and charged with her killing, as was his mother. Anjuman was in her third year at Herat University studying Literature and Humane Science when she died. She left a six-month-old son behind. There is no record of a trial or a conviction.

I first heard her story from a remarkable Afghan student of mine, herself a fine poet, for whom Anjuman had been a continuous inspiration. I won't name this student since she is away from her country. But learning of Anjuman through her younger countrywoman was important. It situated Anjuman for me. I was able, through my student's account, to imagine – at least partly – the courage, the fear, the secret meetings in Herat, the hidden pages. Above all, the determination to succeed as a poet.

But even this knowledge was out of date by the time I got it: I had missed a central biographical detail, published in the *New York Times* in 2005:

Nadia Anjuman, who had been gaining a name for herself as a poet in Afghan literary circles, died over the weekend in the western city of Herat after being beaten by her husband, police officials said Monday.

Inevitably, Anjuman's story, and my student's account of it, made me think back to my own beginnings as a poet. At 25 I had finished a first book, as she had. I was married the previous year, as she was. I was starting to see flaws and silences in my environment in Ireland. I was learning to question the hierarchies and exclusions that were in place there, that I sensed would affect any woman poet trying to define herself . But never once did I feel physically unsafe. I assumed a future in which I could continue to write and publish. Anjuman had neither the assumption nor the future.

Information about Anjuman was scarce at first. It is still not plentiful or detailed. I have no knowledge of Farsi, or of Anjuman's dialect of it which is Dari. In a case like this – a different language, a distant culture – I was painfully aware of chance mistakes or errors. For that reason I'm indebted here to other writers and scholars and poets, whose names I've provided wherever I could. And above all to the translators who have made available the charged, painful lyrics from her first book.

To start with, Fritt Ord, the Norwegian activist foundation, was a platform for details and translations. Later, Marilyn Turkovich, an educational activist, provided information and access to Anjuman's poems on her 'Voices Compassion Education' website.

There has been some actual publication. In 2010 an organisation called HAWCA (Humanitarian Assistance for the Women and Children of Afghanistan) brought out a volume called *Caged Bird: Stories from Safe House and Nadia Anjuman's Poems*. Their annual report states: 'We were able to publish a book "Caged Bird: Stories from Safe House and Nadia Anjuman's Poems" to let the world know about the plight still going on of Afghan women and as a tribute to Nadia Anjuman who was fighting for equality of women in society through her amazing poems.'

Julie R. Enszer, a feminist, scholar and poet, provided an early and thoughtful essay about Anjuman. She opened with a summary of the facts:

The circumstances of her death are contested by her husband and family. Despite that, it seems that she was murdered by her husband. He contends that he only hit her and that she was alive when he left after which she committed suicide; however, confirmation of the cause of Anjuman's death will never be obtained as her family declined an autopsy. More than one western news report noted that some members of Anjuman's family believe that her book with poems about love and beauty 'brought shame to the family.' In spite of the views of some family members, Anjuman's book, *Gul-e-dodi*, translated as

'Dark Red Flower' and published while a student at Herat University, was well received and popular in her homeland.

The journalist Christina Lamb, author of the valuable book *The Sewing Circles of Herat*, added to this: 'Friends say her family was furious, believing that the publication of poetry *by a woman* about love and beauty had brought shame on it'.

IV

Having come this far, I should make clear what this piece is not. My subject is not the Middle East. Nor the politics of Central Asia. Nor is it cultural identity or nationalism. My subject is reading. How we read a poem. How we fail to read it. Beyond that, my subject is the moral responsibility of the poetry reader – an idea without wide currency at this moment.

Surprisingly little time or study has been spent on this reader. Yet this is the same reader who has followed the poem, has shared its history, has endured its disruptions. Who in many ways is a compass point for all that has happened in the past hundred years. Knowing more would surely tell us more about poetry itself. But what methods, what tools do we have to define that reader?

Writers have tried. 'If I read a book and it makes my whole body so cold no fire can ever warm me, I know that is poetry', writes Emily Dickinson. 'The right reader of a good poem can tell the moment it strikes him that he has taken an immortal wound', adds Robert Frost. In both cases the words are eloquent and almost deliberately imprecise. T.S. Eliot assigned a more sober task: 'Pound is not one of those poets who make no demand of the reader'. Adrienne Rich, on the other hand, widening both audience and empathy in her poem 'Dedication', suggested: 'I know you are reading this poem / in a room where too much has happened for you to bear'.

All this falls short of definition. Can we have an exact image of the poetry reader in our mind? Occasionally we are pushed into it when an individual reader comes into sudden focus, as Virginia Woolf does here:

The poem is cracked in the middle. Look, it comes apart in my hands: here is reality on one side, here is beauty on the other; and instead of acquiring a whole object rounded and entire, I am left with broken parts in my hands which, since my reason has been roused and my imagination has not been allowed to take entire possession of me, I contemplate coldly, critically, and with distaste.

As it happens I have a version of the poetry reader in my own mind. And have had for some time. Not a comforting image either; but a contentious one. A figment, certainly; and yet one with which I have kept up some kind of fractious one-sided conversation over many years. One I blame occasionally for what has gone wrong with the transmission of the art.

This version of the reader is familiar enough. It is the one implied by anthologies, articles, biographical sketches, encyclopedia entries. In other words, the nineteenth-century reader. The one who held on tight as poetry careened wildly through that century, when it was a sociable, exciting time to be reading poetry. When the poem was equally welcome at the christening font or the Sunday sermon, at the Victorian court or the novel of courtship. We can even see that reader's shadow when Marianne in Jane Austen's *Sense and Sensibility* dismisses Edward because he couldn't read Cowper: 'To hear those beautiful lines which have frequently almost driven me wild, pronounced with such impenetrable calmness, such dreadful indifference!'

In historical terms, this reader has a fine profile – is seen as attentive and encouraging, a lover of poetry, an enthusiast for its entry into popular society. And always plainspoken about the importance of poetry, even to the extent of blending it with the sacred. 'The strongest part of our religion today,' wrote Matthew Arnold in the middle of that century, 'is its unconscious poetry'.

But there is a critique that can and should be made. To start with, these readers were not outsiders. They were not men and women without a country. Far from it. They thought of themselves as having a country and in some cases an empire. They were creatures of their moment, maybe even abettors of its power. Often they exercised their own: in the early nineteenth century when John Clare began a passage with the line 'accurs'd wealth o'erbounding human laws' Lord Radstock, his patron, immediately protested Clare's 'radical and ungrateful sentiments'. The line was removed from the fourth edition of Clare's work. The story is not unique.

In the tectonic movement that came to poetry after 1800 – the grinding shift from subject to subjectivity – these readers took up their position: editing, approving, disapproving. They shared their world with the poem: their loyalties remained beyond it. Their limitations had consequences. Their pieties collided with their poetry. Which meant that all too often their reading deferred to an external value system – one that intruded on the poem's interpretation and transmission. 'Whatever was the immediate prompting of *In Memoriam*,' wrote George Eliot, 'whatever the form under which the author represented his aim to himself, the deepest significance of the poem is the sanctification of human love as a religion'.

I believe these readers, when they allowed their values to limit their understanding, failed the poem. Is that too harsh? I don't think so. The fact remains that any reader, as soon as they start to read a poem, becomes complicit in the binding and loosing, giving and taking, bestowing and removing of contexts in which a text can breathe, can live. Which leads to the question: does the poetry reader have a moral responsibility? To the text, to the context? The question might seem outlandish given the resistance in any aesthetic discussion to the idea of a moral stance.

For all the contemporary scepticism about poetry, I believe we still want to configure that man or woman who goes to a bookshelf late at night, according to our best hopes. We still believe when they turn the page, and turn it again, that they hold so much more than that in their hands: they hold an encounter with meaning, an act of assent, a compliance with understanding.

This constitutes a moral responsibility. And at this particular moment when poetry is frequently accused of irrelevance or worse, that responsibility persists: to take the poem – both text and context – on its own terms. To remain open to its truths. To step out of the orthodoxies of a familiar world so as to follow Goethe's paradigm: 'Who wants to understand the poem / Must go to the land of poetry'.

Nadia Anjuman's work tests the reader's responsibility. The contexts are unfamiliar. The circumstances are terrible and distracting. There is the additional complication that although we can translate the poem – this is especially true in the Farsi tradition – we might not be able to translate the poet. Anjuman's work is often unsettling: oracular and distant in a way we don't easily recognise. But none of that prevents us having a responsibility to it. New poetry requires fresh resources. From poet and reader, both. Those resources will be necessary if we are to read an emergent generation of women poets whose poems are rising out of the deepest contentions of history. And who need us to listen.

V

As an Afghan poet, Nadia Anjuman plainly cared about her heritage. In the poems in *Gul-e-dodi* she chooses the discipline of the ghazal over and over again. Other poems, other forms are there as well. But she returns to the ghazal for some of her most important statements.

The ghazal, with its ancient patterning of couplet and refrain, was used by Sufi masters such as Jami and Hafiz. And it's plain, even in translation, how deftly Anjuman used the form to explore both affinity and dissent. Her poems deploy the traditional ghazal relations between couplets: strictly connected and as strictly separated, achieving small, beautifully managed shock-waves of repetition and statement as the poem goes forward.

One of these ghazals is simply called 'Ghazal' and is translated here by Khizra Aslam. It stands as a key poem, making a claim both for her presence and entitlement as an Afghan poet.

From this cup of my lips comes a song;
It captures my singing soul, my song.

That in my words is the meaning of ecstasy,
That dies my happiness into grief, my song.

If you see that my eyes say a word,
Then take it as my forgetfulness, my song.

Do not ask of love, O it tells me of you;
My words of love speak of death, my song.

His hope, like flowers, I desire.
No drop of my eyes is enough, my song.

The daughter of this place sings qasida, a ghazal,
But what spoils her strange verses, my song?

O the gardener does not understand my happiness;
O does not ask for many looks of my youth, my song.

From these hands, these feet and words, it looks strange
That my name is written on the slate of this age, my song.

The ghazal also provided a frame for Anjuman's path into a complex artistic consciousness that plainly sensed danger. This poem, also called 'Ghazal', is again translated by Khizra Aslam.

It is night and these words come to me
By the call of my voice words come to me

What fire blazes in me, what water do I get?
From my body, the fragrance of my soul comes to me

I do not know from where these great words come
The fresh breeze takes loneliness away from me

That from the clouds of light comes this light
That there is no other wish that comes to me
The cry of my heart sparkles like a star
And the bird of my flight touches the sky
My madness can be found in his book
O do not say no, my master, O look once at me

It is like the day of judgment
Like doomsday my silence comes at me
I am happy that the giver gives me silk
And all night, all along these verses come to me

Here are lines which go to the heart of her sense of entrapment. This is called 'Poem' and is translated here by Mahnaz Badihian:

No desire to open my mouth
What should I sing of…?
I, who am hated by life.
No difference to sing or not to sing.
Why should I talk of sweetness,
When I feel bitterness?
Oh, the oppressor's feast
Knocked my mouth.
I have no companion in life
Who can I be sweet for?
No difference to speak, to laugh,
To die, to be.
Me and my strained solitude.
With sorrow and sadness.
I was born for nothingness.
My mouth should be sealed.
Oh my heart, you know it is spring
And time to celebrate.
What should I do with a trapped wing,
Which does not let me fly?
I have been silent too long,
But I never forget the melody,
Since every moment I whisper
The songs from my heart,
Reminding myself of
The day I will break this cage,
Fly from this solitude
And sing like a melancholic.
I am not a weak poplar tree
To be shaken by any wind.
I am an Afghan woman,
It only makes sense to moan.

One of Anjuman's most powerful poems is called 'A Voiceless Cry'. Written three years before her death it shows her poise, even as a very young writer, in managing sharp public statements within a lyric pattern. The poem's evocation of desert women, of 'girls brought up on pain' coming in from the road, with dusty skirts and 'joy departed from their faces', makes for a poignant, subversive portrait. It is translated here by Zuzanna Olszewska and Belgheis Alavi.

The sound of green footsteps is the rain
They're coming in from the road, now
Thirsty souls and dusty skirts brought from the desert
Their breath burning, mirage-mingled
Mouths dry and caked with dust
They're coming in from the road, now
Tormented-bodied, girls brought up on pain
Joy departed from their faces
Hearts old and lined with cracks
No smile appears on the bleak oceans of their lips
Not a tear springs from the dry riverbeds of their eyes
O God!
Might I not know if their voiceless cries reach the clouds,
the vaulted heavens?
The sound of green footsteps is the rain.

Universe, an online anthology of poetry committed to teaching and education, carries this poem and another called 'Light Blue Memories'. The poem was written after the Fall of the Taliban and presents one of the difficulties of Anjuman's work. The language, as it comes across in English, is rich and associative, but nevertheless at times seems to inhabit its own dream-world. The idiom of Dari poetry obviously leans that way. But the voice carries through. Here the poem addresses women whose names have been taken away by history. Once again the translators are Zuzanna Olszewska and Belgheis Alavi.

O exiles of the mountain of oblivion!
O the jewels of your names, slumbering in the mire of
silence
O your obliterated memories, your light blue memories
In the silty mind of a wave in the sea of forgetting
Where is the clear, flowing stream of your thoughts?
Which thieving hand plundered the pure golden statue
of your dreams?
In this storm which gives birth to oppression
Where has your ship, your serene silver mooncraft gone?
After this bitter cold which gives birth to death –
If the sea should fall calm
If the cloud should release the heart's knotted sorrows
If the maiden of moonlight should bring love, offer a smile
If the mountain should soften its heart, adorn itself with
green,
become fruitful –
Will one of your names, above the peaks,
become bright as the sun?
Will the rise of your memories
Your light blue memories
In the eyes of fishes weary of floodwaters and
fearful of the rain of oppression
become a reflection of hope?
O, exiles of the mountain of oblivion!

These poems circle back to the same question. Was Nadia Anjuman a woman without a country? At first glance, there seems to be a country, even a nation in her poems. But her work and death suggest something else: the country she wrote about was not the country she lived in. Was she then a citizen-poet? Once again the answer seems in doubt. The citizenship she proposed for herself, part activist and part aesthetic, was not available to her.

Nadia Anjuman's claim to be both an Afghan woman and an Afghan poet put her in the path of danger. If she had really had her own country she would almost certainly never have posed the threat she did when she walked out of objectification into authorship. As it was she appeared to be trespassing on an already existing country – one that was constructed in her absence and made to perpetuate it.

But the issue is poetry and not nationhood. It is easier to think of Nadia Anjuman's death as an honour killing than as a prompt for questions about the art she practised. The truth is that she lost her life in a city whose main square honoured the poem, its practice and history. What Nadia Anjuman forces us to consider above all is that no art is theoretical.

And here, even though it is unfinished, I leave her story. Already poets, translators and commentators are making her work more available: bringing this wrenching allegory of a poet and her poetry – and its cost – into the light of translation and analysis. Much more will be written about her, and should be. In the meantime, in the absence of the living poet, what she and her poetry deserve is what has been the subject of this piece: a readership.

VI

And so I come back to where I started. To the National Library in winter and to the poem by Ted Hughes I first read there. And to the years when I too often read a poem quickly or carelessly – although that was never my intention. But since this piece contains a reproach to poetry readers, it seems only right I should finish it by including myself in that critique.

The poem in front of me that evening was not the one I read. The one I read was clouded by my subjectivity and by a frank sense of my own limits. I felt that the phrase Ted Hughes used – *as deep as England* – was one I couldn't use

about my own landscape, my own country; that it implied an ownership I couldn't claim. Inasmuch as I felt shut out by this perception, I did what I have criticised the nineteenth-century reader here for doing: instead of allowing myself to be changed by the poem, I changed the poem.

I read it as a claim, a separable statement of entitlement, a disclosure of ownership. But of course it's not. Ted Hughes's poem on the pike starts out by invoking a world of nature in which the human element is enhanced but not privileged. It then becomes a subtle unsettling of the whole idea of location. The pike that begins in its own water with its tiger-stripes and clamping jaws has to yield in the eighth stanza to a different habitat. The speaker is remembering 'a pond I fished'. The imagined water in turn becomes an analogue of memory: it has – with its tench and its lilies – survived and shaken off the circumstances of its own creation.

And so the speaker locates that water in a context that provides both identity and disruption.

Stilled legendary depth.
It was as deep as England.

If I had read the words carefully back then I would have seen that the lines imply not a statement of nationhood, but a subversion of it. In nine words the conventions of a national context are stripped back, are exposed to the deep, cold water that has resisted all the directives of origin: that has, in the words of the previous stanza, 'outlasted every visible stone / Of the monastery that planted them'. If I had looked more closely I might have seen that the words come closer to a renunciation than a claim.

But I didn't. I did exactly what I accuse others of doing in this article. I read the poem through my own values and erased its meanings when they unsettled my own. At which point, I ceased to be the poem's reader and became its editor. I have few excuses. I was young. I should have known better. Fortunately I was dealing with one of the most forgiving of forms: all you need to do if you mis-read a poem is re-read it. Which I did.

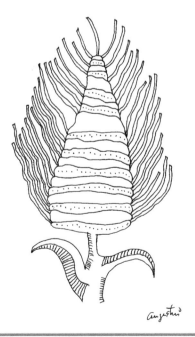

Copyright © Michael Augustin 2014

Reading Eavan

I am pitched to a powerful place:
home:
homes we are warred out of, talked out of, written by omission out of – beaten out of:

'My grandmother lived outside history. And she died there...
Did she find her Nation? And does it matter?'

If the poet hadn't written would it have mattered? What does it take to make those who didn't matter matter? Matter: Middle English **MATERE**, from Old French **MATERE**, **MATIERE**, from Latin material, matter, subject, physical substance, wood for building, from **MATER** mother...

What has the poet done when she asks:

If what was not said was never seen
If what was never seen could not be known

Elie Wiesel talks to millions on Oprah about Nazis throwing babies into the fire
The poet Natalie Handal talks to me from occupied Palestine in e-mail:
Sister after seeing a burnt baby
what else is left? What else? 7/19/147:36:38 PM

What has writing made except a writer?

On my sister's death certificate a middle name appears, I go to correct it thinking something about veracity, official, it should be accurate. What's to be accurate? She is dead, a wasn't, a disappeared, no funeral no nothing: now a name, Rose, appears.

What does Eavan do when she says:

Not a word not a word
Not a word not a word

The secrets our lives were/are ruled by? The silences of hearth, of state. How we are invisible, iced, how they raise billions to control our bodies: who can, who must/must not give BIRTH, must not abort, must abort. Give sex, not give sex.

'You don't need a middle name. You'll get married and take your husband's name.'

Home: one says: I was beaten out of mine
Nation: another says: I was shamed out of mine

Home: the rent man lord of the land landlord takes back home, the army takes back home
The court takes back home, the treaty takes back home, the settlers take back home, the young white wealth take the filth blighted urban spaces that the people were not doing anything nice with anyway (aside from *living* in them – but that gets so complicated in the collapse of support beams and cloud of lead dust.)

Home – the hearth we never owned – to become 'un'-domiciled – or to be bused homeless to an old hotel in the borough of Queens, NYC and have Chinese immigrants stage a protest in eloquent new English: protesting: the black and Latino homeless families who are messing up their we work hard neighbourhood.

Be a lady in black stockings
in the back room of a bath house,
The steam dark
Be a girl in your own fault
Be night falling down
in drops on your back
be pimped pink
t-strap slice a razor
greened eyed alley cat
Be told: get back black
Be fifty and never married,
Be awkward at your desk   feel
the breath on your neck
waiting for you to retire die
be told to get back to that back room
but show up voting day, visiting day, PTA, book club
and wear a gold cross
even though you don't believe in god.
Take a country of the map
cut it up and eat jingoism
and ride the box car to
forever on the border of wishing for more
in the river of almost
in the country of big but not big enuff 4 you
ROOTS – white fibres in a clay pot
stuck to its red sides like long white pin worms
grown round and round in the shape of the pot
hanging in KMART needing water
needing to be paid for
A plant to clean the air.
You are blue eye in one socket
brown in the other –
calico hole childhood –
you were born – not a lot after that
but you liked cats
filled up on them
first one
then ten
and somehow impossibly two hundred

Eavan's:

'The Briar Rose'

Intimate as underthings
besides the matronly damasks –

the last thing
to go out at night
is the lantern-like, white insistence
of these small flowers;

their camisole glow.

Standing here on the front step
watching wildness break out again

it could be
the unlighted stairway,
I could be
the child I was, opening

a bedroom door
on Irish whiskey, lipstick,

an empty glass,
oyster crêpe-de-Chine

and closing it without knowing why.

And I think because that poem is a place, not childhood but its memory, it is a thing that can't be taken, the captured home, they don't even know we have it! The power of the place in our head, that even if we are ousted from it (or even ousted from life itself) it is *written*, the place is written, it exists where it had no name before, and is now a rock of fire, our own Island, our tongue.

This is reading Eavan: Entering a country Entering a home Entering a woman:
Going into forbidden interiors that are controlled, monitored, and defined by the culture at large: army police church school-academy, controlled by imprisonment stoning death shunning impoverishment starvation rape ridicule, sealed by addiction self mutilation silence amnesia isolation anorexia suicide – But are also rocks of fire rocks of fire our own island. Our tongue.

MARK DOTY

'You are dear and stand beside me':
Sappho's Blessing and Sappho's Charge

Night falls twice in 'The Journey', a poem close to the heart of Eavan Boland's work – at once *ars poetica* and lamentation, an interrogation of history's limits and a bold act of claiming poetic legacy. The first dark descends as the speaker finds herself at odds – perhaps after an afternoon of reading new books, or some journal where the sort of poems that most rankle her are on display – with the poetic climate around her. Whether this twilight belongs to a Dublin evening or is an outward sign of poetry's benighted state, she's ready to launch the kind of rhetorical outburst at which all serious readers arrive now and then; *THIS is what a poem must be*, we insist to the bookshelves and the dog, *THIS is what the art requires*. The poem opens

And then the dark fell and 'there has never'
I said 'been a poem to an antibiotic: …

After a few lines describing the way poetry often veils the quotidian in elevated speech, the speaker's aesthetic pronouncement rises to the level of a credo:

Depend on it, somewhere a poet is wasting
his sweet uncluttered meters on the obvious

emblem instead of the real thing.
Instead of sulpha we have hyssop dipped

in the wild blood of the unblemished lamb,
so every day the language gets less

for the task and we are less with the language.

It is not only at their own peril, those fighting words assert, that poets ignore the contemporary and the quotidian; such erasure puts language itself at risk, reducing its capacity to name the conditions of the present. It's easy for poets in our moment to think of ourselves as conservators, guardians of an embattled tongue, but Boland insists that poets fail not by losing the richness of the past but by refusing to forge a vocabulary commensurate with the occasions of the now; it's our work to continually bring language to bear on reality as we know it. (Which is one reason Boland's poems so often want to remind us that we're looking at a suburban home and garden, and the speaker is folding linens or picking up stray toys from the grass; this, as my friend Marie Howe asserts in the title poem of a book squarely in favour of the now, is 'what the living do', in our very particular economic and cultural situations.) And why are we then less with the language? Because if the poet will not struggle to give specific, serviceable speech to the nature of this moment, someone else will. Especially someone who wants to sell you something. I don't think poetry can do everything; how can we accommodate the massive technological reshaping of experience happening now at gigabyte speed? But I believe, as I think Boland does, that our work is to say how it feels to be here, to go as far as we can in the direction of naming and evoking how it feels to be alive in this hour. To retreat is to relinquish the word to engineers, and – far worse – legions of marketers. This is not a lost cause: there's a reason universities on both sides of the Atlantic are full of young people who want to write, and it's not that academia is so deeply magnetic, or that literary fame waits for all; an increasingly large population is hungry for words that will suffice to say what is to be alive, in individual terms, not in the language of the focus group or the committee. There used to be an American literary magazine, back in the hoary old mimeograph days, called *The Unspeakable Visions of the Individual*, a moniker I once found melodramatic and a bit silly, but I don't think that any more. It may be blunt, but it's also dead on. That is poetry's work, to go after the singular, difficult, necessary vocabulary.

The speech ends, the anger fades, dark falls again. This time it seems clearly both actual night, the night in which dreams may come, and something like that dark Dante encountered, at mid-life, when there was no clear way to proceed. Boland is superb at moving her reader between worlds, between levels of reality. Here's the beginning of a tour-de-force of a sentence, broken across 27 lines, in which she descends into the world beneath the world:

> The poplars shifted their music in the garden,
> a child startled in a dream,
> my room was a mess…
>
> … and I was listening out but in my head was
> a loosening and sweetening heaviness,
>
> not sleep, but nearly sleep, not dreaming really
> but as ready to believe and still
> unfevered, calm and unsurprised
> when she came and stood beside me

'She' is Sappho, come to guide a pilgrim and a daughter, and her apparition produces four lines of simple but utterly enraptured anaphora:

> and I would have known her anywhere
> and I would have gone with her anywhere
> and she came wordlessly
> and without a word I went with her

This unpunctuated, ravished speech is the language of enthrallment, and the speaker allows herself to be carried 'down down down without so much as / ever touching down', the unbuttoned syntax evoking the loosened consciousness of that earlier line. 'The light went on / failing' as the descent continues to its eventual ending, at the edge of the river ('the dream water, the narcotic crossing') that separates the living from the dead. Sappho explains the seething crowd visible just across it, the shades of women with their infants ('suckling darknesses') who perished of plague and typhus, cholera and croup, all the virulent diseases of the world before sulpha drugs. No wonder the speaker has wished for a poem in praise of an antibiotic, for here is the alternative, a vast uncatalogued history of grief. Sappho cautions the speaker against understanding these women as types, defined by their work as washerwomen or ladies of the court; she wants the poet to cleave to the stuff of subjectivity, the language of felt experience. The visionary is transfixed; she wishes to be witness to these unwritten lives, but Sappho insists on the unspeakability of what is outside of history:

> 'what you have seen is beyond speech,
> beyond song, only not beyond love;
>
> 'remember it, you will remember it'

But this guiding spirit has not arisen simply in order to point to what cannot be named. She wants to offer encouragement, in the original sense, of instilling heart: '"There are not many of us; you are dear // "and stand beside me as my own daughter."' *You are dear*: what an extraordinary moment in late twentieth-century poetry!

It has been nearly seven hundred years since Dante placed himself in the company of the great Classical poets, in Canto IV, where the Pilgrim and Virgil walk among those dead who were born before Christ, and thus, though without sin, could not be baptised. Here, in Robert Pinsky's translation, is what happens when Dante and Virgil meet Homer, Horace, Lucan and Ovid:

> After they had shared a word
>
> Among themselves, they turned and greeted me
>
>> With cordial gestures, at which my master smiled;
>> And far more honor: that fair company
>
> Then made me one among them – so as we traveled
>> Onward toward the light I made a sixth
>> Amid such store of wisdom. Thus we strolled,
>
> Speaking of matters I will not give breath.

You are dear. They made me one among them. These are remarkable acts of anointment, in which the poet ghosts or puppets an unquestionable authority – in Dante's case five of them! – to testify to the ability of the one writing the poem.

In our time, I'd argue, such gestures belong to the disenfranchised. At its mildest, the impulse takes the form of something like hanging portraits of ancestors in the house: think of Adrienne Rich evoking Ruykeser, or James Merrill (among others) titling poems 'Days of 19__' to import something of Cavafy's dry, solitary, golden-wine eros onto the stage, as well as his obsessive concern with memory. But to bring the beloved ancestor into the poem, and allow her to speak to one directly? That's a strategy for hard times. Frank O'Hara, to the delight of a small group of readers, wasn't writing the mainstream poem of the American 1950s, but he wasn't winning much in the way of prizes either. When he turned to Mayakovsky's hearty, comic account of being visited by the sun while painting revolutionary posters, he chose not the Bolshevik poet to praise him but the celestial body itself, which slyly drops down to Fire Island to confide 'Frankly, I like your poetry'. 'A True Account of Talking to the Sun at Fire Island' is a playfully ironic self-coronation, made charming by the fact that we know and he knows it's a performance, made more resonant and commanding by the darker tones that inflect it. I still remember my shock when a perfectly serious literary critic, writing in an American lit mag in the 80s, dismissed O'Hara's work as 'too faggotty'. Perhaps 'A True Account' grows out of some such internalised insult; it's a poem that wears its gayness – in its wit and comedy, its sparkle and theatricality and swooning emotion giving way to the sincere – on its sleeve.

Boland, in allowing Sappho to say *You are dear to me*, makes a gesture long overdue indeed; where is the woman poet who strode the plains of hell with the men? Where is Sappho, in Canto IV? Too long erased, quietly keeping watch over her daughters, she has come to Dublin, it is clear, to bless and to authorise.

But Boland's dedication to complexity will not allow us merely to shout hooray at affirmation of a woman's right and need to speak. Sappho turns from her verbal embrace to name the problematic inheritance which must be the fountainhead of Boland's poetry:

'I have brought you here so you will know forever
the silences in which are our beginnings,
in which we have an origin like water…'

It's too easy to think that the cure for silence is speech; in fact,

the lives of the women lined along the banks of Lethe cannot be narrated, their grief neither entered nor fully understood. To assume too easy an ability to speak is to deny the depth and reality of their silence. And yet the poet – who wakes to a banging window, rain, her own children sleeping 'the last dark out safely' – has not, obviously, chosen silence. We honour the great dead neither with generalities nor by giving up on the possibility of knowledge; every life is specific, in context, embodied as we are. How much of what it is to be us will also disappear from history? 'Nothing was changed; nothing was more clear', Boland tells us. But I do not quite believe her. It's true that the unwritten history of women was there before her vision and is indeed there when it is done. And it's true, at the end of 'The Journey', that it's not clear how the poet is to proceed, though it seems entirely certain that she will. That is quite enough for a vision to offer. But there's more: the poem gives me the sense that I have been changed; I feel, nearly physically, the unarticulated weight of the past, of suffering human bodies almost without narrative and certainly without particularity, and I'm awake to the bracing lack of clarity attendant in our contradictory responsibilities: to honour the unspeakable and to say what one can.

PAULA MEEHAN

On 'Making Money'

When I first read 'Making Money', in *The Paris Review* in 2001, it was a crystallising experience. The poem did not only speak of the historical moment of its setting, a hundred years ago at the turn from the nineteenth into the twentieth century, but also by implication spoke to what was the particular present moment in turn-of-the-millennium Ireland. We were suffering a turbocharged development cycle that like a juggernaut was powering through the cities and the hinterlands alike.

The poem is set in Dundrum, a topos and a polis already familiar to Eavan Boland's readers: the suburb she made her home in with her husband Kevin Casey, raised her girls in, the suburb at the edge of the city under the mountains, haunted by the ghosts of the last wolves, the suburb that by the time the poem is written has become the site of a massive development project. Here will be built the biggest temple to Mammon, symbol of all the mismanaged wealth of the Celtic tiger, what's now known as the Dundrum Town Centre. The Centre has offered a new slang word to English as she is spoke here in Dublin – *Drummies*, the shopaholic mall rats of all ages who orient themselves by a map of retail opportunities.

'Making Money' traces the journey of the mill workers from their humble mill cottages one dawn, or rather 'the ugly first hour after dawn', at the end of summer. The mill wheel is powered by the braided rivers, including the River Slang (oh what poet could resist), coming down off the Dublin mountains. It's a paper mill and the paper is exported to make money. Literally:

… the crimson and indigo features
of the prince who will stare out from
the surfaces they have made on
the ruin of a Europe
he cannot see from the surface
of a wealth he cannot keep

The women work the hemp waste, cotton lint, linen, flax and fishnets delivered each day by rag wagon. All the details of the noxious and toxic work are in the poem, the alkaline and caustic and soda ash and the sifting and beating and settling and fraying. It's a familiar gesture of Boland's – to use an object, or a process, to make a profound equivalence. The gesture can be recognised in poems such as 'Object Lessons', 'On the Gift of *The Birds of America* by James Audubon', 'Bright Cut Irish Silver', 'An Old Steel Engraving', 'At the Glass Factory in Cavan Town', The Mother Tongue', 'Watching Old Movies When They Were New' – the list grows as the net is cast more widely, and we see that a substantial number of poems set out from a meditation on an object, with or without a meditation on the process involved in its making, and invite us to a consideration of the eternal verity inherent in both object and process. Not symbol of but access to.

The powerful equivalence for me back in 2001 was that 'Making Money' said: we are powerless now. The *poet* says the women workers in their mill jobs are facing the paradox, making money, learning to die of it. But the *poem* says we have no more power in the face of our rulers, the economic rulers and their puppets, their tame politicians, and the war machine they serve, than these women had over the money they made. For someone else.

The vision is cool and cold and inexorable. In an earlier poem, 'Lace', from her 1987 collection *The Journey*, the object of scrutiny is the lace at the wrist of a prince in what Boland calls 'a petty court':

> … he shakes out
>
> the thriftless phrases,
> the crystal rhetoric
> of bobbined knots
> and bosses:
> a vagrant drift
> of emphasis
> to wave away an argument
> or frame the hand
> he kisses;

The description is book-ended between the opening of the poem where the poet, seeking a language that *is* lace, bends over an open notebook in the fading light, and the end of the poem where the lace as object, as ornament, is restored to its part in a human process that has a terrible price:

> what someone
> in the corner
> of a room,
> in the dusk,
> bent over
> as the light was fading
>
> lost their sight for.

The price paid by the maker, the human cost of the craft, the art, has implications for us; it has particular ironies for the poet, the ur-maker, in the temenos that is the poem, in the sovereign state that lies within the poem's boundaries.

The hindsight which we bring to 'Making Money' lets us know that the war is on the way, the Great War at least. Maybe the mention of April draws our own Easter Rising into those cast-off hempen nets: why else have April in a poem that starts in late summer, finishes in rainy autumn? April connotes the Rising for me, important in our own local bother – but that may be the poem reading me. We are clear that that 'terrible century', as Anna Akhmatova called the twentieth century, will be one war after another, and that most, underneath the rhetoric, will be resource wars.

The visionary moment in the poem is when Boland states that the women who make the fine rag paper that will be imprinted with virtual value far beyond their imaginings

> … never will
>
> see the small boundaries all this will buy
> or the poisoned kingdom with its waterways
> and splintered locks or the peacocks who will walk
> this paper up and down in the windless gardens
> of a history no one can stop happening now.

But we see. We are complicit with the century passing. Complicit with the poem passing. We are made to see that what we have been shown is

> … this final proof that
> the past is not made out of time, out of memory,
> out of irony but is also
> a crime we cannot admit and will not atone

Around the time I first read 'Making Money' my partner and I had received Notice to Quit our shabby genteel second-floor flat in Merrion Square. It looked out on the gardens of the Square, a green lung, and we were part of a small, dwindling number of residents who still lived on the Square. A developer from Sligo bought the house our flat was in and even though we had been there for over ten years, we had no legal standing to challenge the Notice to Quit.

We heard on the grapevine that this developer collected art. He obviously didn't collect artists. We were able, just about, for the emotional disruption of losing our home, where we'd had a happy and creative decade. We managed to gather a deposit for a small house that would put us beyond the whim of the landlords, though not, of course, beyond the clutches of the bank. Finding anything remotely affordable in those white-hot tiger years was a miracle in itself.

The property market had ascended into madness. Even the cottages the mill girls come out of, to walk past the

> headlong weir and the sedge drowned in it
> and their faces about to be as they looked down
> once quickly on
> their way to the mill, to the toil

– even those cottages were by 2001 bijou desirable residences and, like the cottages of the fishing community of Howth, say, or the red brick two-up two-downs of the railway workers all over the city, way out of reach of the labouring classes of millennial Dublin, many of whom were newcomers to the city, filling its air with their divers tongues.

And the braided rivers from off the mountain were culverted underground.

> In a spring dusk I walk to the Town Centre,
> I stand listening to a small river,
> Closed in and weeping.

as Boland has it in a more recent poem, 'Re-reading Oliver Goldsmith's "Deserted Village" in a Changed Ireland' (2014).

I read 'Making Money', then, in a strange state of flux and grief and it affected me profoundly. I walked around with the double vision that so many of Boland's poems have offered over the years: the geography of the poem mapping the life as it unfolds in its own processes, and material objects imbued with the kind of aura and force one expects from shamanic power objects, or medicine bundles. That familiar sense of having one's attention snagged and directed with authority and skill.

Not for the first time, an Eavan Boland poem had found the tenor and heft of the times we are living in, found an elegant vehicle to carry the vision, and the pain. I am not equating my small tiger worries with the sweat of the women who worked in the mills. Nor is this poem, as one reviewer has so spectacularly misread it, an exercise in identity politics. It speaks, out of a profound moral sensibility, of what it is to be human, in the present moment, in language that is pure lyric – the clearest and most truthful language can be.

TARA BERGIN

Greenish Silks: Reading Eavan Boland's 'Silenced'

On the road from Dublin to Bray there used to be a big, dismal-looking building, which had a huge sign outside saying YARN FACTORY. I remember passing it in the car as a child, and my dad would tell me that inside there were hundreds of people all working hard making up stories. It was funny to me at the time because of the bleakness of the place, and it was also somehow hopeful to think that such a boring, depressing exterior could be hiding something so exciting.

The ability to tell a story and to spin a yarn in order to create another, alternative world can be central to poetry, and Eavan Boland's 'Silenced', the fifth poem in the sequence 'Domestic Violence', is an example of this. Really, it is an example of what poetry can do, in the sense that it tells its story so succinctly, so suggestively, so objectively and yet so personally, that it is deeply shocking, and – as a direct result of its skill – deeply thrilling at the same time.

The poem re-tells the ancient myth of Philomel, the sister of Procne, who is raped by Procne's husband Tereus, the king of Thrace. When Philomel, in great despair, promises to tell the world about what Tereus has done, he grabs her tongue, and cuts it off with his sword. Afterwards, as Boland describes:

> she determined to tell her story
> another way. She began a tapestry.
> She gathered skeins, colours.
> She started weaving.

She cannot be silenced, in other words, and Boland's use of the word 'skein' here is particularly interesting. Literally meaning 'loosely coiled bundle of yarn or thread', skein can also mean a flock of wild birds in flight (Philomel and her sister turn into birds at the end of the original myth), or 'tangle and confusion'. It also sounds very much like the Irish word *scéal*, meaning story, or tale. And while Philomel weaves her story into the tapestry, the poet herself enters the room ('she never saw me enter'), to stand beside her, and to offer her own account of events. Suddenly, here in the penultimate stanza, the poet manages to weave her own voice – her own colours – into the ancient myth. Being a skilled storyteller, she uses mostly ordinary details; just enough truth to make us believe it:

> An Irish sky was unfolding its wintry colours
> slowly over my shoulder. An old radio
> was there in the room as well, telling its own
> unregarded story of violation.

The presence of these images is as quiet and as disquieting as Philomel's work, and exemplifies, I think, that difficult question of voice in poetry. How do you get your own voice into your poems? How do you know what it is, this voice? Where will you look? Here is one answer, at least: you look at objects, and sounds; you look over your shoulder; you listen to the stories being told to you.

Then for the final, awful, triumphant end; altered by Boland (the white ground on which the original tapestry was woven has been rinsed green here), yet wholly devastating:

> Now she is rinsing the distances
> with greenish silks. Now, for the terrible foreground,
> she is pulling out crimson thread.

Here, in this final stanza, the two voices – the two hands – of Philomel and Boland merge together to create what is ultimately a highly successful translation of a visual image into words. Through Boland's eyes we see the tapestry that Philomel is making. Crucially, the inclusion of the colour green means that the tell-tale crimson creates a different kind of visual effect: a dramatic interaction of colour; a brutality. It illustrates the power of Boland's choices, and the skill of her positioning. This is, as the poem tells us at its start, an 'ancient, gruesome story', re-told with deliberation, and devastating care.

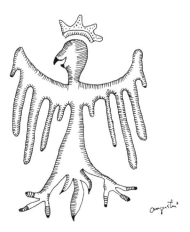

Dictions and Discoveries

What are we going to do with experience? In some poems, the very experience of making the poem itself is conveyed, as though the technical impulse, the urge to find the right words, sound patterns and rhythmical system might be enough to satisfy some need within the poet's nervous system. It matters then what the poem mysteriously does as the poem becomes close to a musical performance. It matters less what the poem says, or what it is about.

There is a beautiful moment in the ancient Irish narrative *Toraiocht Dhiarmada agus Grainne* in which the king, now an old man, has wished to marry the young and beautiful Grainne, who in turn has convinced Diarmaid, one of the king's handsome warriors, to run away with her. As they are pursued across Ireland, Diarmaid, out of loyalty to the king, is unwilling to make love with Grainne. She taunts him as they cross a stream, telling him that the water that has splashed her thigh is braver than he is. And thus they become lovers.

Eavan Boland's version of the story, called 'Song', appears in her 1975 collection *The War Horse*. The first of four six-line stanzas has twenty-seven words, a comma, a semi-colon and a full-stop. Twenty-four of the words have only one syllable. The other three need more time; they take time; they are almost the key words – 'outsleep'; 'water'; 'afraid'. The beat is iambic trimeter, with a variation in the fourth line 'Too fast, too fast' which matches the meaning, catches the speed, not only the speed of the water, but the speed of the voice itself, with the comma denoting a hesitation in the first person singular voice which will declare itself in the last line:

> Where in blind files
> Bats outsleep the frost
> Water slips through stones
> Too fast, too fast
> For ice; afraid he'd slip
> By me I asked him first.

The stanza depends on its rhythm, the single-syllable words suggesting fear, flight, urgency. Although the stanza does not rhyme, there are many repeating sounds, the 'i' sound in 'blind' coming fast in 'file' and again in 'ice'. And then there are the half-rhymes of 'frost', 'fast' and 'first' at the end of the second, fourth and sixth lines; there is the waking echo of 'outsleep' in 'slip'; and the waking echo too of 'bats' in the repeated word, 'fast'.

The last two stanzas of the poem tell the story of the water hitting Grainne's thigh and her taunting Diarmaid, and then his giving in. The third stanza reads:

> My skirt in my hand,
> Lifting the hem high
> I forded the river there.
> Drops splashed my thigh.
> Ahead of me at last
> He turned at my cry.

Of the nouns and verbs in this stanza, there is only one which has an obvious Latin root and that is the last word 'cry'. This mirrors the first stanza, where there are no words with a Latin root, and the other two stanzas where the two words with a Latin root stand out – 'venom' in the second stanza and 'attempt' in the last stanza.

This story of female transgression is not, in Eavan Boland's version, a translation, but rather an attempt to find a mode in English which will not only match the sense of risk and movement of the text it is based on, but will also suggest, using words of Anglo-Saxon origin, a pre-modern time. The song of the title has a prose origin; it manages with concise skill and precision to tell a story in a poem, a story which has its original form in prose narrative.

What does this have to do with experience? For those of us brought up in Ireland with parents or grandparents who belonged to the revolutionary generation, these ancient stories had a special power. Indeed, the act of translation itself into a vernacular by figures such as Douglas Hyde and Lady Gregory at the end of the nineteenth and beginning of the twentieth century gave an impetus to the movement for Irish independence more powerful than, say, any set of economic arguments. Suggesting that these texts belonged to Ireland, and, in Lady Gregory's phrase, added dignity to the country, stirred up a set of strong emotions in what was a sort of political vacuum after the fall of Parnell in 1890.

Some of the ancient stories remained controversial even then, however, because of their portraits of a female sexuality which could not be easily ignored. This was apparent not only in the story of Grainne, but also in the depiction of Queen Maeve in *The Tain*, the epic translated by Lady Gregory in 1902. Lady Gregory, more interested in the heroic elements in *The Tain*, was uneasy about the frank depiction of sexuality in the text and made some cuts. But when the text was again translated in 1969 by the poet Thomas Kinsella, he was unembarrassed by the sexual content.

Eavan Boland's 'Song', then, followed in a tradition begun with Douglas Hyde's *Love Songs of Connaught* (1893) in attempting to find a form and tone for Irish mythology or Irish-language texts which was not itself archaic, which used a diction that was not openly or obviously contemporary, but rather was part of a living speech or tone of voice which suggested something composed now more than translated from then. Also, as a poem about a woman who leads rather than follows, as a poem written by a woman, it matched earlier translations of Irish texts in responding to contemporary and pressing concerns; it allowed the present in from the shadows to make the translation or the re-telling more part of both a exquisite technical experience of making a poem in this form and a personal experience of making a poem which has contemporary resonance.

Experience, of course, shifts and changes, will not stay in place, will not stay still. The distance between Eavan Boland's volume *The War Horse* and her volume *In a Time of Violence* is nineteen years, the distance, in a woman's life, between thirty-one and fifty. Light years. And in a poet's life, more than that. All we have to do is think of the distance between the W.B. Yeats of *The Wind Among the Reeds*, published when he was thirty-four, and the poet of *The Wild Swans at Coole* twenty years later, or the distance in the sensibility of T.S. Eliot over the twenty years between 'The Waste Land' and 'Little Gidding'. This is not about growing older, but about an enrichment and refinement which comes from reading the self, re-creating the self, re-imagining the self, finding dictions to match discoveries.

Eavan Boland's poem 'Love' from the volume *In a Time of Violence* both uses and creates myth; it allows, as the poem's second line suggests, myths to collide. The poet herself is a sort of Orpheus in the poem, charming a loved one with her lines. She invokes Aeneas in the underworld, and Icarus's dangerous flight over the world above, and also Ceres and Persephone, as she remembers a child who recovered from illness. But, to match this, or set against it, she finds a plain-spoken tone that belongs to now; she heightens this tone and makes it taut, but it remains the voice of a woman speaking. History is now and it is in the words she writes. The opening of the poem is in Iowa, a real place in a real time:

Dark falls on this mid-western town

The bridge over the river is seen in dusk, and the dusk 'slides and deepens' to a remembered mythology – 'the water / the hero crossed on his way to hell'. But she wants this myth to collide with the facts of things: 'a kitchen and an Amish table' in 'our old apartment'. And then she invokes the eponymous word – love – and then love becomes mythologised, a thing 'with the feather and muscle of wings'. And then there is a stanza about the child spared, and once more a mythology is evoked, as the hero 'hailed by his comrades in hell' is brought into service, given his due in the poem, only to be tossed aside since the poem wants to swim out to calmer waters. There have been two six-line stanzas and one seven-line stanza. The metrical system is uneven but led by a spondaic sound which lends itself to statement more than song.

And now, Eavan Boland is prepared to make a statement, clear, eschewing myth, or maybe proposing an anti-myth, since the Greek root for the word 'myth' suggests the closing of the eyes or the mouth. To be mute. These next five lines will speak with clear-eyed truth. The first line cannot be read as having two iambic beats, but rather four clear rings:

I am your wife.
It was years ago.
Our child is healed. We love each other still.
Across our day-to-day and ordinary distances
we speak plainly. We hear each other clearly.

These are six sentences. The first four of them admit no word with a Latin root, as though plain speaking requires an earlier tone. There are no flourishes. The plain tone, because of the references to myth in the previous four stanzas, brings with it a sense of casting off one tone to create another one, a tone more urgent, more exact, a tone caught in a strange grip between clarity and cry, between simple statement and a tense undertone filled with the sheer need to make this statement finally.

What to do now? The poem has four stanzas left. Since the tone has become more urgent, the number of lines in each stanza will shorten. Three stanzas of four lines, and one last stanza of two lines. The first of these stanzas is perhaps the most beautiful in all of Eavan Boland's work in its calm eloquence, its discovery of the resonant power of the image, the simple power of the thing. The statement emerges as though from an urgent impulse to state, to say, the poetry surviving in the space between sudden flashing diction and something chiselled from experience, written to be remembered, a sort of monument:

And yet I want to return to you
on the bridge of the Iowa river as you were,
with snow on the shoulders of your coat
and a car passing with its headlights on

It would be easy now to stop the poem here, to let the minor key of the snow on the shoulders of the coat and the car passing with its headlights on create a set of plain single notes for the poem to end on. But just as the poem has earned the right to speak in this tone, it has also earned the right to move the music of the poem into a higher register, to use two exalted words that the poem, even with its delving into what Philip Larkin called the 'myth-kitty', would have earlier resisted. These two words, which belong to mythology and to religion, are 'epic' and 'ascension':

I see you as a hero in a text –
the images blazing and the edges gilded –
and I long to cry out the epic question
my dear companion:

Will we ever live so intensely again?
Will love come to us again and be
so formidable at rest it offered us ascension
even to look at him?

In these two stanzas, instead of allowing two tones to collide, she has found a match for them. She creates an iambic pentameter line – 'I see you as a hero in a text' – to set a tone, filled now with a comfort and ease as the voice stretches itself from the simple business of asking a fundamental question – 'Will love come to us again?' – but insisting also on the right to let the voice soar and the question become more transcendental as the sights rise too, rise to the possible experience of 'ascension', the rising up out of the earth towards the sky, or out of the self towards something that two selves might become.

Once more, it might have been easy to end here, with the daring question, and the sense that even having to ask such a thing implies a knowledge that the answer will never be clear, and might indeed be dark. But there are two more lines. These come as a way of invoking the image in mythology of Orpheus walking ahead in a place of shadows with Eurydice behind, Eurydice being the one who sings. But she cannot be heard now in this place where words are shadows. The poem is resigned now to the way things are, and will be. The lines follow both the terms of a myth and the tone of a voice as though finally there were no distinction between the two:

But the words are shadows and you cannot hear me.
You walk away and I cannot follow.

A Road to Poetry: Eavan Boland Maps the Body Politic

In June 1968, my father and I took a weekend trip to Ireland to see the place from which one or more Wards had left for America during the nineteenth century. As with most genealogies, details were somewhat inexact. We had the locale – Cong, County Mayo – and even the address of a distant kinsman who still lived in or near the house that had been left. It wasn't quite clear, however, when that descendant had left; probably not during the first famine of the 1840s but sometime later in the century. My father was probably the great-grandson of that man, as best I can estimate. Raised the son of a physician – himself lace-curtain Irish in Dorchester, a suburb of Boston; a man of some influence in the community – my father was about as deracinated as you could get for a mid-century Boston Irishman: Harvard, English professor, married a WASP descended from Puritans, sceptical of the shibboleths and rituals of Boston's tribal nationalism. Nonetheless, the pull of the 'auld sod' was still strong enough that a trip, if not a pilgrimage, was thought necessary; we would be *ironic* tourists. But if there was no race memory or sentimentality in my father he was, nonetheless, aware of the ostracism that the Irish had suffered even in Boston. If Ireland was not a homeland, it had been once a home for Wards. Where we were from seemed a question worth exploring. Besides, for an English professor tutoring his son, there was always Yeats.

We were living in London that year, on sabbatical, and the two of us flew to Dublin, rented a car and drove due west to Cong. The visit with the ancient relative was a success. He was hospitality itself in his tiny stone house; he was cared for by the youngest of six daughters, the others all having left home. They still farmed somehow and owned a giant pig. Other snapshots: a sheep-shearing; beagles filling the road while the local hunt milled around; Ben Bulben and Yeats' grave. But the staggering impression on me – I was fifteen – was made by the walls: stone walls not just lining the roads but stretching across fields in a pattern of rational division, but then violating that rationality by crazily continuing up steeply vertical small mountains where no wall was necessary or needed – indeed, where it appeared no wall could even go. At first it was comic: who the hell would build a wall up *there?* But then they began to seem more ominous and scary: bright green lands crisscrossed and marked by stone walls even to and along the ridgelines. We couldn't account for it. It was amazing.

Years later, in my late thirties, when I was picking my way into poetry I somehow discovered Eavan Boland. I'm not sure why or how: a vestigial Irishness at work, an awareness of the Irish tradition (that visit to Yeats' grave had done its work), or did I intuit that she might have something to say to a historian (which is my profession)? All three, of course, but you can see where I'm going with this: to Boland's poems of the Famine and especially 'The Famine Road' or 'That the Science of Cartography is Limited'. Irish roads weren't simply roads any more than those walls were simply walls: they were an enactment of political economy, a marking on the land made by class power:

> 'Might it be safe,
> Colonel, to give them roads, roads to force
> from nowhere going nowhere of course?'

The Famine Roads actually violated the principle of laissez-faire that the English government adhered to when denying aid and relief during the famines. I have no idea whether the walls were also a state project or just a result of the necessity of clearing the land and marking the different tenantries.

Regardless, the connection was enough for me. Retrospectively, I suddenly saw the land we had driven through as American tourists with altered perspective, a new topography that stripped away the natural appearance of the ground. Poetry did that. What Boland's 'Famine Road' (and other poems) meant for me was that poetry could provide another entry into historical time. It's there in the poem's multiple voices. The deadly sign-off of the faceless functionary (quoted above) and expeditor of human misery: 'Your servant Jones'. The alternating stanzas of description of the road-building and the arrival of typhus: 'anything may have caused it, spores, / a childhood accident; one sees / day after day these mysteries' – the word 'mysteries' connecting not only with the Church but with folkways and magic, malevolent fairies. The pathos of the dying man, cast out, the man leaving ('grow / your garden, keep house, good-bye') and the woman left alone:

> Barren, never to know the load
> of his child in you, what is your body
> now if not a famine road?

For someone with a dry, academic understanding of the 'body politic' this was revelatory.

Contrastingly, 'That the Science of Cartography is Limited' surveys the imprinted, historically scarred landscape from a higher altitude. There is only the phrase of the speaker's partner to set the problem in motion: 'Look down you said: this was once a famine road'. And the speaker considers cartography and the world that it surveys and the choice of which terrain is depicted. The mapmaker, in his elegance (the masculine pronoun seems appropriate), cannot render the actual forest let alone a past that has been effaced by History – that is by a history that excludes:

> the line which says woodland and cries hunger
> and gives out among sweet pine and cypress,
> and finds no horizon
> will not be there.

This is a specific, imposed exclusion, not just a forgetting or a failure of the surveyors. History, Boland insists, has been naturalised: 'the line [...] says woodland'.

Boland's image of the woman's body as a famine road is a

powerful one. She has written about how her poetry evolved with a self-conscious shift off the well-travelled road of the Irish literary tradition. Writing herself out from under the weight of that tradition (Yeats, Synge, etc.) necessarily meant a slantidicular look at Irish nationalism itself, especially the romantic tradition of the 'wearing of the green', the pieties of the sentimental song. Her trajectory was not too dissimilar from that of the American poet Adrienne Rich, who found herself unsatisfactorily ventriloquising an inherited diction and world-view at odds with her own emerging voice. In particular, both poets (Rich with the added inflection of her sense of sexual difference) recognised how an established patriarchy, even if politically or nationalistically 'radical', offered them no point of purchase, no viewpoint, no way of excavating a past that would connect with them in the present. Boland's famine poems have a double purpose: they are history poems that recover silenced voices, re-map the past and indict the political economy of oppression, but they are also self-evidently feminist poems. The cartographer is a man. The poet is a woman who uses her marginality, her outsider-hood, to refocus our gaze to see beyond the familiar. In her stylistic evolution, Boland started paring down her verse to long poems with very short lines, a verbal anorexia that matched topics exploring the abuse done to a woman's body, including anorexia itself. Difficult reading and perhaps

too turned into themselves, these poems retained a connection, however fragile, to the famine and the barrenness it engendered, but also to the systems that were imprinted on and internalised by societies past and present.

Eavan Boland now lives part of the year in California, a sere and hilly part of America where the roads are rather different than the ones between Dublin and Cong. Four-, six- and eight-lane freeways, full of cars, carve the landscape up and obliterate the old trail of the Catholic missionaries, El Camino Real, which itself was a trail of conquest. A past that raises the kind of problem that Boland has treated in Irish history. Boland has written poems about America but they tend toward a doubled sense of Irish identity – an Irish American soldier in the Civil War, for instance – or they are about America as a liminal state. They are not as *specifically* grounded as her Irish history poems. Her work does have implications for American poetry, though, and I have learned much from it – as well as from the way that as a woman she wrote herself out from under the weight of the Irish literary tradition. Boland's work has been a sustained, focused effort on the subjects of her poems themselves and the tandem development of her own poetic mind. I owe her a personal debt, shared by many, for opening my eyes, thirty years after the fact, to the meanings of a wall.

JOAN McBREEN

Domestic Interior

The poem 'Night Feed' from Eavan Boland's 1982 collection of the same title has long held a particular place in my own evolution as a poet. The poem also marks a particular place and time in Irish literature. It was a time when Boland was developing her prose critiques and leading workshops across Ireland. While these workshops were open to all emerging poets, those who joined them were mainly women. They were, as the poet Moya Cannon once said, the start of the long process of giving women poets 'the vote'.

So how did this short-lined, warm-toned poem come to occupy such a celebratory but charged space? My own encounter with the poem and the poet during those years will, I hope, provide some context.

This is dawn.
Believe me
This is your season, little daughter.
The moment daisies open,
The hour mercurial rainwater
Makes a mirror for sparrows.
It's time we drowned our sorrows.

I tiptoe in.
I lift you up
Wriggling
In your rosy, zipped sleeper.
Yes, this is the hour

For the early bird and me
When finder is keeper.

When I first read these stanzas in 1982 I was struck by their musical elements. The rhymes, half-rhymes and slant rhymes raised the music. Here we had mirror and sparrows, sparrows and sorrows, dawn and daughter, sleeper and keeper. Then the reader is drawn to the images of the mother quietly entering the nursery, of her lifting the infant, wriggling in a rose-coloured sleeper.

But what struck me most forcefully was how directly this poem spoke to me and addressed my own life as a woman and a mother. I was living in Tuam, County Galway, with my husband, Joe McBreen, and our six children, the eldest being ten years old and the youngest a newborn. I was also teaching at a primary school and so had little time for myself. To consider writing and perhaps publishing poetry, something I longed to do, seemed an impossibility. I had written and published poetry as a teenager in my native town of Sligo. Then, in 1970, I married and started a family and the writing side of my life was, for the most part, abandoned.

Years later, sitting at my kitchen table with Eavan Boland's 1982 book in my hands, I was astonished. Here I was meeting an Irish poet, a woman, married with two young daughters, who was writing poems about her domestic interiors. It was the first time I had encountered a poet using such images as a milk bottle rinsed clear with a hint of winter constellations, jugs and kettles, a washing machine, a nursery light in a suburb window, a baby's fist as damp and tight as a night-time daisy. Ordinary domestic routines such as putting out milk bottles or feeding a new life in the middle of the night were here too:

A silt of milk.
The last suck.
And now your eyes are open,
Birth-coloured and offended.
Earth wakes.
You go back to sleep.
The feed is ended.

In short lyric poems Boland was creating art out of the ordinary. And this had a very profound effect on me.

In 'Night Feed' in particular, the short lyrical lines of plain speech expressed exactly the universal love of mother for child, the vulnerability of both and the already existing sense of separation and loss. The infant will inevitably grow away from the mother and the mother already accepts this in an unconscious way. So the young mother's joy in caring for her child is already tempered with sadness. The last stanza of this poem expressses this very powerfully:

Worms turn.
Stars go in.
Even the moon is losing face.
Poplars stilt for dawn
And we begin
The long fall from grace.
I tuck you in.

In the autumn of 1984, a couple of years after my first encounter with this poem, I was feeding my young baby at the kitchen table, with my copy of *Night Feed* beside me. I had all the collections of poetry that Eavan Boland had published up to then, but it was *Night Feed* I returned to most often. I had heard that the poet was giving a reading in Galway city that particular afternoon. I was determined to attend the reading. With no babysitter I had no choice but to pile my six young children into my battered yellow Volkswagen car. Off we went on the twenty-mile journey from Tuam to the Nun's Island venue in the city. The children were very good and at the end of the reading, too shy to appoach Eavan myself to ask her to sign my books, I sent my eight-year-old daughter, Sarah, up to her with them. Eavan took the books from the child's hands and signed them, then asked her where was her mother. When Sarah pointed towards me and my clutch, Eavan beckoned to me to come up and speak with her. Carrying my baby in my arms, I braved it up to the poet and asked her very quietly, 'How is it possible to be a mother and a poet?' I can still see the tears in her eyes as she looked first at me and then at the children. It would be many years before I came to know what those tears of hers meant.

As she composed herself, I found myself telling her that I too wanted to write poems. She then invited me to attend a series of poetry workshops she was giving that winter at the Irish Writers' Centre in Dublin.

I cannot remember how I managed to attend, but attend I did. It is difficult all these years later to recall many details of those workshops. I do know that in addition to the Irish Writers' Centre ones, Eavan was also criss-crossing the country giving workshops which were, as I have said earlier, attracting women in large numbers. I am still in contact with poets such as Catherine Phil McCarthy, Mary O'Donnell, Clairr O'Connor, Jo Slade and others who were in those Dublin workshops. These poets went on to publish many collections of poetry. Sadly, others who attended have died or have faded from the publishing field. I do remember Eavan making it very clear to the group that she would be an exacting task-master with the poems we would present. We quickly accepted this despite being initially somewhat intimidated, and our poems became all the stronger. Those workshops were to change my life.

I learned that the encouragement and practical advice that I and many other women poets received from Boland was unique. This was, after all, the Ireland of the 1980s and the early 1990s with all the social and cultural injustices suffered by Irish women. This hardship has been well documented in books such as *The Transformation of Ireland* by the historian Diarmaid Ferriter and others such as Margaret MacCurtain. While their work will inform readers who wish to learn more of this period, it seems important to point out that without the generosity of Eavan Boland giving workshops and talking to women of all ages about poetry and publishing, the work of many women poets would never have seen its way into print. A deep debt of gratitude is long overdue to her.

Perhaps it is time that those years be recorded by those of us who can still bear witness, both to the workshops and to how those poems about domestic interiors first found us:

I crook the bottle.
How you suckle!
This is the best I can be,
Housewife
To this nursery
Where you hold on,
Dear life.

Writing this now, in the same room in the same house in County Galway where I once wrote poems surrounded by children, I am again reminded how, as the years went on, the poem 'Night Feed' and all the poems in that collection and in all the subsequent Boland collections continued to feed myself and many, many Irish women poets and gave us the courage to write the poems we needed to write and to find publishing outlets for them where we could. And how we needed that courage!

Eavan Boland's Daring Integrity: A Quick Glance at the Poet's Context

The essence of Irish imagination has been in the provinces: *County Cork, depraved*, as Beckett's Murphy growls, thinking, no doubt, of Daniel Corkery's crowd at a Munster Hurling Final rather than Miss Counihan's lover upon the tomb of Father Prout in Beckett's *Murphy*. Such provincial culture (*think* stories of Daniel Corkery, plays of T.C. Murray, paintings of Seán Keating) is male, sporting, homespun as a Connemara holiday and, sometimes, stupid with alcohol. It is what every Irishwoman has had to negotiate, that lethal conjunction of laddish politics and 'national feeling' – a feeling so alarmingly identified by Yeats in his *Journal* of 14 March 1909:

> So long as all is ordered for attack, and that alone, leaders will instinctively increase the number of enemies that they may give their followers something to do, and Irish enemies rather than English because they are the more easily injured, and because the greater the enemy the greater the hatred and therefore the greater the power. They would give a nation the frenzy of a sect.

And all of this so aptly captured by an editorial in *An Camán* of 6 January 1934:

> We of the Irish-Ireland movement are wholeheartedly behind this anti-jazz campaign. In these columns we have never ceased to stress the dangers, morally and nationally, which jazz music and jazz dance hold for our people, especially in rural areas. The false tolerance towards jazz, speciously advanced in argument by those who advocate freedom of choice in pastimes and recreations, has had its corrosive influence on all phases of national thought.

It is interesting to note, in the context of so much that Eavan Boland has written, how quickly 'freedom of choice' became something un-Irish, unpatriotic. The seeds of our Stasi-like Republic that diminished women were sown long, long ago, and the trail of that national stain goes all the way back to the shrewd and ambitious 'place men' of Daniel O'Connell; the resurgence of Catholic power, that Ibsen-like inertia so brilliantly captured by Joyce. It is too complicated to contemplate at this moment; and, anyway, *Jesus, Mary and Joseph*, it is too depressing for those of us who've tried to live an adult life here: suffice to say that it created a mind-set that dominates Irish commentary to this very day. If I linger too long in any Irish pub I meet Daniel Corkerys thirty years younger than I, and their political and moral certainties frighten me. New media, digital media, that's all very well, but what if the hand pressing the edit button is stilled by the thoughts of Pius XI's *Vigilanti Cura*, 1936, with its insistence on unceasing and eternal vigilance so that film narrative meets 'the requirements of the Christian conscience'. You must understand this: in Ireland the cowed and conventional still laugh loudest, for they are relieved from the burden of conscience. Developing

and protecting the national conscience has been the major nationalist project since the Act of Union. We still act as if we were all Repealers. It is best to see Eavan Boland's work as a singular, visual leap of conscience, away from those curators of national narrative, into a new studio, in order to act upon a fresh canvas. In this great leap of artistic conscience she was most like the visual artists, Norah McGuinness, Mainie Jellett and Evie Hone, who abandoned the dead dialogue of national representation in art and discovered a new conversation with modernism, with Cubism. But, as Paula McCarthy notes in the Ní Chuilleanáin-edited *Irish Women: Image and Achievement*: 'Despite Mainie Jellett's enormous influence, Cubism was never fully accepted in Ireland'. A firm and powerfully resourced Catholic viewpoint had its icy grip upon Irish imagination; it would be decades before that grip was even slightly eased.

'For the senses arise from the essences, they have their origin from the sting of desire, from the sourness; they are the bitterness, and run always in the mind', as Levertov wrote to Robert Duncan in 1959. For Boland, Adrienne Rich and Denise Levertov were the Albert Gleizes and André Lhoté of the revelatory moment. Reviewing the correspondence of Duncan and Levertov, Boland wrote: 'Duncan's way of becoming a poet was essentially – as was Pound's – collaborative. He needed witnesses, companions, an audience.' The great irony of Boland's brave career is that the Irish audience, that crucial parish of rich women, needed her more than she needed them. The audience yearned and Boland became. In becoming herself she created an entirely new field of poetic activity. I was an early witness to her profound effect upon a generation of new women writers. In Cork city in the bleak 1980s she was a pivotal, Messiah-like presence from afar. The poets and fiction writers of the Cork Women's Poetry Circle found in her work, poems and commentary an enabling, moral presence. And she responded to the responsibilities set up by the new expectations in her work; in the mid-eighties she encouraged women leaders such as Máire Bradshaw in Cork by making the long journey south to give readings and preside over workshops. She carried other writers with her, from this land of Ireland to the better land of ideas. The act was gender-aware only because of exclusions based upon gender, for she has always understood, as Robert Graves wrote in his essay '-Ess', that 'poetry should not be an affair of sex any more than, for example, surgery. One says: "Mary Smith is a surgeon," not "Mary Smith is a surgeoness," or even "Mary Smith is a lady surgeon." Sex has no place in the operating theatre. Poetry is a sort of operating theatre.'

For poetry is where we dwell. It is a second country that requires the second map; or, to quote Graves again, 'This nobleman is at home anywhere / His castle being, the valet says, his title' ('The Cloak'). *Object Lessons* and *A Journey with Two Maps* are the double map of that title 'Poet'. They are Boland's attempt at integration, cultural and psychological integration, beginning at an estranged starting-point, that title 'Irish Poet', and ending with political arrival, as described in her essay on Paula Meehan: 'The emergence of women has now made a new space in the Irish poem'. It was Boland, working alone and constantly derided by the male of the species, who created that new space for poetry. She created a new masterpiece with her own name upon it. In writing prose, such work as we find in both *A Journey With Two Maps* and *Object Lessons*, Eavan Boland is answering Yeats' command to the lyric poet: the command that the lyric poet should do everything to explain the life behind the lyrics. The motive of her autobiographical writing is not autobiographical. There is no desperate effort of explanation or personal redress such as one finds in Frank O'Connor's *An Only Child* or Frank McCourt's *Angela's Ashes*. It is exploratory explication, an act of exemplary remembrance. Socially, Boland has no need to explain herself. Like Beckett, she has been blessed with an unfractured upper-middle-class Dublin life. An artist-mother carried her in her womb and she has grown into the full adult life of art. In 1988, in a regular *Observer* review, Anita Brookner wrote:

Autobiography is traditionally a genre peculiar to the upwardly mobile, the socially insecure, those who have no context to explain them. Its purpose is to expunge pain, but more than this, to create a life myth, an alternative support system. In rewriting history and establishing causation a measure of control over circumstances is achieved. It is a daring and agonising task which may not fulfil its intended purpose.

Boland's daring and agonising task has been to call back Irish life, that poor Free State of Austin Clarke living on lack, and to feed it retrospectively with insights of liberation; it is a prodigious effort not just to make the poem but to make the audience learn a little jazz. She has chosen to take on, politically, a society that made boors of educated men and modest creatures of all women. If her mother was an artist, then she is the prodigy, creating a vast studio of new work. I can't help thinking that she belongs with Mainie Jellett and Evie Hone as they scramble to put the last few centimes together for a second Paris latte. She belongs among such Irishwomen, the instinctive and the first-rate who strive for a second kind of representative art.

RITA ANN HIGGINS

The Lost Land

One of the central metaphors in Eavan Boland's work is that of a Lost Land linking Irish history with her own personal experience. She had left Ireland for the first time when she was only six years old. When she came back as a teenager Dublin was a city of smithereens, where she had to collect the fragments of her life and put them together again. The head and the heart were very much affected by the six-year-old leaving home. Memories had to be gathered and sorted and decisions made about how to cope with the child's, and later the teenager's, displacement. The blueprint that would help the poet cope with the seismic jolt she had experienced had not yet been mapped out. She measures the distance between the two worlds with image, metaphor and truth.

In her elegy for The Lost Land the young Boland speaks of herself moving between worlds. She allows us to follow that journey. That sense of displacement is a strand that is carried into individual poems and various collections. What is intriguing about Boland's work is that she doesn't focus only on her own experiences but places them in a wider context of exile. Beyond her personal horizon there are always other people saying goodbye, picking up a suitcase and leaving and maybe never coming back. They are as much in the poems as she herself. She lays out her stall, neatly, concisely, not a word goes astray: a pristine whack of an opening for all its simplicity. You can hear it in the first four lines. The double-spacing makes you stop and take an extra breath. At this point you have no idea how complicated and tiered the loss in the poem is going to be.

I have two daughters.

They are all I ever wanted from the earth.

Or almost all.

I also wanted one piece of ground:

The colon after 'ground' tells us she is not quite finished. She's the poet, she can say more and she must tell us how important the wanted line is. *I also wanted one piece of ground:* Not a plateau, not a field, not a bóithrín, just one piece of ground. She would have ownership of a tiny plot where she might build a house for herself and her family where she would be finally rooted. When you put down bricks and mortar you are of that place. You are not in the shadows then. Yet when Boland went back to her beloved city in her late teens, it was to boarding school in Killiney and back to Dublin at weekends. So the city was still only her weekend home, her Lost Land.

So I could say *mine. My own.*
And mean it.

How important are those few words to her? It could be the heart of the poem but the poem has two hearts. For now we are still thinking about what she wants. She might not want much but it is still a strong yearning and not that unique when you think of it. The poet might have lost out on a country and spent a long time reclaiming it but it will be different for her children. She will make sure that they will not be betwixt and between, that no tempest will scatter their hold on a land, on a country. There is a piece of ground that will have a foundation. Blocks will be added and it will grow into a house with curtains and furniture and domestic objects, and most of all it will be home, *Heimat, baile*. They will have emotional ease in their footfall and no exile.

The poem leaps forward and now the children have grown up, they are far away from her at this point, one still at school in Dublin. *The Lost Land* was the first book that Eavan Boland published after moving to California to work at Stanford. The poet is looking back at the country that meant so much to her. The dislocation is almost complete when memory itself becomes an emigrant. Memory is all we have to draw the picture together in our minds, we rely on memory as our fall-back position, but this is not the case here where memory is roaming around a patch of earth, an unreachable but much-loved landscape. The metaphor has nowhere to go because we are swept along with the storyline.

Then the other heart of the poem comes into play. The poet has always had a strong connection to landscape, real or imagined but mostly painfully real. She does not use landscape as merely a vista to be admired. It becomes more than the place we leave from, or the place to sail back to. Landscape is the canvas, sometimes empty, sometimes populated. Always there.

Now they are grown up and far away

and memory itself
has become an emigrant,
wandering in a place
where love dissembles itself as landscape.

The straight-talking of the opening lines allows us to engage with the personal, but that is just a preamble for something deeper. The poet goes on to weave her own life and her country's history of emigration together. You can hear her distinctive voice when you are reading it.

The reader is now aware that in this layered poem a dual imagery lives side by side; the poignant and the wretched. We have established that the personal is only part of the poem's make-up. When we read how 'they' must have seen it, it gives us a flicker of the poem's otherworldliness. In the 'shadows falling' we are back in Boland's enchanted territory, an element that we are used to. We have the poet as witness 'searching for the last sign of a hand', thus creating

a broad spectrum between lost land, state of mind and the historical element that the poet draws on as centrepiece.

At night,
on the edge of sleep,
I can see the shore of Dublin Bay,
its rocky sweep and its granite pier.

Is this, I say
how they must have seen it,
backing out on the mailboat at twilight

She does not need to say too much here. She has created the scene and she lands it with a perfect pitch. I read a piece by her once[1] where she said: 'some territory that can never be claimed, held, kept, has for me, become more enduring than any of the places I've called home'. To the poet The Lost Land holds a deeper meaning than a mere country, a landscape. The Lost Land takes in all the losses the poet has experienced. The losses are viewed from whatever side of the Atlantic she happens to be on, they do not have a built-in harmony that makes this a cosy poem. The poem will do its work on the senses and the imagination. The poem will stay with you long after you have finished reading it. This is partly because of the evocative imagery. Other reasons are more complex. The dislocation and exile woven in the poem are greater than the poet's – and the country she feels exiled from. For the most part we are in elegy territory. The slip roads into the poem facilitate a deeper meaning through clues rather than road signs. Boland gives us the clues but holds a tight rein on the losses, and in time they dissipate and all she can do now is name them. Whether she does it with elegance or grace or with a darker motif, the result is still the same.

I see myself
on the underworld side of that water,
the darkness coming in fast, saying
all the names I know for a lost land.

Ireland. Absence. Daughter.

1 In *Don't Ask Me What I Mean: Poets in Their Own Words*, edited by Clare Brown and Don Paterson (Picador, 2003).

Language as Truth Serum in Eavan Boland's 'The Oral Tradition'

Mother earth. Mother tongue. Mother wit. The artist, especially the poet, must acknowledge or give credence to what one comes out of – in relation to time and human existence. As evidence, one can consider the creation myths. Eavan Boland, in her poem 'The Oral Tradition', renders a contemporary creation myth by which the rural world – 'across the fields at evening / and no one there', 'in an open meadow', with 'the bruised summer light' and 'mauve eaves on lilac' – and the ordinary people who inhabit that world invoke the primal as an act of becoming. But it is through the poet's rendering of this 'overheard' world which roots in the psyche of the speaker, and thus in the psyche of the reader, that language creates an almost biblical garden as folklore – perhaps an echo of the word made flesh.

The poem begins with perfect casualness – 'I was standing there / at the end of a reading / or a workshop or whatever' – a seductive tactic that forges an intimacy with the reader. Boland situates the reader in the contemporary context of the poetry workshop. She continues: the others in the room walk 'out into the weather', and the speaker is left there 'only half-wondering / what becomes of words, / the brisk herbs of language'. Already the poet is approaching the heart-mechanism of poetry and discerning the psychology of everyday language contrasted by the exactness within pastoral imagery. As the poem later teaches us, Boland believes that the expected scents and hues of nature must contrast with something more worldly and, thus, spiritual to become poetry. She reminds us that poetry happens, not in what the poet has to say, not in what is invented, but in the lives of everyday people, and in this poem, everyday women. Poetry exists in the tradition of passing on such stories.

By the fifth stanza, the poem shifts from the internal atmosphere of the speaker and the external atmosphere of the room ('a firelit room' described only by impressions of light and colour) to the observed gestures of others – two women whose conversation, first through the movement of their hands, and then through fragments of language, lures the poet-speaker into a rumination, one that conjures an old world of truth-telling. Here the poem directs the reader back to the title.

Boland knows a lot about feeling through observation. She also shows how silence is a natural element of the narrative. Through juxtaposition the poem rises from a moment of 'only half-listening' into a state of profundity, of being in the world. Through this fragmented language the speaker (and the reader) is transported.

> They talked to each other
> and words like 'summer'
> 'birth' 'great-grandmother'
> kept pleading with me,
> urging me to follow.

The three words in quotation marks resonate. They are universal, but they depend on a process of association and on the collaboration of the listener to interpret them. The raw, natural music draws us closer, and already we are there in the open field with this great-grandmother as a young woman, watching the moment as it is about to unfold. In the following stanza time constricts and expands:

> 'She could feel it coming' –
> one of them was saying –
> 'all the way there,
> across the fields at evening
> and no one there, God help her'

Time is happening in two realms – the present moment of telling and the past where the woman is somehow forever in the field alone about to give birth. 'God' is an instrument of initiation: the woman bears the full brunt of nature, which is unmerciful, but the invocation of 'God' reminds the listener, who is listening from the future, that there is a dimension of spirits, and in the listener's knowing this, the woman receives a blessing – her humanness.

But in the ninth stanza, Boland's genius manifests itself with the same casual certainty she depicts from the first line of the poem. In a totally imagistic moment, perhaps different from any other in the poem, the tangible becomes metaphorical and may momentarily seem discursive:

> (Wood hissed and split
> in the open grate,
> broke apart in sparks,
> a windfall of light
> in the room's darkness)

She has placed the listener and the reader in at least two places at once, giving light to a deeper, more profound truth. We pause. Is the speaker still in the room, about to exit? Though we are still 'in the room's darkness', contained, held between the parentheses, there is, however, 'a windfall of light' that echoes the natural world.

Here, the imagistic foreshadowing is tonally exact, just right, especially when we arrive at the climactic tenth stanza:

> ' … when she lay down
> and gave birth to him
> in an open meadow.
> What a child that was
> to be born without a blemish!'

The passages between quotation marks have the appearance of being excerpted from the body politic of a national archive. This vision is partly word of mouth. For the poet, elements of 'the oral tradition' are overheard, participated in, and memory is underscored – an unspoken commentary on the naturalness of the spoken. Boland embraces the past to understand the present and future. Truth is straightforward, 'without a blemish'; it is also heroic, melodic, and spiritual.

It reaches for that which can be sung or spoken to the light of day without pretence, but always with raw grace and hints of grandeur. In that sense, our stories have created us. But, what's more, birth may be considered the ultimate act of creation, and here Boland passes on to us the story of the birth of an unblemished child.

'The Oral Tradition' reminds us that we, especially poets, are indeed indebted to cultural memory. The poem aligns memory and imagination. The speaker, standing there, has been touched by 'the bruised summer light'; this moment of 'birth' is also the delivery of feeling through believable language. It's the moment where 'the oral song' incarnates, where the 'superstition' embedded in the act of retelling and in the very nature of 'the wreck of language' becomes the 'remnants' of a people. Indeed, what would a people or nation be without its stories, folklore, dreams, and songs? By the final stanza of the poem Boland teaches us that what a listener carries away – what resonates – is truth. The folkloric is stripped down naked in a merciless light, and the reader can't help but see and know the inner workings of history. For Boland, one feels, poetry has to be honourable and natural, though at times as terrifying as giving birth alone in the open meadow, and that it is also made of blood and the guilt of being human.

THEO DORGAN

Eavan Boland, the Good Manager

When I was a child, my mother and her women friends had a term for a capable woman: she's a good manager, they'd say, the circle of faces acknowledging the accuracy, the justice of earned praise. A good manager kept a good house, was provident, foresaw what would be needed, put money and other resources aside against the rainy day that was all too often literal – keeping your children shod against winter was a recurring care.

They had a kind of watchfulness, these women, an air of attentive quiet, a stillness around the eyes, an atmosphere of clarity in their houses and about their persons that was almost visible. When they looked at you, you felt yourself considered. When they thought about something, you trusted their conclusions.

The good manager in our small community was a resource; resourceful herself, and known to be so, she had the power and the capacity to help resolve situations, to inspire, to give good counsel; to be, if needed, a clear-sighted champion.

I have always loved and admired the way Eavan Boland manages her thoughts, her perceptions and her poems. How she carries herself in the world, how she moves in language, and in our lives as readers, with a cool air of consideration about her person and in her work.

Justin Martyr, a Christian apologist of the second century, says of Athene, protector of the city, that 'when the god had in mind the making of a world through a word (*logos*) his first thought was Athene' – and there is something of Athene's authoritative calm in Eavan's contemplation of her own life and work, in her marshalling and deployment of her resources, in her consideration of the *polis* – in our time and in the deep backward of history. As the good managers of my childhood disposed the resources they commanded, so, too, Eavan is always considered and sparing as she moves in the sphere of *logos*, examining and building her world with care, always prepared to be silent, to let the world disclose itself.

To all those qualities I would add one other, the instinctive natural courtesy of her imagination, her acknowledgement that we hold language in common, that the reader must have a way into and out of the poem. In his poem 'Dance of Words', Robert Graves enjoins: 'To make them move, you should start from lightning', and goes on to say that the 'choreography' of words, and the theme, should always be kept 'plain'. In one of my favourite Boland poems, 'Irish Poetry', the lightning flashes from an emphatic opening line – 'We always knew there was no Orpheus in Ireland' – to strike ground in a place that has been, we see at the end, always the end that was coming, the only possible way out of the poem and back into the world. The word-hoard of the poem, to speak of that, could scarcely be made more plain.

The poem is dedicated to the late Michael Hartnett, a fated poet if ever there was one, and between the title and the dedication lies not alone Hartnett's famous and short-lived turn away into writing in Irish but the half-life of a language that is our truth, in part, but no longer our chosen speech. In this way, with a fine economy, Boland signals from the outset that this is a poem of woundedness, of lack and scarcity and absence – and at the same time, of healing.

The opening stanza makes a stark claim of fact:

We always knew there was no Orpheus in Ireland.
No music stored at the doors of hell.
No god to make it.
No wild beasts to weep and lie down to it.

This is a large register for an opening, invoking the classical Greek story that underpins so much of the European tradition; if we have no Orpheus, is our poetry, then, somehow a lesser poetry, a more minor utterance? If no god has made it, what are the limits of what our poetry can claim? Are we, in Austin Clarke's words, to 'live on lack'?

The next move, the second stanza, clears the board with a clean gesture:

But I remember an evening when the sky
was underworld-dark at four,
when ice had seized every part of the city
and we sat talking –
the air making a wreath for our cups of tea.

The flick-back of 'underworld' and 'wreath' is a neat, economical way of keeping the classical frame of reference going; the winter tea-house is sparely established, the full stop is an arrest in time that does not impede the flow of thought (and anticipation) into the next stanza:

And you began to speak of our own gods.
Our heartbroken pantheon.

From the gods to a Dublin café to the gods again, a quick sweep that gathers so much in, and then the minor shock of that 'heartbroken', the prefiguring of grief that is so much more than personal – so much in so little compass, how well-managed this is.

Then on and out in the fourth stanza to the illuminations of Attica, the meticulous recordings of the first great Western historian, set against stark Hyperborean poverty:

No Attic light for them and no Herodotus.
But thin rain and dogfish and the stopgap
of the sharp cliffs
they spent their winters on.

Winter again, the span from the café to the western shore, poor diet of a marginal people, their gods exiled with them, their cancelling from history, their having no record or recorder – the speed and economy of this leading fleetly, and with seeming finality, into the first line of the next stanza: 'And the pitch-black Atlantic night'.

I hear behind all this the familiar *ullagón* of a subject people whose narrative of recourse is pitched between loss and self-pity. I am intended to hear this, of course, since so much of Irish poetry, for a very long time, was tuned to just such a keening edge, and Hartnett, Boland's interlocutor, the explainer in the poem, was intimately familiar with and translator of Ó Bruadair, Ó Rathaille and others, the masters and authorities of that mourning note.

So far it has been all loss, now comes:

… how the sound
of a bird's wing in a lost language sounded.

You made the noise for me.
Made it again.
Until I could see the flight of it: suddenly …

Such deft invocation here – the poet invoking the bird, the bird's wing invoking a language, a poetry, we might have thought lost.

No Orpheus in Ireland? 'You made the noise for me', and 'suddenly' Boland, and we the readers, are given the vision evoked:

the silvery lithe rivers of the south-west
lay down in silence
and the savage acres no one could predict
were all at ease, soothed and quiet and

listening to you, as I was. As if to music, as if to peace.

It seems to me that Eavan, the good manager, has here managed something quite special. In a short compass, in the neat, spare English of her considered and considering attention, she has set aside with precision and tact the self-wounding colonised mind that sees in our small island a marginal and minimal culture undeserving of serious regard. In its place, she proposes a posture of listening, of respectful listening to the music of what actually happens in a language that is not lost while it lives in the mouth, in the breath, of a poet.

That she speaks in the language of the former colonial power is neither a political nor an aesthetic impediment; the English language is become another source, a resource, and it is in English that Eavan makes her poem. Hartnett, by speaking in Irish the sound of a bird's wing, can call up music and peace in a spell of invocation, and his Irish, also, is both source and resource – it is out of the word-music of Irish that the bird flies up, up and out into Eavan's imagination, and out of the poem into ours.

It is, at least, a point of view: that for Irish to live as a language it is only necessary that some people continue to guard and use it, continue to think and speak in it, continue to make poems in it.

I think it impossible that Irish will ever again be the everyday language of the Irish people – but this is not at all the same thing as saying that Irish is fated to join the long and growing line of languages that have fallen, are still falling, into the abyss of extinction. Absolutism and compulsion have not worked to stabilise or expand the use of the language; these strategies have indeed, unsurprisingly, sparked a rolling rebelliousness and resistance across a spectrum from shame and boredom to, effectively, a willingness to countenance linguicide. Boland's short and exquisitely managed poem proposes a resolution on a scale that is deceptively intimate and domestic; a mutual listening, quiet conversation over cups of tea.

If this invitation to civility were all that the poem proposes, we might be satisfied – but there is more. There is a proposition here about poetry and its powers that will be resisted by all those whose response to a poem is an impulse to paraphrase.

You made the noise for me.
Made it again.
Until I could see the flight of it …

What was it that was said of Orpheus? That he could make stones live, charm birds out of the trees, make wild beasts 'weep and lie down to it'. The 'it' was the music he made, and the music had meaning. This is what is proposed in the myth, that sound, coded and ordered and shaped by and with intentionality, is in itself capable of carrying and importing meaning. What else, if not this, is Boland proposing or claiming when she tells us that, having no Irish herself, she 'could see the flight of it'?

I am conscious that I am stepping into a minefield here, and am minded, having drawn the reader's attention to this aspect of the poem, to do what any sensible person would do in such a situation, and stop marching. I will content myself with saying that this is but one of many instances where Boland has, with deceptive quietness, introduced radical, even explosive, propositions into what seems on the face of it a modest poem.

I am reminded of a particular occasion, a late autumn afternoon when my mother and a friend were speaking with gratitude of a neighbour, one of those famed good managers, who had by tact and quiet common sense resolved a fractious and complex dispute to do with our local Credit Union. 'Do you know what, Rose,' the friend said, 'that woman should be given a small country to run.' What was I, nine, ten? Hovering invisibly, as usual, on the edge of adult conversation, I picked up the phrase and packed it away for future consideration. I knew it for a high compliment, but I was sufficiently attuned to the actual lives we led to know that such power, the kind wielded by teachers and Guards and politicians and officials, was beyond the reach of the likes of us. Beyond the reach, even, of our neighbours the good managers. I think I packed the phrase away because I sensed that, beyond all unlikely dreams of what could actually happen, the words were intended to salute and honour a certain, not unattainable, level of personal capacity and authority. Power of a different kind.

It has been her and our good fortune that Eavan Boland's natural capacity has been for a poetry of authority, that she has proved such a good and exemplary manager of her gift.

MÁIGHRÉAD MEDBH

Expressing the Source: Eavan Boland and Adrienne Rich

I have always been affected by Eavan Boland, though we probably appear to be opposites. At a time when I was trying to strike out for what I saw as liberation by speaking of the intimate disaffections, she spoke of diurnal femininities too, but often with a noble, transformative acceptance or love of them. Even so, she was and still is a powerful voice for women's freedom. She wrote suburban domesticity in a way that enabled other women to live it –

> to wed our gleams
> to brute routines:
> solstices,
> small families.

('Monotony')

The domestic world she presented was startlingly sparse and oddly adequate, even when she spoke of its irritations and complained, as many of us did, about the demands of motherhood that seemed to arrest our hopes of flight and tether us to repetition and the ministrations called love. I hadn't read her work for some time when by chance I recently encountered one of her poems on a library shelf. 'Indoors' begins:

> I have always wanted a world that is cured of the outdoors.
> A household without gods.

My old responses were instantly recurred. A direct, honest voice, lines loaded with conceptual ramifications. The style is conversational but also lyrical. That is, it has prosaic syntax but a tone of deep contemplation. This intimate touch, the feeling of being spoken to from underskin to underskin is one of the things I value most in poetry.

> I have two daughters.

> They are all I ever wanted from the earth.

> Or almost all.

('The Lost Land')

A voice that comes honestly from oneself is something that must be achieved in a poem. It's a commonplace by now to say that the self is not a homogeneous unit. In the manner of string theory, perhaps, the perceiver is not a point but a series of effects with many dimensions. So it's always hard work to convey the most salient inner truth in written form, to make it the sphinx-voice of the poem. In Eavan Boland, the sphinx-voice is born of a careful examination of feeling, often beginning with a personal statement, then broadening out to find echoes. Refer to Jung's theory of synchronicity: that many things happen at once doesn't mean they are mutually causative, just that they are relational. I experience Eavan Boland as a relational poet whose referential scope is wide, and who never embellishes for the sake of effect. She speaks to the underskin because she speaks a calm, passionate, independent truth in a disciplined manner.

I moved along the library shelf and picked up one of my own books, *When the Air Inhales You*. A poem leapt from the page in energetic display. It was mapped, musical, somewhat posed, conscious of its body. How different. Like a door swinging open to a colder climate, or two incompatible flavours. But I also intend to be true to my experience in a way that both examines and illumines. I live in my poems and they in me. Or so I thought. Suddenly a stranger to my own work, I asked myself, 'Who or what is writing my poems? What is she/it trying to do?'

> For one moment when you express the source,
> when the hard chatter of your tongue
> turns to silver silk and slides you to the wind;
> for a moment when the air inhales you
> and you rest in its transparency like a
> thought you don't know you're thinking –
> wouldn't you live this jacketed life?

('Unified Field')

Inspirational, you might say. Declarative, you might assert. Musical, maybe. Distant, you might say. Or intimate, but does it draw you into the mind of the speaker as 'Indoors' does?

These lines are from 'Womb' in *The Making of a Pagan*, my first book:

The return journey is
the only journey there is;
from light and teeming space
in search of the dark place,
back.
But there is colour here,
treasures hung high on the walls,
a cave that would be black,
but they and the hint of a door
prism it.

Again the element of declaration, almost the positing of an argument. The first five lines constitute a premise, as the first two lines in 'Indoors' are a premise, but mine implies a pre-existing process leading to a position. Eavan is confessing.

Am I an aphorist? Do I take the journey and then offer my readers the map? I love aphorisms – the poetic and philosophical sort – but I intended these poems to be directly spoken experiences. Ah! I remembered. Transported by the particular gift of Eavan Boland, I'd forgotten my home ground.

my hands began it
and now I love it
my cunt is swelling
thinking of it
thinking of a tongue on it
                                        ('Coming Out')

If that's not confessional…
    Eavan Boland's tendency is to conceptualise the physical. Mine is to embed the concept in the body.

… for intellectual creation too springs from the physical, is of one nature with it and only like a gentler, more ecstatic repetition of physical delight.
        – Rainer Maria Rilke, *Letters to a Young Poet*

I seem to constantly bring that physical delight to the forefront in my poems, regardless of subject matter. My poems have been strongly rhythmic because they emerge not just from my brain but from the other organs too, literally, palpably. I quite often search for the rhythm (or arrhythmia) of the experience first, and then hunt the words. Maybe that's the reason why I took to performance poetry. My poems were dramatic, organic monologues, songs of the underskin, conflating sense impression with fact and analysis. I've also wanted to verbalise in the raw, name events and parts of the body as they are colloquially named, instead of placing them within specific cultural contexts. Another matter is the question of attention. I can lapse into mindmull very easily, so I've given what I wanted myself – a sense of drama. But I might be changing.

A writer who connects with Eavan Boland in my mind is Adrienne Rich. Both are very open and expert in communicating pain, though Adrienne Rich's pain was greater and more imminently political. Existential and political pain does not appear to be so prevalent a topic in poetry these days, and wasn't exactly common currency when Adrienne Rich began writing either. Both poets had to battle with a resistant poetry establishment consisting of 'a congeries of old boys' networks', as Rich described it in her essay 'When We Dead Awaken: Writing as Re-Vision'. The difficulties, coupled with their educational advantages, engaged them and made them both expositional and skilful at once. Learned, and perfectly able to work in formal poetry, they devised their own individual voices, bedded in uncompromising observation. I have never opened a collection by either poet without sensing an immanent integrity underwriting the lines – an integrity of style, form and expression – the poetic kind. Even in topographical sprawls such as 'An Atlas of the Difficult World', which defies a centre, there are vortices that keep you there.

I don't want to hear how he beat her after the earthquake,
tore up her writing, threw the kerosene
lantern into her face waiting
like an unbearable mirror of his own.

Such pain is as prevalent as ever, and our wrestling with our condition just as global to us, but reading a poem like this in 2014 feels like visiting a slightly strange literary country. Jorie Graham is of a different nature when she looks at a socio-political concern, as in 'Guantánamo':

Waning moon. Rising now. Creak, it goes. Deep
        over the exhausted continents. I wonder says my
        fullness. Nobody nobody says the room in which I
        lie very still in the
darkness watching.

There is currently a certain resistance to the overtly egocentric, aching voice, as if the popular impatience with earnestness and lament has infiltrated the arts. Are we in danger of becoming too focused on procedure, to the detriment of experience and self-exposure? There is integrity in procedure too, but Boland and Rich were spokeswomen for their generation and for women who were not like themselves, whom they absorbed into their first-person voice. When you marry style with empathic self-exposure and political intent, as Rich does here, you reach, after a journey through a scatter of difficult landscapes, a closing stanza with lines like these, that will reach your reader in a place where she is afraid to be seen –

I know you are reading this poem
in a room where too much has happened for you to bear
where the bedclothes lie in stagnant coils on the bed
and the open valise speaks of flight
but you cannot leave yet.

and

I know you are reading this poem because there is nothing
        else left to read
there where you have landed, stripped as you are.
                            ('An Atlas of the Difficult World')

– and she weeps.

LORNA GOODISON

'Making Money'

Another poet might have taken this quarrel with others into the arena of rhetoric, but Eavan Boland has chosen instead to speak in calm and measured tones of the poor Irish workers who produced the high-quality paper on which their colonial masters printed bank notes.

Hers is a poetic voice that is both ancient and modern, one that speaks for people who had no voice but who need to have their story told clearly while keeping the mystery at the heart of it.

I had the great good fortune to hear her read 'Making Money' on a BBC radio programme recorded during the Commonwealth Writers' Conference held in Manchester in 2002; and her dignified recital of a poem on a subject that might easily have produced a rant or an incendiary diatribe against historical injustices filled the recording booth with an air of reverence and respect due. I remember the silence that came after she finished reading that poem; the silence of respect given.

I am deeply moved by the way that Ireland, the country itself, the material world, is the subject of the poem, with references to the rivers, the mountains, the air, the plant-life, all of which are lovingly rendered.

The people, namely the women who 'came out in the ugly first hour / after dawn', move through the poem like other-worldly mysterious presences cooking the natural hemp waste, the cotton lint, the linen and flax and fish nets – all of which speak to the old ways of making money: agriculture, cottage industry, fishing and washing. When alkaline, caustic soda and soda ash is added to the backwash 'suddenly / they were making money'. They make the paper that makes the money, but

> ... they do not and they never will

> see the small boundaries all this will buy
> or the poisoned kingdom with its waterways

> and splintered locks or the peacocks who will walk
> this paper up and down in the windless gardens
> of a history no one can stop happening now.

I always stop when I get to 'a history no one can stop happening now'. I believe that if the poem had ended there it would have done its job; but thankfully it goes on to offer up more riches in the form of clear-eyed wisdom:

>   if you can keep
> your composure in the face of this final proof that
> the past is not made out of time, out of memory,
> out of irony but is also
> a crime we cannot admit and will not atone
> it will be dawn again in the rainy autumn of the year.

That this poet is confident enough to employ the word 'irony' is a gift.

That this poem waits until the very end to remind us that women's work often generates wealth for others but not for themselves makes it one of my favourites among her many fine poems.

> ... the women are walking up
> as they always did, as they always will now.
> Facing the paradox. Learning to die of it.

I am grateful to Eavan Boland for reminding me again that there is no need to write as if our readers are hard of hearing. I am grateful to her too for demonstrating that when you are moved to speak on behalf of people who have no voice, it is necessary to keep mystery and paradox at the heart of what you write or say.

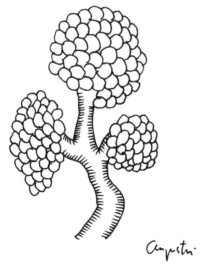

MEDBH McGUCKIAN

Birds and their Masters

When Eavan Boland's first volume, *New Territory*, appeared in 1967, I was buried up to my A-levels in Wordsworth. My desire to be a nineteenth-century English poet was too sexual to dream that an Irishwoman young enough to have been my school prefect was at that moment publishing, in 'The Winning of Etain', as sumptuous and learn-offable-by-heart a sublimation for my palate as *The Eve of St Agnes*. I was desperately aware that an Ulster Catholic was miraculously, with his *Death of a Naturalist*, recharging the poetic imagination of the colony as well as the cultural centres. Suddenly there were poetry readings advertised in the local press and, armed with my copy of *Death*, I remember a crisp walk in the snow, from our house on the upper Antrim Road, down to my first one, in St Malachy's Old Boys' Club on the Crumlin, a symbolically apt setting. My coat was lincoln green, military style, also aptly enough, with epaulettes and braided buttons; but my walk was virginal and soldierless, and perfectly safe then, before the Troubles. I was the only woman in the room, apart from an elderly lady in furs. I knew nobody, spoke to no one, understood not a word. There was as always a long table with water from which two older men and a pristine youth with Grecian curls, whose names went over my head, performed their baffling rite. Maybe one of them wondered what my buttons were doing there, looking for death, there.

My next inauguration was when Cecil Day-Lewis (no Daniel) gave a reading at the University, where I was not yet a student, and my sense of alienation was complete. I penned the following verses in my maid's garret, just to show you how wide the five years were between me and *New Territory*, or any territory at all:

On a Poet-Laureate

I loved him, sitting high above us all,
remote and god-like in his golden strength.
He had raised my face to see me in the hall,
and I was young and small beneath his length.

He read his poems quietly and slow;
but all his solemn fervour was pretence.
He turned my love to lust, I turned to go –
his pen was prodding at my innocence.

Had I come across Eavan's book then, it would have 'blown my mind' in a different way, as it still does, as it does now, in its out-of-print dragonfly dress from the locked larder of the Linen Hall Library. I am not saying if or how much my life would have altered. I am just saying, I wish somehow I had discovered it, or it me; it would have meant everything as an influence. It was not till *The Penguin Book of Irish Verse* in 1970 that any inkling of the existence of women poets in the South filtered through to me, and not till Eavan's second collection in 1975 that I began to feel there was a Jean-Baptiste about. What would I, at a gauche and ignorant seventeen, have made of the fact that a twenty-two-year-old

was addressing, with more arrogance than mere confidence, even with aggression, in stanzas of classical, mandarin, impersonal perfection, not just the contemporary Irish male poets whose names I hardly dared know, on equal terms or as competitors, siblings, possibly with contempt; but also, on their own Petrarchan ground, such sonneteers as Yeats and Shakespeare. That in addition she was translating from the best of the Gaelic poets brilliantly, could allude casually to both Oedipus and Aengus, while looking through seductive mascara as if she was not averse to the Beatles. That she was passionately concerned with the problems of Irish history – 'The dour line of North and South' – 'So are we left / Writing to headstones and forgotten princes' – and that her principal achievement was her facility with the curse.

When I recall the chastening, illuminating effect upon me, as upon us all, of Paul Muldoon's undergraduate debut in *New Weather* (1973), how its originality of style, angle, vocabulary, opened so many doors of possibility in the language, I cannot help but feel that to have missed Eavan's early voice when it happened was to have missed an irrevocable gift. Perhaps I might have found the technical expertise overpowering. Eavan herself has more or less at present repudiated, as precociously precious, her initial male-orientated formality for its lack of warmth. As Mandelstam acknowledges, the iambic is an exclusively masculine development and precludes intimacy. She has discarded requiems and dedications to explore in shorter lines and freer rhythms the rawness of female experience: 'somewhere a poet is wasting / his sweet uncluttered metres on the obvious / emblem instead of the real thing'. Yet I now find an incredible authority expressed in that whirlwind challenge of the Sixties, and under the control of the surface coldness, 'This woman's secret history and her loves – '.

Twenty years later, in the Poetry Book Society Choice selection, *The Journey*, she was to rework that same theme, the function of art, into 'Self-Portrait on a Summer Evening'. The poem 'From the Painting, *Back From Market*, by Chardin' is one of the most haunting from the first group, and the only lyric, apart from the narrative investigations conducted in the version of the Etain legend, whose beautiful mysticism seems to have offered the poet a way of talking openly about herself, the only lyric to have a woman as its central subject, even though the mediator is still a man:

Dressed in the colours of a country day –
Grey-blue, bue-grey, the white of seagulls' bodies –
Chardin's peasant woman
Is to be found at all times in her short delay
Of dreams, her eyes mixed
Between love and market, empty flagons of wine
At her feet, bread under her arm. He has fixed
Her limbs in colour, and her heart in line.

In her right hand, the hindlegs of a hare
Peep from a cloth sack; through the door

Another woman moves
In painted daylight; nothing in this bare
Closet has been lost
Or changed. I think of what great art removes:
Hazard and death, the future and the past.
This woman's secret history and her loves –

And even the dawn market, from whose bargaining
She has just come back, where men and women
Congregate and go
Among the produce, learning to live from morning
To next day, linked
By a common impulse to survive, although
In surging light they are single and distinct,
Like birds in the accumulating snow.

The title's naming of the painter pays obeisance to his importance. The 'I' is an unobtrusive, offered opinion rather than a personal distortion or re-vision. In sentiment and style it follows the tradition of Auden's 'Musée des Beaux Arts', a philosophical meditation on the morality of aesthetic detachment, which Mahon brought to a high political level. It is almost as if every poem in this first parading ground is a one-off exercise demonstrating her expert education in the craft, with the performance correctness of a three-point turn. The final bird image coalesces with bird imagery woven through the text to suggest that the market is the public buying and selling of poetry and its cut-throat competitive laws, as opposed to the private inner life that nourishes it, is nourished from it. Although there is irony in the adjective 'great', a suppressed violence in the game that has been slaughtered for the day's meal, the attention to the sequence and detail of the canvas for more than half of the poem imply an acceptance on the whole of authority, an unrebellious reading.

The mature comment is subtly addressed to the other woman previously subsumed into the artist's cosmos:

Jean-Baptiste Chardin
is painting a woman
in the last summer light

All summer long
he has been slighting her
in botched blurs, tints,
half-tones, rinsed neutrals.

What you are watching
is light unlearning itself,
an infinite unfrocking of the prism.

Before your eyes,
the ordinary life
is being glazed over:
pigments of the bibelot,
the cabochon, the water-opal
pearl to the intimate
simple colours of
her ankle-length summer skirt.

Truth makes shift:
The triptych shrinks
to the cabinet picture.

Can't you feel it?
Aren't you chilled by it?
The way the late afternoon
is reduced to detail –

the sky that odd shape of apron –

opaque, scumbled –
the lazulis of the horizon becoming
optical greys
before your eyes
before your eyes
in my ankle-length
summer skirt

crossing between
the garden and the house,
under the whitebeam trees,
keeping an eye on
the length of the grass,
the height of the hedge,
the distance of the children

I am Chardin's woman

edged in reflected light,
hardened by
the need to be ordinary.

The rhymes throughout 'Self-Portrait on a Summer Evening' are subversive and ridiculing rather than slavishly imitative. 'Light', the male medium, is paired with 'slight', 'afternoon' or male time with 'apron'; Chardin is deposed from the title to rhyme mockingly with 'garden', 'woman', 'children', 'hardened' and 'ordinary', so he is reduced to size. 'Self-Portrait' plays between the meaning that the painter is expressing his own anima, and that Eavan herself is not only his woman but *him*, his equal in art. In the first poem the act of creation is forever complete, as in 'Ode on a Grecian Urn'; here it belongs in a continuous present, not some eternity. The artist himself, not abstract art, is accused of falsification, denigration, giving the subject less than her due. All deference is gone; the colours which before seemed romantic are now sexually wrong. Eavan is unfrocking herself of the ornamental poetic vocation. Her questions are no longer rhetorical; the hallucinatory drama of the scene enacts the illusion she describes, 'before your eyes' is repeated to emphasise the wearing routine of domestic duties preventing the free, observant range of vision. Tsvetaeva's first line, 'We are keeping an eye on the girls', comes to mind. Yeats's lazulis lose focus, the length of the grass replaces the obsession with the skirt-length, 'edged' rhymes with 'hedge' and 'woman' this time with 'children' in a bitter restoration of the reality that has been sacrificed. The 'surging light' of the Sixties dawn narrows to the measurements of a light that is reflected only.

I am indebted to my friend Anne Coleman of University College Galway for these concluding quotations from Sandra Gilbert and Susan Gubar:

The female poet's basic problem is an anxiety of authorship; a radical fear that she cannot create, that because she can never become a 'precursor', the act of writing will isolate or destroy her. [...] Her battle is not against her (male) precursor's reading of the world but against his reading of *her*. In order to define herself as an author she must redefine the terms of her socialization. [...] Frequently, moreover, she can begin such a struggle only by actively seeking a female precursor.

What distinguishes Eavan Boland is that, far from suffering such anxiety, she managed to somehow be her own precursor and thus, without my knowing it, also mine.

This essay is reprinted with permission from *The Irish University Review*, where it was first published in a special issue on Eavan Boland (issue 23.1, Spring/Summer 1993).

GABRIELLE CALVOCORESSI

Library Hours

Suddenly
I wanted
to stand in front of it.
I wanted to trace over
and over the weave of my own country.
('In Which the Ancient History I Learn Is Not My Own')

The first time I met Eavan Boland, I was working at Library Hours Bookstore in Wallingford, CT. The store was down the road from the elite boarding school I attended. It was a school I was woefully underprepared for, coming, as I had, from a fairly terrible public school in a rural part of the state. Every day I lived with the knowledge I could fail out. I didn't have the study skills the other students had. I didn't have the languages and the poise. People tried to help me and people told me I'd be better off leaving. That was a lesson I learned there: some people will help you and some people simply don't have the time. What I knew was that place was saving my life. I wasn't being threatened and bullied as I had been in my other school. More importantly, I had this job in a bookstore that allowed me to read all day.

Weekdays or weekends it was always the same: I'd walk in through the back door and say hello to Pat. The store was almost always empty. It was just far enough from school that neither the students nor the teachers ever seemed to go there. Most sources of industry had left the town so books weren't as much of a priority as figuring out how to put food on the table. Sometimes someone would come in and return a hardcover and when I went to give store credit they'd say, 'Oh, no. Pat let me borrow it.' That's how I learned that Pat let people borrow the hardcovers if they promised to bring them back in perfect condition. When I asked why she said people had lost their jobs, as if that was all the explanation needed. For my part, I asked to be paid in books. She'd suggest I should be saving some money and then sigh as I would take the cash she gave me and ask how much the stack of books I'd collected through the day would cost. Sometimes she'd ask me how school was going. 'Fine,' I'd say, feeling the knot of worry and shame in my stomach. 'You're a great reader,' she'd say. 'That's really important. You're curious and you love to learn.'

I remember I was alone in the shop when I met Eavan. I liked to go over to the poetry section as soon as I got in and pick out a few books to spend the day with. Seamus Heaney had come to read at my school and then Donald Hall had come. I wanted to do 'that', I thought to myself. I don't think I really knew what 'that' was. It seemed different from what the poets we read in English class did. Of course, I know better now but then it felt like something utterly new. A kind of life of the image and experience I thought only lived in my daydreams and in the movies. 'Do we have Seamus Heaney or Donald Hall?' I asked Pat. 'We've got a whole section of poets,' she said. 'Have at it.' I moved in and moved on deeper into the shelves. *Outside History* sat there looking at me. Eavan Boland. What kind of name was that? How would I pronounce it? I said it over and again. I asked Pat if she thought I should say it with long 'e' or like an 'a'. I'm pretty sure I said that this looked liked the thickest book we had by a woman poet. 'She's important,' Pat said. I paid my whole day's wages for the book at some point after carrying it around the store for ages. When someone did come in they'd say, 'What are you reading?' 'Eavan Boland,' I'd say. Sometimes saying her name right, sometimes only thinking I was. I liked to carry the book in my school bag. Somehow the weight made me think I could do it, could make it through exams and French class. It made me think I could stay.

***

I went off to college. Library Hours shut down so when I was home I went to Atticus instead. I bought *In a Time of Violence* there and drove it across the Middletown bridge, past the farm stands, the Dairy Queen, past Cobalt Market and my grandparents' house, to the rocky outcrop on the river where I liked to go read. If I turned my head back I could see the small house my mother lived in before she met my father, before her precipitous decline. I liked to read with my back to that house, with the river in front of me, the power plant kitty-corner downriver from where I sat. One time when I was little I found a part of a clipper ship lodged in the ground. Sometimes I'd look up from my book and try and remember where that was. I read 'In Which the Ancient History I Learn

Is Not My Own', aloud to myself and the river:

> The linen map
> hung from the wall.
> The linen was shiny
> and cracked in places.
> The cracks were darkened by grime.
> It was fastened to the classroom wall with
> a wooden batten on
> a triangle of knotted cotton.

How did she do that? I'd actually ask the question out loud. How did she speak like everyone else spoke and still make it sound like a poem? In those first years at Sarah Lawrence I slowly tortured my patient and steadfast teachers with poems that somehow just didn't sound anything like me. I was trying and yet, again, I just wasn't making the grade. Not to myself, at least. And not to the older students who said my poems sounded like pop songs (the horror!) and suggested outside of class that maybe I should think about not writing poems and try… something else. I'd stare at this poem until the sun started to go down. 'The linen map … hung from the wall … The linen was shiny … and cracked in places'. The effort of it. The way she made the picture (*image*, I'd remind myself) come to me at just the pace my own mind

would make it if I were remembering. It wasn't just that I could see it, that I had the very same map (I thought) in my third-grade classroom at St. Thomas. She was making it old and new at once. She was doing this thing with time where the past and the present all happened at once. How? I sat on the rocks with my mother's life looming behind me and wondered. How did she do it? I stared at the page itself. For the first time I looked at the white space, at the pressure of the white space. I'd shut the book and stare at the cover. Who was this person who could do this? 'Fastened' and 'batten' and 'cotton', I'd say as I stared at the cover. 'Fastened' and 'batten' and 'cotton'.

Some people will help you. There's a whole other part of this story where I learn to pronounce Eavan's name because I say it to her in person every day. There's a whole other part of this story where I listen to her teach me how to talk about poems in a whole new way and how to teach and how to be a stronger person. There's the story where I sit in an orchard in Ojai today and try to say her name wrong and start laughing at how funny it sounds. And then I think of myself back at the bookstore and how Eavan wrote for that girl who is still me. Some people will help you. And, more importantly, some people will save you and keep saving you so you can help others. Fasten and batten and cotton. My whole life was right there in front of me.

JEE LEONG KOH

The Other Eavan Boland

This short piece will not do for Eavan Boland what Randall Jarrell did for Robert Frost or what Boland herself did for Sylvia Plath in her essay collection *A Journey with Two Maps*. It will not rescue a different Eavan Boland overlooked or ignored by critics. Its ambition is laughably much smaller. As I re-read her *New Collected Poems* in order to write this tribute, I was struck by the consistencies in the long and well-known course of this poet's development. What were they? The high-mindedness, for one. For another, the tolerance of ambiguity. For a third, the feeling for others' suffering. These were the qualities that first drew me to her poetry, and that still engage me.

And so I thought I would write about the great help Eavan Boland gives me, a gay Singapore poet, in resisting and re-envisioning a patriarchal and colonial literary heritage. Now that would be a suitably weighty subject for a tribute. But as Boland has taught me to ask, what gives me my sense of what is suitable and what not? Whose dictates and decorum am I obeying? So, flipping back and forth in the book, I began to entertain a somewhat impertinent question: does Eavan Boland have a sense of humour?

Of course I mean in the poetry, having met the person only for a minute in the dazed atmosphere of a poetry reading. And I am happy to report after a conscientious search that

in the tome of *New Collected Poems* there is at least one poem that induces a case of the funnies. For that reason, if not for any other, 'The Fire in Our Neighbourhood', from the 1987 volume *The Journey*, is rather special.

The title is less than promising, fires being, after all, no laughing matter. But the first line suggests otherwise, with its odd locution. The sign factory 'went on fire' last night, as if a conflagration is a kind of labour dispute. This is, however, not to be a socialist poem, for the factory, as the speaker corrects herself, is not really a factory. It is more like a workshop where they painted window signs 'when times / were good'. It is no dark satanic mill. Sure, the poem goes on to refer to sawmills, but they are the rehearsal studio of the local rock band – made up of ageing poet-rockers? – who practise on Saturdays 'with the loud out-of-tune bass guitar'.

If the places threatened by fire refuse to become signs of seriousness, the same goes for the fire. Although the paint cans went off 'like rifle fire', the only guns involved here are paintball guns, thank goodness. In the flickering light of the flames, ordinary things such as garden walls and pools of rain received a 'violent ornamentation' that would disappear the moment the fire was put out. The violence would not take hold. The speaker even makes fun of poets', her own, love for exotic words. In the world elaborated, or ornamented, by flamelight, simple cloth and wood became 'gimp and tatting, guipure and japanning'. How absurd to be thinking of Japan as Rome burns!

But we knew the fire brigade were on their way; we knew it as far back as stanza two in this poem of six stanzas. And when they arrived, they made short work of the fire. 'It didn't take long' is the shortest sentence of the poem. The next shortest is 'And the flames went out'. This fire brigade knew what they were doing. They even turned their hoses on the sawmills, which might or might not be burning, so that no stray spark could mate with a mote of dust.

Pity the ageing rockers, excited as schoolboys, when they arrived at their rehearsal studio after a week's wage slavery only to find damp ash. Perhaps we would not be blasted by that tuneless bass guitar for one glorious Saturday, the speaker thought, as the night became dark again. The fire was exciting enough. Pity the neighbours 'who slept through the excitement'. The poem ends with what almost amounts to glee at what the neighbours missed. The ending is, however, shot through with humour directed at oneself. The night 'belonged', after all, to the sleeping neighbours. Unlike the speaker, they would have their uninterrupted rest. The neighbourhood had been safe from the fire all along.

The sly humour in the poem is not merely a matter of tone but is finally a place – the speaker's window – from which to view the fire, the destruction of things. Painfully aware of the fires of the past, Boland is determined to rescue suffering lives from the inferno by giving them voice and shape in her poetry. I think of her fever wards and stabbed stars. The other Boland, at least in this one poem, knows that in some grand scheme, everything will be all right. Such knowledge, the daughter of comedy, is rightly elusive.

ELLINE LIPKIN

The Books We Hold More Closely to Us

When I was first introduced to Eavan Boland's poetry I knew I had discovered someone whose aesthetic, voice, and vision would matter deeply not just to me, but to a generation of poets still troubled by gendered struggles within the poetry world. As a graduate student in creative writing in New York City in the mid-90s, I was often frustrated by the conservative biases of my programme and stunned at how male-centric the reading lists I was handed often were. When I picked up Boland's first book of prose, *Object Lessons: The Life of the Woman and the Poet in Our Times*, I didn't devour this book so much as I inhaled it. Here was a woman writing eloquently about unnamed issues I knew were real, articulating the ambitions of many other female poets who were also stymied by invisible barriers, the press of tradition, and the need to know one's voice mattered.

Still prominent on my bookshelves, my text is interleaved with colourful flags of Post-it notes and the marginalia of my more youthful self who was gratified by what Boland was offering – awareness of her own gendered experiences, and her struggle to find her place within the history of poetry. Her taut prose adapted her lyric gift as she parsed the past, with sympathy for her former self and an outstretched hand beckoning along the next generation of women poets. All of this felt like a balm to me.

During my years in New York City, I met Eavan in person on several occasions. At the request of my teacher, Alice Quinn, she visited our poetry workshop where she offered the counterbalance of her voice to the curriculum, which, albeit 20 years ago, was still heavily biased in favour of male writers. More memorably, I heard her read with Adrienne Rich at the DIA Foundation. When Eavan spoke of her own reverence for Rich and remarked that she would remember this reading for all of her life, I was struck by her homage and the necessity of making visible a legacy of foremothers who had built a foundation so that others could enter. I felt deeply indebted, in turn, to both Boland and Rich. It was clear how necessary this work still was.

When Eavan writes, in the preface to *Object Lessons*, 'I know now that I began writing in a country where the word *woman* and the word *poet* were almost magnetically opposed', she opens a discussion about the ways in which women were made invisible by a tradition that she also honoured. How to find oneself, as a burgeoning teenager, a young adult, and then a mature woman who was ambitious enough to want a life in poetry and the fulfilment of a family is one of Boland's chief themes – one that spoke deeply to me, and to my cohort of graduate student friends, as we discussed between classes what was never addressed during – questions we didn't dare to ask. Boland's recollection of the difficulties she faced, some only reconcilable in hindsight, was both moving and inspiring.

At the start of *Object Lessons* Boland describes how much she wanted, when she returned to her student flat, to hear stories about other women poets:

> I wanted to read or hear the narrative of someone else – a woman and a poet – who had gone here, and been there. Who had lifted a kettle to a gas stove. Who had set her skirt out over a chair, near to the clothes dryer, to have it without creases for the morning. Who had made the life meet the work and had set it down: the difficulties and rewards; the senses of lack. I remember thinking that it need not be perfect or important. Just there; just available. And I have remembered that.

Enfolded into this book is just such a story, with its doubts and worries as well as its triumphs. As she ends her book, Boland is prescriptive and direct. Her articulation, particularly in her essay 'The Woman Poet: Her Dilemma', felt as relevant then to me as it is now. She exhorts, 'women should break down barriers in poetry in the same way that poetry will break the silence of women'.

Years have gone by. I have graduated with a doctorate in Creative Writing, specialised in feminist literary theory, and volunteered to teach creative writing to teenage girls. When her second book of prose, *A Journey with Two Maps: Becoming a Woman Poet* came out in 2011, I could not read it fast enough. Once again, I experienced the joy of finding challenges made clear that I had long sensed, but couldn't quite articulate.

In *A Journey with Two Maps*, Boland further traces the genesis of her identity as a poet while growing up in and outside of Ireland, always aware of the heavy weight of canonical history that relegated women to a far corner of the conversation and how its press informed her education and first attempts at writing. Her taut, clear statements, rendered with rhetorical force, make her case for how women poets need to reapproach history and reappropriate tradition.

The title's inclusion of the word 'maps' is both metaphorical and literal – as Boland creates a palimpsest that includes a feminist viewpoint about what can broaden the topics that enter into a poem, never mind which writers enter the canon, crossing from object to subject within. Boland writes movingly of the masters – all men – offered to her throughout her education in England, America and Ireland, and how she recognised there wasn't room within these poems for a female presence who wasn't decorative or objectified, and the effect this had on her emerging work.

Within the second section, 'Maps', Boland traces a matrilineal legacy that connects with the subject matter central within her life and that she no longer wants to deny. Her tributes to a range of female poets, including Rich, and an anonymous 'dream-vision lyric' written in Latin, presumably written by a woman, reveal again the importance of knowing one's history and of homage. Boland also signals her commitment to recovery of women's voices within a chapter that describes her intensely moving project translating the work of post-war female German poets, anthologised in her volume *After Every War: Twentieth-Century Women Poets*.

When I got to the final section, 'Destinations' – a single chapter entitled 'Letter to a Young Woman Poet' – I realised again the intimacy and the obligation of Boland's mission. A riff on the Rilke title of similar name, Boland offers the story or the letter that she first mentions longing for in *Object Lessons*. Here, Boland proposes that the young woman poet must claim a past that has traditionally excluded her, and closes the book by thanking the women poets in the generation before her whose strength bolstered her when she started out. She writes, 'But I believe words such as *canon* and *tradition* and *inheritance* will change even more. And with all that, women poets, from generation to generation, will be able to befriend one another. And that, in the end, is the best reason

for writing this letter.' Through her activism and commitment Boland has rewritten a relationship to history. In her insistence, she holds the door open wide for other women to pass. Her openness, intelligence and dignity are simply galvanising.

Not long after it was published, I heard Boland read from *A Journey with Two Maps* at the Huntington Library. I was six months pregnant at the time, nervous about the impending birth of my first child, my desire to continue writing poems and teaching, and how to make these weave. When I returned home that evening I reread her chapter 'Reading as Intimidation' in which she writes about the period after her first child was born and she learned she would have to authorise herself to write about the emotional and sensual territory of caring for a child.

I paused when I found her lines about wanting a life in which she 'lifted a child, conscious of nothing but the sweetness of a child's skin, or the light behind an apple tree, or rain on slates' and she realised this could become part of her subject matter. The thought echoed lines I remembered from *Object Lessons*: 'As a young woman and an uncertain poet, I wanted there to be no contradiction between the way I made an assonance to fit a line and the way I lifted up a child at night.' Finally, she realised, as she writes in *A Journey with Two Maps*, that there didn't need to be a disconnect between her life as a mother and her work as a poet, and her charge to rewrite, remap, and remake spurred my courage for what was soon ahead. Boland insists, despite the canon-makers, that 'whatever I lived as a woman I could write as a poet', including her life within a darkening suburb which includes 'a child's antibiotic on a shelf and a spoon beside it'.

That evening at the Huntington, Eavan concluded by reading her beautiful poem 'Anna Liffey', which includes the lines:

In the end
It will not matter
That I was a woman. I am sure of it.
The body is a source. Nothing more.
[...]
In the end
Everything that burdened and distinguished me
Will be lost in this:
I was a voice.

The reverberations of these final words resonated with all the myriad commitments about making a life in poetry that Boland makes explicit throughout her prose – yet, in the end it is her vision and voice that will define her. I know I will continue to return to her work as these texts become part of a genre of necessary books through which one generation speaks to another, beckoning, encouraging, to make an essential and inspiring difference.

LINDA GREGERSON

'Quarantine'

Some vistas of human suffering put eloquence to shame. That's wrong. Some vistas of human suffering put those of us who have been spared to shame. And demand eloquence of nearly mineral austerity:

> In the worst hour of the worst season
>   of the worst year of a whole people
> a man set out from the workhouse with his wife.
> He was walking – they were both walking – north.

The poet forswears ornament; ornament would be obscene here. But she also, searingly, forswears the alluring deceptions of artlessness. Ruthlessly distilled, the suffering and the history that outstrip our ordinary powers of comprehension are rendered in a single 'hour' and a single pair of human beings. Ruthlessly distilled, the formal cadences and echoing alliterations that can make words lush are trained to something sterner:

> She was sick with famine fever and could not keep up.
>   He lifted her and put her on his back.
> He walked like that west and west and north.
> Until at nightfall under freezing stars they arrived.

Arrival in a kinder world might signal hope, or shelter at the very least. But in a world where the powers of cold and hunger and ordinary suffering have been vastly multiplied by endemic hatreds and learned indifference, arrival is a bleaker proposition:

> In the morning they were both found dead.
>   Of cold. Of hunger. Of the toxins of a whole history.
> But her feet were held against his breastbone.
> The last heat of his flesh was his last gift to her.

At the midpoint of the middle stanza of an unrelenting 20-line poem, the poet wrests from a vista of desolation her miraculous 'but'. We call such moments turning-points, but this is root and branch: the sweeping away of lesser measures.

My morning newspaper has for months been a chronicle of horrors: an elderly woman sitting amidst the rubble that was once her home, seven members of her family dead. The body of a weeks-old infant wrapped in bloody winding cloth. The scattered belongings of passengers killed when their plane was shot out of the sky. Tear gas in the streets because another unarmed black man has been shot dead in America. Each irreplaceable lost one lost forever. How do we begin to take it in? The part that prior suffering plays, and loss of hope? The part that we have recklessly allowed to happen? The part we might ameliorate, if only we knew how?

In the meticulous stanzas of 'Quarantine', we see the poet's counter-argument to the deadlock of baffled despair. If there is to be any help for us, it must first be imagined. Amidst the wreckage of history, its traces must be found. So Eavan Boland's act of homage to the tenacity of human connection is also an *ars poetica*, a gift of warmth and fierceness in a frozen world. The gift is one she refuses to call by its usual, easy name:

> Let no love poem ever come to this threshold.
>   There is no place here for the inexact
> praise of the easy graces and sensuality of the body.
> There is only time for this merciless inventory:

> Their death together in the winter of 1847.
>   Also what they suffered. How they lived.
> And what there is between a man and woman.
> And in which darkness it can best be proved.

My students, the best of them, struggle with the relationship between ethics and aesthetics. Who am I, they say, to speak about the harm endured by others? And worse: who am I to prod among the wreckage for the sake of a poem? And on the other hand: who am I to speak about anything else? As though my little turmoils and enlightenments could matter in a world so harsh. Is silence better after all? – the an-aesthetic or emotional quarantine of speechlessness?

One of the realms in which they struggle most productively is style: poetic style, they come to believe, is an ethical practice. During the process of composition, they can feel it in the nerves: a misstep in any direction and the poem comes crashing down. Effusion is vulgar, didacticism deadly; even restraint can smack of piety. As the smallest syllable can destroy a metric, leaving it mechanistic or hopelessly botched, so the smallest move (a miscalculation of tone or duration, for example) can destroy the proportions that constitute good faith.

As a matter of faith, 'Quarantine' adheres to and prescribes a 'merciless inventory'. We feel its purity of style, its allegiance to the strictly denotative, as a purity of intent. And yet, the poet in her wisdom allows the grace note of those modest indentations. The second line of four, five times, affords the smallest concession to beauty of form, and its lineaments come like sustenance.

What is poetry for? That is the questions my students are really asking, and if there is an answer it sounds and looks something like this: the careful alignments of cadence and auditory echo, the ameliorating variant in a regimen of stern flush-left, remembrance and exactitude erected against the forces of oblivion. The ancient business of poetry has always been straightforward: to praise, to lament. 'Quarantine' makes a secular sacrament of both.

SANDRA M. GILBERT

In the Suburbs of Modernism

Not suddenly then, but definitely and gradually, a place
I lived became a country of the mind. Perhaps anywhere
I had grown used to, raised my children in, written my
poetry about would have become this. But a suburb by its
very nature – by its hand to mouth compromises between
town and country – was particularly well suited to the
transformation.
          – Eavan Boland, 'The Woman, the Place, the Poet'

In the late eighties, I went to lecture at the Yeats International
Summer School, where I was thrilled by the company
of brilliant colleagues and delighted to visit the sacred Yeat-
sian sites – Knocknarea, the Lake Isle of Innisfree, Thoor
Ballylee – to which my husband and I had also made a
pilgrimage a decade earlier. I still remember how everyone
in the town of Sligo seemed to me to be literary, and in
particular how there was such an overflowing audience for
a reading by Seamus Heaney that we 'faculty' had to sit on
stage, behind the great poet, so we couldn't see his face as he
read. But another memory catches me too. One night in the
pub to which we all retired after the evening's public events,
I was approached by a vivid woman who introduced herself
as a poet, and eagerly began to discuss feminist theory with
me. She was Eavan Boland, a writer whose art and thought
I would come to value deeply within the decade, although I
didn't yet know much about her work.

I've only met Eavan in person a few times over the years,
but I will call her by her first name because I consider her a
sisterly companion in poetry, criticism, and in what I suppose
I should call gender politics. As I reread her books of prose
and verse – quite a few of them stacked up right now next to
my laptop – I'm repeatedly struck by the parallel paths we've
taken in our aesthetic concerns. The very titles of her works
(*In Her Own Image, Outside History, Night Feed, Against
Love Poetry*) dramatise the perspective from which she has
consciously and deliberately viewed the world throughout
her career, one that I too have sought to adopt. Like Adri-
enne Rich, whose feminist poetics shaped so many artists of
our generation, Eavan has consistently defined herself as 'a
woman [who chooses] to walk here. And to draw this circle.'
And besides our mutual devotion to Rich, Eavan and I also
share a fascination with a number of other key precursors
and contemporaries, including such different figures as Anne
Bradstreet, Edna St. Vincent Millay, Elizabeth Bishop, Paula
Meehan, and most notably Sylvia Plath.

My title here, however, is meant to emphasise some-
thing else that the author of *Outside History* and I have in
common: what my recent re-reading of Eavan's work has
taught me to think of as a *suburban consciousness*. Literally, of
course, this writer has frequently, in both poetry and prose,
recorded the details of her life as a denizen of the Dublin
suburb of Dundrum. The observations are acute, bringing
the quotidian to the page in flashes of attention that trans-
figure domesticity: the 'silt of milk' left in a baby's bottle,
the 'bran fur of the teddy bear', a 'sumptuous / trash bag

of colours' waiting to be patched into a quilt. All these, as
Eavan so brilliantly noted in 'Domestic Interior', a kind of
early poetic manifesto, are radiant 'in the sort of light / jugs
and kettles / grow important by'. For Dundrum isn't – if
you'll forgive a bit of wordplay – humdrum. With its new
houses rising, its 'purpose-built shopping centre' (whose
offerings I just discovered on a website), its kids and kittens
and flung-down bicycles, it's as a place a type of the modern,
even though, or perhaps precisely because, it's not all that far
from the nineteenth-century workhouse that Eavan visits, in
a search for family history, in her superb essay 'The Woman,
the Place, the Poet'.

Like many of Eavan's women contemporaries, I have lived
in that place, earnestly writing and studying while raising
children, tidying toys, simmering soup, and sometimes
despairing in the pantry. My son and two daughters – less
than two years apart from each other – were pre-schoolers
when I was in my mid-twenties, ensconced in a creaky old
house in Kew Gardens, Queens, New York, probably more
humdrum than Dundrum, while commuting several times
a week to Columbia University, where I did graduate work,
and Queens College, where I taught remedial composition.
My husband commuted to even more places than I did in
his efforts to keep us going, and when I was home (which
was most of the time) I typed his doctoral dissertation while
scribbling vaguely Lawrentian short stories in spiral-bound
notepads and scrawling poems not just in the same notepads
but, as I sometimes even now discover, in the novels and
critical works I was trying to memorise for my orals.

I remember the details of that housebound domesticity
too, though I don't believe I ever transcribed them as metic-
ulously as Eavan has: the tricycle abandoned just beside the
front stoop, the day lilies by the fence, the playpen next to
the battered umbrella table in the backyard, the high chair
with its smear of apple sauce. And I remember the odd
disconnect that now connects me to Eavan herself, and that
even then, in the sixties, connected me to the near-precursor
who meant, I think, as much to me as to Eavan: Sylvia Plath,
whose *Ariel* I read with the same fervour that I devoted to my
researches into Dr Spock's *Baby and Child Care.* The discon-
nect between dailiness and desire, between the small world
of the suburban household with its clatter and clamour and
what seemed to me the great world of the Columbia library,
where I once wrote of seeing Gawain's Green Knight in an
impassioned vision of – of what? of aesthetic fertility? of
phallic pride?

Like Plath, I believe, but unlike Eavan, I didn't consciously
know I was what came to be called a feminist. I'd read *The
Second Sex* in college, and been vaguely nauseated by it: I
didn't want to meditate on Beauvoir's insights! And though
soon enough, in my suburban dwelling, I was to read Betty
Friedan and Kate Millett and come slowly to articulate that
perceived disconnect between dailiness and desire, it was
in the pages of *Ariel* that, like Eavan, I found not only an
aesthetic model but a newly conceived subject matter, a *topos*

as the literary historians would say, that gave me permission to live an examined life of my own under my own suburban roof.

And the spaces under that roof, as Eavan has so luminously explained, were not just literal but truly symbolic spaces, spaces only apparently outside history that constituted an alternative architecture in which women, writing in rooms of our own, began to reimagine and revise the supposed centres of literature itself. In that time – the sixties, the seventies – in those places, for those of us who were aspiring writers these locales were, yes, types of the modern, but not of the modern*ist*. Indeed, as Eavan makes clear, these realms in which we young mother-poets lived were the suburbs of modernism.

Here's what the dictionary says about *suburb*:

A "residential area outside a town or city," from O.Fr. suburbe, from L. suburbium "an outlying part of a city," from sub "below, near" + urbs (gen. urbis) "city." Close to crowds but just beyond the reach of municipal jurisdiction.

True, as Eavan notes, the suburb was 'by its very nature' a space of compromise between town and country. But consider the etymology of the word, which haunts much of her thinking about its significance. *Sub urb*: below, not really beside, the city. Outside history. The liminal, outlying, maybe *sub*ordinated zone, the work zone of transformation, where babies are metamorphosed into teenagers, and suppers are cooked, and fabrics are quilted together. But poetry? Doesn't poetry belong in the city of intellect? Surely poetry is born in the city where, as Eavan's magisterial compatriot Yeats wrote in his tribute to the heroes of 'Easter 1916', the great are to be met

> ... at close of day
> Coming with vivid faces
> From counter or desk among grey
> Eighteenth-century houses.

But if the great are in the cities, scorning or celebrating its winding streets that follow 'like a tedious argument' but really lead to 'overwhelming' questions, who inhabits the sub urbs? Why, needless to say, the women and children, and now – in many cities (for instance Paris and San Francisco and London) – the immigrant 'others', the new ones, the different ones. And as Eavan has taught us, it is these unlike, even unlikely populations who have changed and will change the centres of literary power, or so we must hope, those of us who have lived under the outlying roofs. Perhaps what Eavan calls, in one of her many fine discussions of Sylvia Plath, the 'stresses and fractures between a poet's life and a woman's' might become, for those who survive and celebrate the suburbs, empowering. A painful argument, perhaps, but it can be made, and Eavan has compellingly made it.

Nearly, now, two decades, ago – in 1996, when as the President of the Modern Language Association I was asked to mount a Forum for the organisation's annual convention – I invited Eavan to be one of the speakers at that occasion. The theme I had proposed focused on the upcoming millennium: 'What Was the Future? What Will the Past Be? Reading and Writing at the Turn of the Century'. And here are some of the words Eavan said, in an eloquent voice that comes straight from the suburbs of modernism, and too from the feminist suburbs of the Irish literary tradition so magically embodied in, of course, William Butler Yeats and his Celt-icist contemporaries – and now in Eavan and her feminist counterparts:

I was a woman in a male, bardic, hierarchical poetic culture: that past had been made in my absence and might well exclude my presence. Therefore my relation with it could only become more and more volatile and contentious, and at the same time less informed, if I could not change it. Only gradually did I learn to use a given identity which was my womanhood, to subvert an inherited one, which was that poetic past. In the process I saw that if I could change the past, I need not, after all, be imprisoned by it.

Not imprisoned by it? Absolutely not. On the contrary, Eavan has been liberated by her own transformations of the past and of the suburb to which so many women writers have been consigned. Along with Plath and Rich and Bishop and the others she so keenly admires, after all, Eavan has helped move the suburb, the city below the city, to the centre – to what may become a community of commonality. The 'past and future are no longer stable zones in poetry', she added in the same talk. And she should know. She is one of those who has rethought the past and reimagined the future, remapping what were once liminal regions so that they have become cherished countries of the mind.

A Conversation with Eavan Boland

SHARA McCALLUM: *Over the years, your poems have portrayed 'unheroic' individuals, often women, who are absent from the grand historical narratives of empire, nation-building, and the like – who stand 'outside history' as you describe them. This is true in your most recent poem sequence, 'A Woman Without a Country', as well. What is the hold this subject has had and continues to have on you as a poet?*

EAVAN BOLAND: I've spoken before about the difference between past and history. And it's a way of looking at things that's still true for me. The past still seems to be a place where lives were lived that just couldn't be translated into what you call the grand historical narratives. History seems different when you start to look at it like this. When you read it through its absences – through women who didn't even have a walk-on part in it – you see it differently again.

In your last five books you have included long poem sequences. Among other things, I'm interested in the dedication to this new sequence: 'This sequence is dedicated to those who lost a country, not by history or inheritance, but through a series of questions to which they could find no answer'. This spoke to me very personally and also gave me the feeling that whoever is being (indirectly) addressed is essential to the telling of the story of the grandmother's life and the poet's reflections on culture and history.

The dedication was there from the beginning. My own grand-mother, who's referred to in the sequence, lived on a margin of history. She also died there far too young. But there are many other people who for one reason or another lost their place in the continuum. Or else never had it. Some years ago I translated some German-language poems by women who lived before and just after the Second World War. These were poets who lost a country suddenly or gradually. Their poems struggled around that loss. Because a boundary was re-zoned or an army marched in a different direction they were stripped of a terrain where people not only live but where they also get a chance to name themselves. A country, a nation, a national identity sound like such public things. But the loss of them can be private and very bitter. That was in my mind, both with the poems and the dedication. I remember in an interview you spoke about poetry being something that could explore 'complex notions of identity'. And I agree. For me the complexity is partially stored in this.

What you say about a 'public loss' becoming 'private' is perhaps one of the reasons the dedication spoke to me, as did the figure of the grandmother. I'm curious – did you create her based on family memory and stories or were the details of her life more invented?

There's almost no invention. But of course there's subjectivity. The details of her death are accurate. The death certificate is quoted from the actual document. I deliberately wove in the factual with the subjective because I think that's what happens: events and people get caught in a subjective mix.

Reading the poem, I feel as if the grandmother is almost a mythic figure. What does myth-making afford this poem?

It's not myth – because myth can be a defence mechanism against a reality rather than revealing it. But I did want to show something emblematic about her experience. This was a young woman who lived in the maelstrom of what would later be called the struggle for Irish freedom. It was important to me to put a text and context together to show how those realities missed one another.

To shift gears for a moment, I'd like to ask about your process with writing sequences. Do you first write individual poems and then collage them once you see that they might work as all-of-a-piece or do you know you want to write a sequence from the start and develop the material with that in mind all along – or use some other compositional method?

It's more or less fragmented. Although I usually have some sense of direction while I'm writing. The poems I finish when I'm thinking of a sequence don't just have an individual life. They have a collective edge to them, a kind of sociable shimmer. I see them as belonging in a context and I want to see them that way. Which is not to say there isn't some place-setting and rearranging as well. Sometimes I finish a group of poems and I can see clearly that one or two don't belong there. Then I just remove them and work on. That's the best thing about sequences – they're plastic and malleable. To me they seem like modern-day cast-offs of larger lyric or narrative plans that wouldn't work today. *The Prelude* or *Childe Harold* wouldn't find any oxygen in the here and now. But a sequence is a workable sort of a compromise, with lyric and narrative ghosts popping up here and there.

I love the idea that individual parts of a poetic sequence have a 'sociable shimmer' when arranged. I think in some of your earlier long sequences, like 'Colony' and 'Against Love Poetry', individual parts work as stand-alone poems (even when informing the whole). This seems different than in the new sequence, where the prose parts take on their 'shimmer' by virtue of the personal narrative as context; and vice versa, where the personal lyric-narrative sections obtain a more political 'edge' by their proximity to the prose interspersed.

One of the reasons I like sequences is because of their have-your-cake-and-eat-it features. They do work by juxtaposition. But the poems are easy enough to detach. Poems I've written like 'That the Science of Cartography is Limited' or 'Quarantine' were once parts of a sequence. But as time goes on they turn up here and here, without the sequence. They have a life as single poems. The truth is poems are never compromised by sequences. But a sequence can be compromised by a strong poem which reverts to the page with no folk memory left of being in a sequence. In the current sequence I do fasten the poems a bit more to the page with the prose disruptions. But I'm fairly sure the same thing will happen.

Thinking more of the poetic modes you use in this sequence, what is the relationship between the prose-like 'lessons' and the lyric-narrative sections?

Just that I wanted to disrupt the sequence. In my previous ways of arranging a sequence, say for 'Outside History' or 'Domestic Violence', I relied on the pauses and spaces between poems to do the work of dis-connection or connection. This sequence had more voices in it, and one way of bringing in those other voices was through the prose 'lessons', with their choppy pieces of information. In fact those 'lessons' are pieces of prose migrated from an earlier book of mine, *Object Lessons*. That book was involved both with ideas of a nation and of being without one. So I felt the prose extracts could be brought in as a micro-chorus.

Most of the poems in the sequence are in couplets, tercets, and quatrains, when not in a single, block stanza. What did the choice of a uniform stanza offer you in writing these and when, in the compositional process, did you decide on the stanza-length for each?

I often work in stanzas. I think they have a blunt, coping-stone sort of value in building a poem. Sometimes I prefer verse paragraphs. But stanzas were better suited for what I was doing here. I'm comfortable in different line lengths, with different forms. And the form of the stanza on the page is often your clue as to what pauses you can get, what room for rhetorical intervention you have. I don't always decide on a stanza length in any very conscious way until I'm well into a piece. I've sometimes taken a poem out of one stanza, when it's nearly done, and tried something else.

I know your mother was a painter and that in your recent book of essays you've written about ideas of authorship and individual expression through meditating on her own work as an artist. Do you find though that you draw on visual forms as analogues for poetic forms?

I never did that. At least not in that way. My mother was indeed a painter. She studied in Paris. And she became the private student there of a Cubist painter, Leo Survage. She also exhibited in Dublin during the thirties and forties, when she came back to Ireland. One of the vivid memories of my childhood is of a room with a paint-covered easel and brushes soaking in turpentine. That was in London. I remember fog outside the window and dull afternoons and these incongruous splashes of paint. I still could almost reach out and hold those tubes of paint, with their squiggles of carmine and yellow. But it's not translatable. My mother's world was visual. It dealt in images. It transferred them through paint. I never felt that had much to do with my world as a poet. I don't proceed through visual forms. I'm not even sure what they would be in poetry. I have a practical interest as a poet in the mathematical side. I've always been more numerate than literate, in some odd, off-kilter way. I can't remember an address. But I can remember a number. In fact, I can sometimes imagine numbers better than words. So forms for me when I write a poem are numerate if they're anything. Certainly not visual.

You've written poems about being a mother, wife, etc. Is it possible to say how your sense of your own identity has been informed by writing about these roles?

I've written poems about marriage and about my children. But I haven't done so with any sense of 'roles'. In fact even the word pulls me back into some of the controversies of the sixties and seventies when subjects like that were put under pressure from several sides. In fact, just about the time I was setting up some of those poems, male writers were arguing that poems about children or marriage showed women settling for niche subjects, with a clear implication that larger themes eluded them. In a way I expected that sort of thing. When I published a book called *Night Feed* at the start of the eighties I ran into that criticism. And I wasn't so much concerned because it seemed to me a continuation of a mixed-up critique – a sort of putting on of canonical pince-nez in order to standardise and exclude. What troubled me more – in a way it troubles me still – was that women poets were arguing towards something equivalent. Even a poet I admire as much as Adrienne Rich was making the case that writing as a wife and a mother could undermine imaginative energy. In her essay 'When We Dead Awaken' she writes: 'to be a female human being trying to fulfill traditional female functions in a traditional way *is* in direct conflict with the subversive function of the imagination'. Here's another sentence from that essay: 'to be maternally with small children all day in the old way, to be with a man in the old way of marriage, requires a holding-back, a putting-aside of imaginative activity, and demands instead a kind of conservatism'. I disagreed then and do now. As a poet I didn't view marriage or motherhood as institutions designed to oppress a creative energy, but as choices that had consequences. Being married and having children shaped myself and my life and gave me access to the language and perceptions that shape-changing events give. It still troubles me that writers like Rich who otherwise brought such adventure and clarity to poetry, could encourage certain women poets to see a primary part of their experience – their families, their children – as being in conflict with the other primary source of their experience, their imaginations.

I'm glad you note that about Rich as I think her essay comes out of a schism in herself that seems accurate to how she felt as a woman living in the 1950s in the US, yet it separates spheres of our lives and wants to hold them apart in a way your work does not. Your poems often engage with personal and public histories at the same time, for instance. Do you think the notion that aesthetics and ethics are separate aspirations for the poet persists? And, if so, how do you respond to that as someone who has spent a career (in my view) troubling that distinction?

There's definitely still a view out there that if a poet holds to an ethical view sooner or later it will undermine aesthetic values. I don't agree. Personal histories are rooted in memory and self-awareness. Public histories are constructed in a selective way. When they meet – and they often do in poetry – the issues have to be ethical as well as aesthetic. The old purist argument that poetry needs to be free of the ethos of private feeling or moral crisis makes no sense to me. I do recognise the risks of didacticism and the heavy layer that polemic can put on a poem. But the ethical imagination doesn't have to involve itself with either of those. And the idea that aesthetics can exist without being troubled and confirmed by an ethical perspective just doesn't seem practical to me.

I think even before I met you I always felt a strong connection to your work (poems and essays) because you were collapsing divisions that I wanted to feel were not always going to be in conflict (country and woman; mother, wife and poet; for example). Do you ever think about the ways in which the meanings of your work might speak to readers in another country, another place, another time?

I don't really think of that. But I'm aware how much easier it is now to have an idea, a phrase, a poem travel across boundaries. And I want to be able as a poet to speak across divisions and set identities. When I think of poets who spoke to me when I was young I'm conscious of barriers that vanished when I read, say, Yeats. I was very young when I began reading him. In fact I was a convent school girl, sheltered in the same Irish middle class he so distrusted, without any obvious connections to him in terms of faith or tribe. But for all that his poems found me. And still do.

I don't mean to presume too many shared experiences and erase important differences, but as a Caribbean woman poet I've also wondered if you see a connection between you as an Irish woman writer and other women writers from the 'margins' of empire (Caribbean or elsewhere)? You've spoken a lot about how American women like Plath were influential for you, and I wonder if there are other ties you feel to women poets from other regions?

I'm always drawn to the work of other women poets, especially to those you describe as on the 'margins' of empire. But it's not exactly empathy that brings me there. It's more a process of translation. A writer like Louise Bennett looks at first like she would be inaccessible to a poet like myself. But I think her achievement is translatable in my terms. I look at it through my curiosity about performance, about the politics of the vernacular, about the resistance of a literary world to both those values – which for a long time meant she didn't receive her due as an exemplary artist. Above all, it translates into my sense of the poet's responsibility, as does Lorna Goodison's work. There's an essay by Allen Tate published in 1951 called 'To Whom is the Poet Responsible?' This is a direct quote from it: 'To *whom* is the poet responsible? He is responsible to his *conscience* in the French sense of the word: the joint action of knowledge and judgement'. I've always been dissatisfied with that answer. And I like the fact that women poets in the last half century and more – from Akhmatova to Rich to Levertov – have been widening and revising the idea of the poet's responsibility. I see that in women poets from the Caribbean. But also very much in poets from the Middle East, where the work of Forough Farrokhzad – she died in the sixties – really opened my eyes to the possibility of new definitions.

Do you think the emergence of women writers in countries where they have not been strongly represented in the literature is necessarily political?

I'd use 'inevitably' rather than 'necessarily'. A woman writer, finding her voice in a country where she has been in the literature rather than of it, should be a literary figure. But it doesn't always work that way. Representation is itself political. It often signals the stake-holding of the dominant culture. I remember in Ireland as a young poet being surprised at how vehement the opposition was to poems I wrote about my daily life as a woman. As if I was violating some code. It struck me that I must be trespassing on something – or maybe just intruding on a series of biases, all the way from subject matter to the shape of a poem. Nevertheless it's important to emphasise something. I did at times feel exasperated and even isolated back then. And I had fairly well worked-out views about standing on the margin of a literature – and I could be vocal about them. But I also felt safe in a civic and physical sense. And that's the difference. That safety can't be taken for granted for certain women poets emerging right now from real historical contention. I could always continue with what I was doing, no matter what anyone said or wrote. But I could see even back then, reading Haight and Reeder on Anna Akhmatova, how dangerous representation and restriction could be for women in certain places, at certain moments. There's a wrenching story of Akhmatova's distress when the Writers' Union censured her in the late forties, because she knew she would lose her ration book. We've now moved further again – partly through technology and travel – so we can see the lack of representation for certain women in certain situations goes much deeper than silence. That it can end up in danger and exclusion and even physical harm. Important stories like those of Forough Farrokhzad in Iran in the sixties and Nadia Anjuman in this decade in Afghanistan prove it. So in this more limited sense, the emergence of women writers in countries where their work puts them at risk is political. And should be.

You make a crucial distinction between the politics of exclusion and that which leads to exile, bodily harm, and even death, as in the case of Anjuman. What can poetry do – or does it have a role or purpose – in the face of the most extreme forms of injustice?

I don't think poetry has a role. But the poetry reader does. And I think that role reaches from just opening a book and paying attention all the way to the moral responsibility of rethinking what a poem says and who a poet is in our time. Over the past few decades there has been a definite tendency in certain critiques – some of them reflected in poetry workshops – to talk about the politicisation of poetry as if it was a disruption of its purity. I think it's been limiting and damaging. It's allowed for a conversation that suggests the political poem is somehow un-poetic. That's enough to make poets like Nadia Anjuman less visible than they should be. I understand that it's difficult to make literary decisions about poets in other languages and from other cultures. But our contact with the rich European poetry of the post-war period – from Montale to Bachmann – should be enough to show that these poets are of consequence for all poetry, not just for their own language and culture.

Reviews

THE PITY OF WAR

OWEN SHEERS, *Pink Mist* (Faber and Faber) £8.99
ANDREW MOTION, *The Customs House* (Faber and Faber) £9.99
TOM PAULIN, *New Selected Poems* (Faber and Faber) £14.99

When we are effectively at war, albeit at a distance and by proxy, the actual fighting delegated to a professional army, how are poets to respond? Hardly any of us have had any experience of combat, or come under the kinds of economic pressure that drive people to join up. Owen Sheers' answer was to embed himself among those who had, spending time with returning soldiers and their families. The result is *Pink Mist*, a verse-drama broadcast over five nights on BBC Radio 4 and widely acclaimed in hardback, not least by Ross Cogan in this magazine. Its appearance in paperback gives us a chance to examine the qualities that make it such a compelling piece of writing.

The first thing to be said is how specific it is. Commissioned by Tim Dee, a BBC producer based in Bristol, it makes vivid use of Bristol settings; the *Thekla*, the cargo ship turned into a nightclub that has a Banksy sprayed on the hull, 'a death's head with a hood, / the prow of his canoe breaking the Plimsoll line'; the estate of post-war prefabs where one of the young soldiers grew up, 'roads all over the place – Outside your door, through your garden, / a motorway over your roof. But the ones in front of you? / They're narrow and few'; the cliff by the suspension bridge where the three boys engage in a succession of dares, 'pushing each other further and further / out…'.

The second is how well Owen Sheers uses the medium. The three boys join up together and it's the interplay of their voices, and the voices of their families, that lends the play its momentum, each realisation given just enough time to dawn before another voice breaks in. We are taken into their confidence, we hear them thinking out loud, an intimacy peculiar to radio that Sheers exploits to deliver a final surprise – though it works almost as well on the page, where reading creates its own intimacy.

Pink Mist does not just build up layers of detail ('A sudden tree of earth and smoke' when an IED goes off, 'the ground dropping and rising, / like a heartbeat under the soil'), it strips them away too, showing how in combat any thought of 'queen or country, the mission or belief' simply comes down to 'keeping your mates alive, / Or avenging the ones who've already died'. In so doing, it lays bare the emotional dynamic that politicians are always ready to harness from a safe distance: 'Cos that's what fuels war, though no one will say it, / Love, and grief, its rougher underside.' The play drives the point home in its closing lines: what the soldiers are fighting for – or fighting from – is 'an abuse of love'.

An army doctor makes a similar point in one of the found poems from the First World War that open *The Customs House*: 'Naturally it can save a good deal of time if men, / before battle, have pictures from the Hate Room hung / in their minds of things the enemy have already done…' – the barbarity of which

Andrew Motion offsets by introducing us to 'Captain John Buxton, a prisoner of the German army / for all five years of the Second World War', who kept his sanity by studying the redstarts on the camp perimeter: '*The chief joy / of watching them is to prove they inhabit another world*', a note struck again in 'Whale Music', where we are warned that what we may be left with 'will be the silence of your own creation'.

Startling as the detail is in the found poems, what lifts the First World War sequence is 'The Death of Harry Patch', the 'Last Fighting Tommy', whose life Andrew Motion recounted in *The Cinder Path*, complete with some of his characteristic turns of phrase. Now he imagines one final parade of the 'hundreds of thousands of dead' who 'immediately rise up, straightening their tunics' and Harry Patch 'running quick-sharp along the duckboards' to join them:

> When he has taken his place, and the whole company
> are settled at last, their padre appears out of nowhere,
> pausing a moment in front of each and every one
> to slip a wafer of dry mud onto their tongues.

In the same way, 'Home Front', a sequence of three short poems in which Motion imagines a soldier's dying thoughts in Afghanistan and his wife's thoughts as she walks beside the coffin at Brize Norton, is worth far more than the half-a-dozen found poems that precede it. The soldier's death is subtly refracted through biblical allusions, the grove of mulberry trees where he lies transporting him to the brook Cedron and Gethsemane, and these are echoed in the deep Amen of the Hercules' engines as it comes in to land; but the poem is brought to rest, as it were, in the wife's voice, which has a piercing naturalness:

> He detested the rain all his life although I adore it,
> and was soaked through the instant I took my place
> alongside him in our procession across the tarmac.
> Dry sand would still have been glittering in his hair.
> And in the corners of his eyes, his ears, more sand.

What this poem offers that the found poems, of their very nature, cannot is what Heaney called 'the redress of poetry', resolving the loss through the tenderness of its expression.

Tom Paulin came of age as Northern Ireland was turning into a war zone and, though higher education swiftly teleported him out of there, ironic glimpses of what he saw when he went back as 'the owl of Minerva in a hired car' became a feature of the poetry:

> A Jock squaddy glances down the street
> And grins, happy and expendable,
> Like a brass cartridge. He is a useful thing,
> Almost at home, and yet not quite, not quite.

Politically, Paulin's sympathies were with the United Irishmen of 1798, the largely Protestant leaders of the first Irish rebellion against British colonial rule, and in 'The Book of Juniper' he made a determined effort to 'dream / of that sweet / equal republic' and mythologise it with a richness of verbal texture that approaches Heaney's. But the contemporary reality was very different. As he was forced to concede in 'Desert-martin', the poem that gave us that glimpse of the Jock squaddy,

> It's a limed nest, this place. I see a plain
> Presbyterian grace sour, then harden,
> As a free strenuous spirit changes

To a servile defiance that whines and shrieks
For the bondage of the letter,

a psychology that Paulin equates, in a comparison that seems prophetic now, with 'Masculine Islam, the rule of the Just... A theology of rifle-butts and executions'.

But there was another inheritance that he could carry forward, the Ulster speech he had grown up with, 'a language that lives lithely on the tongue', as he argued in the first Field Day pamphlet of 1983, *A New Look at the Language Question*, but is 'homeless' and 'derelict', 'a language without a lexicon'. *Fivemiletown*, his collection from 1987, saw him drawing on this resource and finding his own distinctive style. He may have chanced on it as he recalled his adolescent misadventures, 'for I felt dwammy sick / at the face of meeting you again', but it serves him equally well when he comes to remake an iconic poem like Akhmatova's 'Voronezh':

But that tin lamp
on the poet's table
was watched last night –
Judas and the Word
are stalking each other
through this scroggy town
where every line has three stresses
and only the one word, *dark*.

One of the discoveries of this *New Selected Poems* is how brilliantly Paulin remakes the work of poets who had to live, like him, through dangerous times.

In the same spirit, his empathy with the outsider heightened by his own marriage to a Sikh, he imagines 'Chagall in Ireland' refusing to be intimidated by 'a bad baste running down the boreen' after throwing a half-brick through his window but 'like someone signing a letter *with love*' painting him 'into the far corner'. It's a pity the *New Selected* could not find room for 'Vitebsk', where Chagall first had to confront the bigot, 'let him know that I'm not / going to die / for a long long time', only to warn us, 'hold to your doubts', that 'his children's children / will seed the earth with our sorrows'.

Paulin's recovery of his childhood speech and his exploration of the subtle differences it conveyed – 'I mean we live in two streets / off the same road / – the Ormeau Road / why should we say it different?' – reaches its climax in *The Wind Dog*, a freewheeling radio poem that spins from sound to sound until it has taken us from 'the bulgey river' of Paulin's earliest memories to 'the poet who died / in the same asylum as Lucia Joyce', that poet being John Clare, the unexpected resonances of whose 'homeless' speech Paulin has always championed as a critic.

The Wind Dog, which the *New Selected* rightly gives in full, was one of the radio poems commissioned by Tim Dee to celebrate the fiftieth anniversary of Radio Three. One cannot help wondering how much better *The Invasion Handbook*, Paulin's recreation of the events leading up to the Second World War, might have been if that had been written to a performance brief. The *New Selected* hints at what might have been, giving us in the voices of Stalin, Clemenceau and Churchill the vivid impression of a play about to take to the air, and no indication of what awaits the reader in the book itself, page after page of characterless, short-lined free verse, as if Paulin had published the notebook rather than the final work. He knew the risk he was taking:

now I plunge my hand again
into a wallet that's greasy
and without the frame
– no the idea –
of form or shape

and in the end 'that slimy wallet [...] time has on its back' proved just too 'slippery', a 'drecky sack'.

The selection ends with poems from *Love's Bonfire* that take us back to the territory and the voice of *Fivemiletown*, and that's the voice that will attract future readers. The champion of Hazlitt and Clare will matter to scholars but the young will identify with the young Paulin, 'bare as need, poor guy, / or the sole of that trainer', and the experience of being 'on edge [...] like rubbing one finger / along the dulled blade / of a penknife, / then snapping it shut'.

ROGER GARFITT

VITAL WORLD

MAURICE RIORDAN, *The Water Stealer* (Faber and Faber) £12.99

From 'The Lull' at its opening – where the deftly controlled syntax generates a measured whirlwind, and every word bristles with the expectation of whatever is poised to answer the stillness at the centre – to the unpunctuated, uncanny monologue 'The Face' which ushers the collection to a thrilling close, the poetry in *The Water Stealer* storms, rattles and glitters on the pages, as Maurice Riordan channels the unmistakable natural energy he finds in the language of real people and things.

Sometimes it's dream-language, with its 'full coherence', and the images and sentences come tumbling out, recreating the speaker's confusion, while adhering firmly to its own special logic and structure: as in 'The Age of Steam',

where I'm young again, alone, home for holidays
or about to fly to Canada – running this time
for the plane (the airport's in the farm next to ours)
while carrying a shorn Christmas tree and worried
will I be allowed to board, when I wake ... then drift
to a house I've lived in years it seems, [...]

only to wake again, properly, to 'a dawn / of dampened sun [...], and in my chest / the hissing thumping piston – 14 years on – of grief'. Sharing his dream-complex in a number of poems, Riordan lets us in on a vital world we wouldn't otherwise know, and the experience excites because it's all so close – as though it's unfolding for reader and poet simultaneously. This sense of involvement is not only due to the content (who isn't intrigued by dreams, their own or other people's?), but to the long, taut, muscular sentences, frequently sustained over multiple stanzas – as in 'The Larkin Hour', which leads us along with the speaker into 'a city whose patois escaped / my competence, whose skittish moods and laws / of tense were too crafty-quick, its misshaped / coven of vowels devised, it seems, to taunt / my ear'.

Riordan acknowledges the 'disablement' that results from not always having access to precise linguistic labels, but which can also be mind-opening:

And watching the bubbles now like cells
in a petri dish, it's hard to think one pulse
of code sent brain to brain would bring to mind
their wisp-fire on the creosoted wood,
together with wind and sky this end of day […]

('Irish')

There are a few elegies in the book, for friends and fellow poets, including a moving homage to Gregory O'Donoghue, 'The Hip-Flask', which captures shared settings and snippets of conversation so vividly that it's a relief when the poet admits 'The heartache of it all goes to my head'. Other, less

emotional, nostalgia-trips – to an earlier world where everyone smoked everywhere ('Sweet Afton') or to a generic summer holiday resort ('Postcard from San Benedetto del Tronto') – exhibit the well-honed wit of Simon Armitage's best poems. There are also wry ones in which the poet, at 60, looks back or addresses the matter of ageing, and tells it like it is: the (again dreamlike) forgetting of names and pop-culture trivia in 'Gone With the Wind', for example ('Why does one good woman now hide behind another? / Is there some kink occurring, a hindrance in my brain?'), or the quotidian belligerence registered in the short confessional poem 'Habits'. On the rare occasions he pretends to be writing axiomatically, as in the two-liner 'Quits'

BUTTERCUP FESTIVAL

Buttercup Festival © David Troupes www.buttercupfestival.com

('Life's short – a blink. The wise owls tell us so. / But it's the longest span you or I will know'), Riordan makes the white space around the lines bloom with the things he's deliberately not mentioning.

Facts and instructive bits of science are seamlessly woven into the lyric perspective, as in 'August', 'the month of strenuous bad-omened dreams / when the sun has steadied but the heat / keeps arriving on its own momentum' and the poet's vision is filled with ants: 'When a male latches onto a queen, they'll tumble / back to earth *in flagrante* – she'll shed her wings / and burrow below ground, fertile for the winter. / I've never seen one but it works. There's no end of ants.' Or the beguiling, strange, tender tribute to the female water spider, who 'goes, a bauble of mercury, / shimmering like a fish lure / and at risk from the carp / until she reaches the tangle of weeds, / where she's hung her silken tent'.

There are pure, illuminating observations and interrogations of nature, too; as in 'Stars and Jasmine', which places in new relation three otherwise indifferent creatures, 'cat, hedgehog and – our summer interloper – the tortoise': 'A perfect triangle, they can neither eat / nor marry one another. / And tonight they are gods / under the jasmine under the stars.' Also in the title poem, which negotiates bewilderment and grief while brimming with the practical facts of garden management:

Where were the carp? Sunk in the mud
or ferried into the dawn by the cormorant?
Or was it a town fox that chewed
through the tarp so it bled while I dreamt,

while my brain worried old scars,
the saucer of streetlight grew brighter
overhead and neared the huddle of carp
– who'd have jumped and bitten in terror,

gorping helplessly in the poisonous gas.

This is unmistakably Hughesian territory, and Riordan enters with ease – armed with the same mastery of nostalgia that powers MacNeice's best poems, and an invigorating originality of expression that allows the twenty-first-century spirit into the lyric landscape.

REBECCA WATTS

THE SONG CARRIES

NIALL CAMPBELL, *Moontide* (Bloodaxe) £9.95

When an author opens his first collection with a poem called 'Song', he's making two clear statements. He's claiming allegiance to a major tradition: English Renaissance poetry is full of songs, often to be accompanied by that blameless lute; so, later and luteless, is the work of Romantic poets such as Blake. And he's gently insisting that he possesses a poetic ear, an organ apparently absent or at least defective in some of his contemporaries. He gives himself eight lines to prove the point:

What sweeter triumph can there be
than the match lit in the grain-cellar,

no moon in the dark gallery
below the sleeping house. It's better

when I'm alone – can freely handle
those older tools for harrowing
and planting, turn the bent seed-cradle,
or thumb the axe-blade like a harp string.

If that isn't quite what we were expecting, so much the better. In two quatrains, Niall Campbell creates part of the world which informs so many of his poems – the islands of South Uist and Eriskay in the Outer Hebrides – and, better still, finds exactly the right tone for it: intimate but unfussy, rapt yet practical. There's a hands-on authenticity here: he knows these tools so well that he could probably do without the lit match; and he knows how to thumb an axe-blade 'like a harp string'. The movement of the poem towards its final sharp surprise is perfectly controlled: consider, for instance, the deft way in which a single well-placed adverb, 'freely', suggests both the inhibiting constraint of company and the physical ease of solitude.

Other kinds of song are both described and exemplified in *Moontide*. 'And This Is How It Started' takes us back to the time of competing Scots makars; 'The Songs of Kirilov' belong to a character in Dostoevsky; 'A Song for Rarity' is a charming little epithalamium; while 'Walking Song', a deliciously functional poem, has precisely the rhythm for the walker to intone while making, or mistaking, Frost-like choices between alternative roads. 'Concerning Song/Silence' explores the creative tension and balance which lies at the heart of Campbell's work, ending with the head gathering 'some of what / the heart already knew of quiet: // the hush, the burr, the meadow-weed, / that this is all, and this enough'.

When, in 'Black Water', Campbell describes the Chinese image of sleep, 'the sleeper drinking from the night sea', he adds with winning simplicity: 'A fisherman's son, I'm drawn to this.' He seems enviably at ease in his own skin, yet he can inhabit some surprising alternative personae. In 'Fleece', he imagines himself in 'the stock frame of the shearsman / at Colchis', the one who created the Golden Fleece, which is a sort of mythological side-step from his more familiar world; but in 'The Work', having begun by seeing himself plausibly as 'the whaler poet', he moves through a series of wry transformations which end with 'the waiter poet', 'offering the choice wine, polishing to the light, / the bringer of the feast and the bill'. It's a lovely image: apt, affectionate and undeceived. And there are geographical dislocations too for the fisherman's son. Several poems find him in Grez sur Loing – where the expected song is, unexpectedly, Edith Piaf's – or in urban Glasgow, misty and smoky on Bonfire Night, with the 'marvellous forest' of an 'awed crowd' and a benevolent red sky: not so far from home, after all.

Campbell's most subtle modulations of mood and cadence often occur in his shortest poems. Here's another of just eight lines, this time from near the end of the book, called 'Kid':

This is it, the true time, when little matters;
when the sun's dropped so low behind the hill
that the light fails, and doesn't mind its failing;

and art is just the kid by a now pink river
kicking stones out to mid-stream. Hey kid, dreamer,
here's a road and a tune, just whistle out

to dusk-fall – sometimes, the song carries; sometimes,

the shadow casts out longer than the man.

The familiar, and therefore tactfully under-described, dusk-scene is immediately enlivened by two quietly articulated thoughts, that 'the true time' is 'when little matters' and that light 'doesn't mind its failing'; here, as usual, Campbell's control of diction and verse-movement seems to me impeccable. Then, in the second stanza, there's that unexpected touch of skittish cuteness in 'Hey kid, dreamer…' – surely addressed to the poet's younger self – but it doesn't outstay its welcome; instead, the poem modulates again to its carefully paced and almost elegiac final couplet. Yes, 'sometimes, the song carries': it certainly does in these wonderfully enjoyable poems.

NEIL POWELL

WITH TEETH MARKS

ILYA KAMINSKY, *Dancing in Odessa* (Arc Publications) £8.99

I came across the American paperback of *Dancing in Odessa* in 2007 and was immediately impressed. Here was a rare poetry not drowning in neo-classicism, circumscribed by tax dollars or indeed thirled to a finely honed sense of self such as to be exemplary – and dead. The verse was pitch perfect, the images exacting and tender, the structure playful and precise. Perhaps the most astonishing thing was the biographical note. The poet was in his thirties and English his second language – he had arrived in the US in 1993 at the age of sixteen without a word of it.

The themes of Kaminsky's poetry are familiar. They speak with delicacy of a debt of tutelage to Tsvetaeva and Mandelshtam. Joseph Brodsky too remains a cynosure. What is most striking is that Kaminsky's eye and ear for poetry is unerring. Indeed in 2010 he co-edited (with Susan Harris) the *Ecco Anthology of International Poetry*, a book that is an education in itself.

Adam Zagajewski astutely observes that Kaminsky's achievement in these poems can be traced to the way in which he grafts the Russian literary tradition onto 'the American tree of poetry and forgetting'. Indeed. The graft works for reasons that are both modest and miraculous. The poems are enabled – and hedged – by a language that thickens tender experience with a spoonful of genuine insight. To that insight might be added something like wisdom. The qualification is precious because it reintroduces the notion of poetry as a system of eternal deferrals, or 'vowels with teeth marks' as Kaminsky notes in *Musica Humana*, his elegy for Osip Mandelshtam. Such lupine vocabulary is a statement of faith in the reader. It is also Kaminsky's nod to Brodsky's influence on his own development, an influence beautifully rendered in the poem 'Elegy for Joseph Brodsky' which is included here. In it, Kaminsky imagines Brodsky's lines buffeting – and being buffeted by – New York's granite rock. What might be a poem about exile is actually a poem that celebrates the preservations of memory where the act of remembering is a kind of delinquent feat, circuitous, unburdened, defining ('your poems are wolves nourishing us with their milk'). This is sustaining, brilliant poetry – not everyone's cup of tea of course, but we are the better for it. The stage lights are underfoot.

GERRY MCGRATH

CONTEMPORARY EPIC

JENNY LEWIS, *Taking Mesopotamia* (Carcanet/OxfordPoets) £9.95

Two epigraphs open Jenny Lewis' *Taking Mesopotamia*, published this spring by Carcanet/OxfordPoets. The first is an excerpt from Lord Grey of Falloden's *Memories and Reflections* (1919), the second, lines from Tablet III of *The Epic of Gilgamesh*: 'As for humans, their days are numbered, / whatever they do is like a puff of wind'. Both passages suggest man's hubris, the inherent futility of certain undertakings. Weaving personal and military history while paying tribute to the epic tradition, *Taking Mesopotamia* layers conflicts and losses – the death of the speaker's father, the devastation of Iraq, once known as Mesopotamia ('the land between two rivers'), and the lives of those who have travelled there throughout the ages. Part lyric meditation, part work of historical research, *Taking Mesopotamia* offers the best of both kinds of considerations, reaffirming the intersection of the personal and political.

Central to Lewis' collection is her research into her father's part in the Mesopotamian Campaign of World War I. Tom Lewis' journals inspired the loose narrative structure of the collection's poems. Lewis seamlessly integrates facts from past and present military operations into musical, fully imagined poems that transcend the subject of warfare to reflect on cultural heritage and human inheritance. By juxtaposing poems in her father's voice against those in the voices of contemporary combatants, Lewis actively confronts the dichotomy of past and present, skilfully constructing lyric and thematic echoes. A poem in Tom's voice dating from 1916 recalls:

> only reeds,
> about two foot high, for a makeshift cover. Each
> battalion had sixty bellums to cross the waters.
> Five hundred of us British and Indian soldiers
> practising punting – a strange regatta! We needed
> to find Noah and his ark before we started to go
> slowly, one by one and two by two, into the dark.

On the opposite page, the companion poem dating from 2010 considers the clearing of those same marshes:

> Reeds are like lungs filtering and cleaning water […]
> When Saddam cleared them and drained
> the marshes people said Iraq has stopped breathing.

The contrast between the two poems, uttered in different ages but united by place, suggests what poetry can do to exhume, recast, and re-energise history, our recent past enlivened by the less recent, and vice versa. Lewis reminds us of the sacredness of Mesopotamia's war-torn grounds and the palimpsestic nature of violence and beliefs.

Tom utters one of the most poignant revelations, an admission of the war's spiritual context: 'We can still / trace our beliefs back here, where our own God / roared from the burning bush *thou shalt not kill*'. This proves one of the collection's remarkable strengths: Lewis ensures that the poems are never weighed down by their research, but given additional urgency and vitality. The factual details work in the service of rather than against lyricism, and the entries complicate our assumptions about war and those who wage it.

One of the most haunting poems in the collection derives its power from a semiotic tension, the disconnect between a word and its meaning. The language of the title itself, *Taking Mesopotamia*, suggests a euphemistic effort to soften the act of conquering. Lewis weaves this concern throughout the collection, confronting the subject head-on in 'Non-Military Statements':

> Neutralisation [killing soldiers] is part of any war
> as are soft targets [bombing civilians].
>
> Life deprivation [killing anyone] and surgical strikes
> [shelling and bombing] can be justified.
>
> Extraordinary rendition [kidnapping] of illegal combatants
> [people we don't like] is necessary in the war against terror.

In this purposefully anti-lyrical poem, Lewis exposes a catalogue of military terms to their human cost. She unassumingly captures the shiftiness of language, the jargon that covers its tracks with euphemisms: 'neutralisation', 'soft targets', 'life deprivation'. This poem, so antithetical to Lewis' gorgeous lyricism, evokes an uncomfortable truth. But it also reminds us how vital poetic language is to counteract the numbing, desensitising language it condemns.

Contrastingly, in 'Father', the connection to Lewis' own legacy clicks back into focus:

> My face is made from yours –
> your jaw, your weak right eye:
> my shin bone's from your leg,
> shattered in the moonlight
> as you supervised the digging
> of the trench at Kut-al-Amara.

Moments like these highlight the many stakes the collection juggles successfully. The vastest wars and empires are, at their core, composed of and fed by relationships between individuals. The collection's final poem, 'Epilogue', returns to the epigraph from Tablet III of Gilgamesh, 'whatever they do is like a puff of wind…'. It's a humbling reminder, and one that befits a collection that pieces together, in the epic tradition, so many voices, myths, histories, heroes and failures. But where landscapes, nations and rulers may not endure, the poem's survival serves as a testament to the power of writing.

Taking Mesopotamia offers the depth of an epic with the tight curation and lyricism of the best contemporary poetry. A topic this ambitious in scope necessitates an original execution. The storytelling that Lewis undertakes pays tribute to this tradition in its complexity, reminding us that poetry was at the heart of ancient Mesopotamia and remains a part of Iraq's culture.

MAYA C. POPA

A BELIEVABLE FOOTHOLD

PETER GIZZI, *In Defense of Nothing: Selected Poems 1987–2011* (Wesleyan) £21

Besides being a collection of the most compelling American poems of the last thirty years, Peter Gizzi's *Selected Poems* is the story of how a poet schooled in the radical deconstructive tradition of Language poetry ended up reimagining the lyric for the twenty-first century.

Proceeding backwards, *Threshold Songs* from 2011 is one of the most striking sets of poems the century has produced so far. The fragile self-examination of this book, motivated by the deaths of his parents and his brother, the poet Michael Gizzi, is such that a new voice entirely seems to have entered the language. The work's stress on contingency and flux, combined with a commitment to the lyric so refused by the traditions of radical American poetry Gizzi emerges from, creates a living form of soul-making – forms of enquiry, hesitance and failure that articulate for grounding in the contemporary's 'changing light':

> now
> that you're gone
> and I'm gone what
> did we learn
> what did we take
> from that oh
> always dilating
> now that you're here
> and also gone
> I am just learning
> that threshold
> and changing light
> a leafy-shaped blue
> drifting above
> an upstate New York
> Mohican light
> a tungsten light
> boxcar lights
> an oaken table-rapping
> archival light
> burnt over, shaking
>
> ('Analemma')

There is not simply change in Gizzi's world, but a metamorphic way of seeing; we are 'always dilating'. Gizzi seeks a place on the 'threshold' of the present, sounding an anxiety broader than the psychological – a tensile, vigilant sense of becoming and unbecoming. Nothing is taken as given, as shown in the preceding volume, *The Outernationale*:

> If we just ask that every song touch its origin
> just once and the years engulfed
>
> If problems of identity confound sages
> derelict philosophers, administrators
> who can say I am found
>
> ('A Panic That Can Still Come Upon Me')

As always with Gizzi, the destination is the journey, and the trajectory of his career before his most accomplished work is its own achievement. Having become accustomed to Gizzi's style over the last decade, however, it can be difficult to acclimatise to the slightly different poetics of work before. Reading the first poem of *Some Values of Landscape and Weather* (2003), 'Objects in Mirror are Closer than they Appear', for example, one mistakes the backward glances at a photo's 'eyes of the dead' for the threshold of personal loss so typical of the later work. One must adjust to the more direct political cast of thought in these earlier poems, to realise that this is a poem about history and the 'unquantifiable' proximity of the past, 'closer than power lines' compared to its distant appearance in old militaria and curious specimen jars (with links to US imperialism and 9/11 that are unavoidable). Such baroque symbolism is a constant throughout the earlier collections. 'New Picnic Time', 'Lonely Tylenol', 'Some Values of Landscape and Weather' are among the finest of these charged allegorical landscapes (another of my favourites, 'Last Cigar', from *Artificial Heart*, has not made the cut).

This perspective cuts both ways, however. Though the very first poem of the book, 'Song of the Interior Begin', seems rooted in the Language poetry of Gizzi's apprenticeship – fragmented, dissonant and constructivist – one can witness the marks of a different ambition in hindsight, as the poem uses these techniques to express processes of consciousness:

So the tree for even
a twig   O branch   O earth

there is too   (psalm)
Neither a pool nor
a crown   And day spills
to where is   O water

Begin! Begin! So sing
of lever   Are eyes
shy?   O iris   O onyx
Into blouse of

    Air go there!

A chaos of impression is on the cusp of cohering here: momentary attempts to grasp being (in the George Oppen poem this references: 'That they are there!') are the subject here more than the usual 'materiality of language' we might associate with such a style. Other early poems state this ambition explicitly: 'Periplum', for example, citing Pound's notion of a voyaging, critiques the 'accurate study' of mapping, setting 'Still // satellites' against 'everyday distances', urging self and reader to 'Put your map right with the world'. Typically with Gizzi, to put right is to put *right in*, knowing is dependent on living with, though one might end 'at sea'. The two types of poem here, radical mimesis and Oppen-like statement, synergise in the later work, where statement becomes affect and vice versa.

Gizzi's *Selected* shows that space can be cleared for lyric thought in the twenty-first century, but that the lyric itself must undergo reinvention. Reading one after another of the 70-odd poems here, where even long works are split into short, lyric sections, the reader never has the expected sense of completion the form implies, that any poem has 'ended'. Gizzi has made it seem that the lyric (rather than the sequence, the New Sentence, the serial poem or the conceptual opus) is the form that can best articulate the thresholds of our lost, dispossessed, fluid modern

experience: it is precisely the fragility, the apprehension, the momentariness of its small capacity that can offer us a believable foothold again.

BEN HICKMAN

OUT THERE

DERRICK BUTTRESS, *Welcome to the Bike Factory* (Shoestring Press) £9.00
JAY RAMSAY, *Agistri Notebook* (Knives Forks and Spoons) £6.00
TOM CHIVERS, *Flood Drain* (Annexe Press) £4.00
WILLIAM PALMER, *The Paradise Commissionaire* (Rack Press) £5.00
CHRISTINE DE LUCA, *Dat Trickster Sun* (Mariscat Press) £6.00

Which elements of the world 'out there' remain dark to poetry? Although, after the banking crash, economists now praise skilled engineers, most English poets ignore industry. Derrick Buttress is a praiseworthy exception. His pamphlet, *Welcome to the Bike Factory*, explores the bitter roots of British industry. Buttress, who also writes prose and radio plays, has a keen ear for the facts of others' speech. He pares down the words, published in 1842, of Patience Kershaw, 17, who hauled coal wagons: 'I go to the pit at five o'clock / and come out at five in the evening'. A different route 'out' is found by the 'stockinger' who, in Buttress' telling last line, 'taught himself to read and write'.

Buttress hits home with his account of school Shakespeare: 'We were not chosen for our thespian gifts, / but because we could read'. (This is still the poetry of our world, with 5.2 million English adults 'functionally illiterate', according to the National Literacy Trust.) The post-war 'Bike Factory' offered work at its most numbing, mechanically rhythmic: 'clocking on, clocking off'. Though Buttress occasionally labours points, his account of the arrival of a new car is subtly ominous. The bike factory workers (who knew their metals) 'searched for a flash of chrome, found none'. The discovery that the 'brand new Ford' was a 'cheap tin toy' quietly undercuts the declaration: 'the car was definitely a sign / of the good times coming our way'.

Affluence may betray. Buttress' poems do not. They are wise, energetic and humorous. When a limp is 'assumed' to be a war wound, 'the truth was, I had fallen off my bike'. 'Feel its pulse', Buttress' final words command. His poems' sympathies pulse outwards, from 1840s 'working girls' to 'the smart girls' who 'rush [...] light as dancers / away from me / like daughters / leaving home'.

The pulse of Jay Ramsay's pamphlet, *Agistri Notebook*, is quickened both by 'your txt' and Heraclitus' sayings: 'Change is rest'. I suspect that its visionary ambitions may alienate readers who do not wish a poem's opening to reach out to 'The emptiness beyond name'. But Ramsay's work is metrically secure and habitually musical, even as it celebrates change: 'everything which is / new is lighter than we know'.

There are glimpses of a loved woman, observed with measured clarity: 'slowly climbing your white staircase through the early / afternoon heat, hair up, all in black, to the room above'. The 'one love' flares out in other insights: 'this icon of St John, surely a woman'.

Ramsay's writing opens out into unguarded insights, often in a kind of free-flowing prose. 'The best kept secret must be how fragile men really are. [...] It was when you said, while working for the police, that you realized *how easy it is for a man to be killed.*' The poems are often sharply sensual: 'the man with his salt-dried matted hair'. They are also unexpectedly funny: 'graffiti-sprayed [...] Maria – well, it's Jana, actually – '

The *Notebook*'s vision of Greece is unusually benign: 'the bars below / are full of the innocent on holiday'. I was absorbed, almost dazed by this collection's 'sun [...] in the great wheel of its blazing'. These are poems which would warm winter: 'a story no one can imagine'.

Poems can illuminate little-known facts of the world outside. Although I grew up near Hull, I never knew that it was named after the small river which runs through Tom Chivers' long commissioned poem, *Flood Drain*. Chivers mentions, in a helpful introduction, that the Hull is left to 'snake through the industrial landscape'. His short lines funnel, admirably, the brisk activity out there: 'joiners & welders / hauliers & packagers / the makers of pipes / tanks, tubes & drums [...] this is our business'.

Though the present's business includes the past, Chivers' pouring of Middle English into his *Flood Drain* may make its appeal less wide than the Humber. But his lines are beautifully fluent and flashingly contemporary, as Chaucer uploads to Facebook: 'a temple ymad of glas / framed for a selfie'. Langland's dreamer updates into recession: 'I shoop me into shroudes / a pair of fingerless black gloves / from Poundland'.

I occasionally thought the poem's rhythms slightly underpowered on the page, but the poet's voice might lift their flow, with the little river 'again / & ever / rising'. Chivers' abbreviated lines can also have a lovely elegiac fall: 'btwn the river / & the wrecking yard'. There is humour in *Flood Drain*'s briefest encounters: 'can you give a horse an ASBO?' It is vivid with the voices of Hull's people, experiencing earthquake: 'I hear my daughter screaming MUMMY MY BED IS SHAKING [...] I was sat on sofa and it started moving'. Chivers is a fine editor, of word and world.

William Palmer's 'Paradise Commissionaire' displays a cosmic energy:

With moons as medals on my breast,
and stars for pips, earth's atmosphere
broad navy blue across my chest [...]

Still more disarming is his story's end, as the film goes into reverse: 'On a yard-wall, backward into view, / walks a young boy, comically sad'.

There are only nine poems in Palmer's pamphlet. But each is a small world, drawing the reader out of familiar orbits. 'The Hidden Hero', apparently about 'writing a novel', expands its scope and lines into ferociously funny, then sorrowful accounts of a rogue character, haunting a life. 'The somebody who stole / your girl. And gave her back' transforms the writer/reader into the 'poor landlord' 'cupping your ear to catch the sounds of love'.

In Palmer's account of a death, rhymed with quiet art, the wilder excesses of poetry are cast aside: 'nothing is to be, from now, / like anything else at all'. These shapely, profound poems finally mourn 'The Lost Music': 'What it is to be *there* – not with the dance forgotten / and all of the jokes and half the world gone'. It is hard not to love a poetry whose rhythms seem to finger the pulse of the world outside, and the beat of its time: 'What it is to be *there*'.

The sun was still there when I opened Christine De Luca's smouldering yellow pamphlet. On the first page, set in prickle-sharp fonts by Gerry Cambridge, was the title poem. Britain's poetry, increasingly, draws on the richness of its different languages. But which language is this?

You could aa but lay a haand apö dem,
licht troo silence: a holy hubbelskyu

da foo spectrum o taer-draps; a slow air
ta turn you inside oot, ta brak a haert.

(Happily, the poet provides her gloss: aa: all; apö: on; troo: through; hubbelskyu: uproar (it would be worth reading the poem for that alone!) foo: full; brak: break.)

In *Dat Trickster Sun*, De Luca marries what I would call, hesitantly, phonetic Scots with – the yellow cover assures us – 'Shetlandic, her mother tongue'. Her lines are spiky with life. 'Iceland's haert [...] flames spunkin fornenst ice' (spunkin: igniting; fornenst: against). A fresh lyricism sparks her English phrases: 'tink [think] o da doo [dove], her baffled lullaby'. (The poems teem with birds: 'stirleens', 'peewits'.)

De Luca's writing in standard English has an acute simplicity. A Shetland child, with whooping cough, needs 'the boat that brought the doctor'. 'You held me upside down to get my breath'. Her poetry is memorably contemporary: 'dis gödless googlin'. Yet it is at home in the universe : 'sib [related] tae da hale wirld'.

The sun was gone when I closed De Luca's poems. But I was left with the conviction that more fine poems waited, as yet invisible, out there on the darkening air.

ALISON BRACKENBURY

NEW THINKING

JOHN REDMOND, *Poetry and Privacy: Questioning Public Interpretations of Contemporary British and Irish Poetry* (Seren) £14.99

In this impressively written and thought-provoking collection of essays, John Redmond artfully explores a critical tendency to involve poetry interpretation with public spheres of value which, as he shows, often have little to do with the original text. Across seven chapters Redmond addresses Derek Mahon, Glyn Maxwell, Robert Minhinnick, Plath as an influence on Heaney, John Burnside, Vona Groarke, and, finally, David Jones and W.S. Graham. Each chapter takes up a familiar or previous critical reading of a poet, indicative of a 'public' framework of interpretation, and then proceeds to provide a concise overview that challenges this reception, ending with a more thorough and demonstrative analysis through which to stake a renewed perspective.

Before taking up this task, Redmond's introduction condenses a wealth of incisive observations pertinent to his discussion – all of which are immediately and excitingly relatable to anyone with an interest in the 'role' and 'representation' of contemporary British and Irish poetry. I put these terms in inverted commas, as they are the shifty harbingers of much ambiguity, cynicism and reproach, and rightfully so: what 'role' should definitively be assigned to a medium so indebted to the indefinable and what, once enrolled in its chosen (nay, given) role, should and can it represent? Unlike music or visual art, both of which are freer to inhabit and construct abstraction as a basis for emphatic communication, poetry has to strive in a medium of reference. Granted, it can break up, bend, tangle and 'tell it slant' but ultimately, as language, its reading often still falls prey to the impulse to 'explain' ('role'/'representation') in a way that both music and art are more frequently excused from. At just over a decade into this new century, Redmond diagnoses a distinct *fin-de-siècle* mood: in globalised economies, financial collapse and political fall-out from 'the implosion of New Labour' our secularised society and Americanised culture has become besotted with its own sense of an ending. The journalistic attraction to apocalypse being more compelling than what comes after has lured both Giorgio Agamben and Paul Muldoon (as Redmond notes) to write books entitled *The End of the Poem*. As Redmond suggests, in 'public life as in literary life, we have entered a period of deleveraging and disavowal, of recanting and retrenchment', at which point he wryly observes that now 'seems to me like a good time for emptying out some old ways of thinking about poetry'.

So, what of 'role' and 'representation' now? Is, for instance, the poet laureate embodying a belief that 'bards should say wise and Delphic things in the neighbourhood of power' or is this 'role' an ornamental reduction of the poet 'to a kind of stage turn wheeled out for the sake of variety, somewhere between a contortionist and a spirit medium'? How does the relationship between poetry and academia manifest the interaction of public structures in an interpretation of role? Does the legacy, or hangover, of the 'New Generation' find its influence in Creative Writing as an institutionalised position strangely hostile to intelligent scrutiny? Is this then touting a workshop sensibility that responds to the over-intellectualism of critical theory with an anti-intellectual championing of the parochial, the regional and the anecdotal, as somehow more authentic? What does it mean when universities are 'nurturing a poetic class' within academia that opposes the analytical rigour *of* academia, and then what is the role of the poet-academic in his or her 'spiritual hyphenation'? Nestled in the founding swamp of all of this, as Redmond persuasively articulates, are the 'excessive claims made for the public orientation of poetry'. It is this nervous over-determination of utility in a public sense that leads to Redmond's description of both the poet laureateship and the position of Oxford Professor of Poetry, in which it is 'not the poet who fills the role, but the role the poet fills'. It is this 'displeasing symmetry' between claims and reality that each separate essay addresses.

While every chapter offers a reliably stimulating and cogent discussion of its particular poet, the analysis of Derek Mahon stands out as perhaps the most memorable and convincing. 'Derek Mahon: Student Prince' explores Mahon's writing as a sustained immersion within a student sensibility; withdrawn from the responsibilities of labour and adult interaction to conserve instead an insular refuge in thought and writing: 'literary consciousness turned in upon itself'. It is a privacy divorced from the Troubles that critics so often extrapolate as a latent commentary in his poetry. This observation lends Mahon's work the fragile and more personal nature it most readily communicates, but that has been previously bypassed in favour of political readings. In his attempt to deflect the external in his poetry, recreating the sealed intellect and aspiration of student life, Mahon's nostalgic poignancy is wonderfully articulated by Redmond: 'the ideal state is to spend your days dreaming about the days spent dreaming of a future. The model literary life is a dream of the literary life.' This romanticised reflection is also traced in Mahon's autobiographical prose, in which he reveals a kinship with J.P. Donleavy, another student from Trinity. In quoting Donleavy in an epigraph to his poem (one which has moved through a series of revealing titles: 'Dog Days', 'Dream Days') 'J.P. Donleavy's Dublin', Mahon reveals the heart of his own philosophy:

When you stop to consider
The days spent dreaming of a future
And say then, that was my life.

Redmond extends this analysis to culminate in a close textual reading of Mahon's seminal poem 'A Disused Shed in Co. Wexford', interestingly continuing a critical dialogue with the interpretations of Tom Paulin and Hugh Haughton. Here he highlights the significance of that poem's titular adjective, 'disused', contrasting it with the lively reverie of working that sparks through Frank O'Hara's *Lunch Poems* (a poet Mahon parodied). Redmond finds instead that 'Mahon's poetry begins where labour ends – in refuse: the flotsam and jetsam of discarded articles, heaps of scrap metal, "the terminal democracy of hatbox and grab."' Unlike the famously social and open poems of O'Hara and their celebration of the 'occasional' joy of New York in its bustling present, Mahon's work looks to what is past ('disused'), moving from introverted seclusion into a later creeping doubt that such self-sufficient silence is not enough. As the first stanza of 'A Disused Shed...' introduces its 'slow clock of condensation, / An echo trapped forever', Redmond's assertion, of Mahon as the melancholy 'Student Prince' aligned with the famous mushrooms in the poem ('Magi, moonmen / Powdery prisoners of the old regime'), becomes all the more hauntingly astute.

By challenging the dangerously default path of poetry hermeneutics, where 'the figure of the writer is hazily aligned with a desirable social goal' leading to exaggerated claims in which 'poetry emerges in the face of "ideology" and, suitably reassured, the writing gleams with moral uplift', Redmond encourages a more sensitive and patient reading. Rather than retroactively assigning a programmatic utility to poetry in order nervously to justify its relevance, be it 'representation' or 'role', this book manages intelligently to acknowledge the subtle movements between frames of public and private that poetry can explore. It is a reading that allows for the poem or poet as flawed, confused and difficult in a way far closer to an experience of 'real' than critical claims that loudly map over the poem, to the detriment of clearly seeing its terrain.

DAVID SPITTLE

SOME CONTRIBUTORS

TARA BERGIN's first poetry collection *This is Yarrow* is published by Carcanet Press, and has just been awarded the 2014 Seamus Heaney Centre for Poetry Prize.

EAVAN BOLAND's most recent volume of poetry *A Woman Without a Country* is published this autumn by Carcanet Press and W.W. Norton. She is the Mabury Knapp Professor in the Humanities at Stanford University.

ALISON BRACKENBURY's eighth poetry collection is *Then* (Carcanet, 2013). New poems can be read at her website, www.alisonbrackenbury.co.uk.

MILES BURROWS began life as a child actor. He studied Russian during National Service, then Classics and Medicine at Oxford. He has won several awards in the Hippocrates competition for poetry in medicine, and won a prize this year in the Brontë Society short story competition. He is collecting poems for his second collection.

GABRIELLE CALVOCORESSI is the author of *The Last Time I Saw Amelia Earhart* and *Apocalyptic Swing*. She is Senior Poetry Editor at *Los Angeles Review of Books*.

PAUL DEATON's poems have appeared in *The Spectator*, *The London Magazine* and anthologies including *The Echoing Gallery* (ed. Rachael Boast). He was runner-up in the 2010 Arvon International Poetry Competition.

THEO DORGAN is a poet, novelist, essayist, editor, librettist and broadcaster. His most recent publications are the novel *Making Way*, and a new collection of poems, *Nine Bright Shiners*.

MARK DOTY's new collection of poems, *Deep Lane*, will be published in April 2015 by W.W. Norton and Jonathan Cape. A National Book Award and T.S. Eliot Prize winner, he lives in New York City and teaches at Rutgers University.

ROGER GARFITT lives just under the Clee-Clun Ridgeway. His *Selected Poems* is published by Carcanet and his memoir, *The Horseman's Word*, is a Vintage paperback.

SANDRA M. GILBERT has published eight collections of poetry. Her prose books include *Wrongful Death*, *Death's Door*, *Rereading Women*, and, most recently, *The Culinary Imagination: From Myth to Modernity*.

LORNA GOODISON has won numerous awards for her work in poetry and fiction. She teaches at the University of Michigan in Ann Arbor, and her most recent book of poems is *Oracabessa* (Carcanet, 2013).

LINDA GREGERSON's *New and Selected Poems* will be published by Houghton Mifflin Harcourt in autumn 2015. She teaches Renaissance literature and creative writing at the University of Michigan.

BEN HICKMAN is Lecturer in Modern Poetry at the University of Kent. He is the author of *John Ashbery and English Poetry* (Edinburgh UP, 2012) and *Poetry and Real Politics: Crisis and the US Avant-Garde* (Edinburgh UP, 2014).

RITA ANN HIGGINS has published ten collections of poetry, a collection of essays and poems, *Hurting God* (Salmon, 2010), and a prose memoir, *Ireland is Changing Mother* (Bloodaxe, 2011).

AMANDA JERNIGAN is the author of two books of poems (*Groundwork* and *All the Daylight Hours*) and a monograph on the poetry of Peter Sanger; she is editor of *The Essential Richard Outram*.

HENRY KING has completed a PhD on the poetry of C.H. Sisson. His poems have been published in *New Poetries V* (Carcanet) and a number of journals. He blogs at henrymking.blogspot.co.uk.

JEE LEONG KOH's fifth book of poems *Steep Tea*, forthcoming from Carcanet Press in 2015, is inspired by the work of Eavan Boland and other women poets.

YUSEF KOMUNYAKAA is a poet and professor in the Creative Writing Program at New York University.

ELLINE LIPKIN is a Research Scholar with the Center for the Study of Women at UCLA and teaches poetry for Writing Workshops Los Angeles. Her poetry book, *The Errant Thread*, was chosen by Eavan Boland for the Kore Press First Book Award.

JOAN MCBREEN has published four collections of poetry and edited two anthologies. *The Mountain Ash in Connemara*, her CD of poetry and music, was released in 2014.

SHARA MCCALLUM is the author of four books, most recently *The Face of Water: New and Selected Poems*. She directs the Stadler Center for Poetry and teaches at Bucknell University.

THOMAS MCCARTHY was born in Co. Waterford and for many years was a public librarian in Cork. His last collection was *The Last Geraldine Officer* (2009). His new collection *Pandemonium* is due in 2015.

JAMES MCGRATH's poems appear in various magazines. He lectures in English at Leeds Beckett University. His first monograph, *The Naming of Autism*, is forthcoming from Rowman & Littlefield International in 2016.

MEDBH MCGUCKIAN teaches at the Seamus Heaney Centre, Queen's University. The winner of many literary awards, she publishes with Gallery Press where her most recent collection is *The High Caul Cap* (2012).

MÁIGHRÉAD MEDBH is a poet with seven published books and a reputation for dramatic readings. Most recent works are *Savage Solitude* (Dedalus) and *Pagan to the Core* (Arlen House).

PAULA MEEHAN, poet and playwright, lives in her native Dublin. She has most recently published *Painting Rain*, from Carcanet Press. She is Ireland Professor of Poetry 2013–2016.

JOSEPH MINDEN's poems have featured in *Iota*, *Magma* and *The Frogmore Papers*. He won the John Kinsella and Tracy Ryan poetry prize in 2013.

CHARLES MUNDYE teaches in the Humanities Research Centre at Sheffield Hallam University, and is the editor of Keidrych Rhys, *The Van Pool: Collected Poems* (Seren, 2012).

HORATIO MORPURGO's work has appeared in many magazines. He writes on literary themes, the environment and European affairs. His last book was *Lady Chatterley's Defendant & Other Awkward Customers* (Just Press, 2011).

ANDRÉ NAFFIS-SAHELY's poetry was featured in the *Oxford Poets 2013* anthology (Carcanet). Forthcoming translations include Émile Zola's *Money* (Penguin Classics, 2014) and Honoré de Balzac's *Physiology of the Employee* (Wakefield Press, 2014).